Computation and Estimation Strategies

Building on Numbers You Know

Grade 5

Also appropriate for Grade 6

Marlene Kliman
Susan Jo Russell
Cornelia Tierney
Megan Murray

Developed at TERC, Cambridge, Massachusetts

Dale Seymour Publications®
White Plains, New York

The *Investigations* curriculum was developed at TERC (formerly Technical Education Research Centers) in collaboration with Kent State University and the State University of New York at Buffalo. The work was supported in part by National Science Foundation Grant No. ESI-9050210. TERC is a nonprofit company working to improve mathematics and science education. TERC is located at 2067 Massachusetts Avenue, Cambridge, MA 02140.

This project was supported, in part,
by the
National Science Foundation
Opinions expressed are those of the authors
and not necessarily those of the Foundation

Managing Editor: Catherine Anderson
Series Editor: Beverly Cory
Revision Team: Laura Marshall Alavosus, Ellen Harding, Patty Green Holubar, Suzanne Knott, Beverly Hersh Lozoff
ESL Consultant: Nancy Sokol Green
Production/Manufacturing Director: Janet Yearian
Production/Manufacturing Supervisor: Karen Edmonds
Production/Manufacturing Coordinator: Joe Conte
Design Manager: Jeff Kelly
Design: Don Taka
Illustrations: Susan Jaekel, Carl Yoshihara
Cover: Bay Graphics
Composition: Archetype Book Composition

This book is published by Dale Seymour Publications®, an imprint of Addison Wesley Longman, Inc.

Dale Seymour Publications
10 Bank Street
White Plains, NY 10602
Customer Service: 1-800-872-1100

DALE
SEYMOUR
PUBLICATIONS®

Order number DS47047
ISBN 1-57232-800-2
7 8 9 10-ML-02

Printed on Recycled Paper

INVESTIGATIONS IN NUMBER, DATA, AND SPACE®

TERC

Principal Investigator   Susan Jo Russell

Co-Principal Investigator   Cornelia Tierney

Director of Research and Evaluation   Jan Mokros

Curriculum Development
Joan Akers
Michael T. Battista
Mary Berle-Carman
Douglas H. Clements
Karen Economopoulos
Claryce Evans
Marlene Kliman
Cliff Konold
Jan Mokros
Megan Murray
Ricardo Nemirovsky
Tracy Noble
Andee Rubin
Susan Jo Russell
Margie Singer
Cornelia Tierney

Evaluation and Assessment
Mary Berle-Carman
Jan Mokros
Andee Rubin
Tracey Wright

Teacher Support
Kabba Colley
Karen Economopoulos
Anne Goodrow
Nancy Ishihara
Liana Laughlin
Jerrie Moffett
Megan Murray
Margie Singer
Dewi Win
Virginia Woolley
Tracey Wright
Lisa Yaffee

Administration and Production
Irene Baker
Amy Catlin
Amy Taber

Cooperating Classrooms for This Unit
Betsy Hale
Arlington Public Schools
Arlington, MA

Hilory Paster
Brookline Public Schools
Brookline, MA

Technology Development
Douglas H. Clements
Julie Sarama

Video Production
David A. Smith
Judy Storeygard

Consultants and Advisors
Deborah Lowenberg Ball
Marilyn Burns
Mary Johnson
James J. Kaput
Mary M. Lindquist
Leslie P. Steffe
Grayson Wheatley

Graduate Assistants
Richard Aistrope
Kathryn Battista
Caroline Borrow
William Hunt
Kent State University

Jeffrey Barrett
Julie Sarama
Sudha Swaminathan
Elaine Vukelic
State University of New York at Buffalo

Dan Gillette
Irene Hall
Harvard Graduate School of Education

Revisions and Home Materials
Cathy Miles Grant
Marlene Kliman
Margaret McGaffigan
Megan Murray
Kim O'Neil
Andee Rubin
Susan Jo Russell
Lisa Seyferth
Myriam Steinback
Judy Storeygard
Anna Suarez
Cornelia Tierney
Carol Walker
Tracey Wright

CONTENTS

WHERE TO START

The first-time user of *Building on Numbers You Know* should read the following:

When you next teach this same unit, you can begin to read more of the background. Each time you present the unit, you will learn more about how your students understand the mathematical ideas.

Investigations in Number, Data, and Space® is a K–5 mathematics curriculum with four major goals:

- to offer students meaningful mathematical problems
- to emphasize depth in mathematical thinking rather than superficial exposure to a series of fragmented topics
- to communicate mathematics content and pedagogy to teachers
- to substantially expand the pool of mathematically literate students

The *Investigations* curriculum embodies a new approach based on years of research about how children learn mathematics. Each grade level consists of a set of separate units, each offering 2–8 weeks of work. These units of study are presented through investigations that involve students in the exploration of major mathematical ideas.

Approaching the mathematics content through investigations helps students develop flexibility and confidence in approaching problems, fluency in using mathematical skills and tools to solve problems, and proficiency in evaluating their solutions. Students also build a repertoire of ways to communicate about their mathematical thinking, while their enjoyment and appreciation of mathematics grows.

The investigations are carefully designed to invite all students into mathematics—girls and boys, members of diverse cultural, ethnic, and language groups, and students with different strengths and interests. Problem contexts often call on students to share experiences from their family, culture, or community. The curriculum eliminates barriers—such as work in isolation from peers, or emphasis on speed and memorization—that exclude some students from participating successfully in mathematics. The following aspects of the curriculum ensure that all students are included in significant mathematics learning:

- Students spend time exploring problems in depth.
- They find more than one solution to many of the problems they work on.

- They invent their own strategies and approaches, rather than rely on memorized procedures.
- They choose from a variety of concrete materials and appropriate technology, including calculators, as a natural part of their everyday mathematical work.
- They express their mathematical thinking through drawing, writing, and talking.
- They work in a variety of groupings—as a whole class, individually, in pairs, and in small groups.
- They move around the classroom as they explore the mathematics in their environment and talk with their peers.

While reading and other language activities are typically given a great deal of time and emphasis in elementary classrooms, mathematics often does not get the time it needs. If students are to experience mathematics in depth, they must have enough time to become engaged in real mathematical problems. We believe that a minimum of 5 hours of mathematics classroom time a week—about an hour a day—is critical at the elementary level. The scope and pacing of the *Investigations* curriculum are based on that belief.

We explain more about the pedagogy and principles that underlie these investigations in Teacher Notes throughout the units. For correlations of the curriculum to the NCTM Standards and further help in using this research-based program for teaching mathematics, see the following books, available from Dale Seymour Publications:

- *Implementing the* Investigations in Number, Data, and Space® *Curriculum*
- *Beyond Arithmetic: Changing Mathematics in the Elementary Classroom* by Jan Mokros, Susan Jo Russell, and Karen Economopoulos

This book is one of the curriculum units for *Investigations in Number, Data, and Space.* In addition to providing part of a complete mathematics curriculum for your students, this unit offers information to support your own professional development. You, the teacher, are the person who will make this curriculum come alive in the classroom; the book for each unit is your main support system.

Although the curriculum does not include student textbooks, reproducible sheets for student work are provided in the unit and are also available as Student Activity Booklets. Students work actively with objects and experiences in their own environment and with a variety of manipulative materials and technology, rather than with a book of instruction and problems. We strongly recommend use of the overhead projector as a way to present problems, to focus group discussion, and to help students share ideas and strategies.

Ultimately, every teacher will use these investigations in ways that make sense for his or her particular style, the particular group of students, and the constraints and supports of a particular school environment. Each unit offers information and guidance for a wide variety of situations, drawn from our collaborations with many teachers and students over many years. Our goal in this book is to help you, a professional educator, implement this curriculum in a way that will give all your students access to mathematical power.

Investigation Format

The opening two pages of each investigation help you get ready for the work that follows.

What Happens   This gives a synopsis of each session or block of sessions.

Mathematical Emphasis   This lists the most important ideas and processes students will encounter in this investigation.

What to Plan Ahead of Time   These lists alert you to materials to gather, sheets to duplicate, transparencies to make, and anything else you need to do before starting.

INVESTIGATION 2

Multiplication and Division Situations

What Happens

Sessions 1 and 2: Multiplication and Division Strategies Students find different ways to solve problems that can be modeled with multiplication and division. They discuss how to think about remainders in a way that makes sense in the context of the problems.

Session 3: Division Strategies Students share what they know about notation for recording division equations and remainders, and they discuss relationships between multiplication and division. They discuss different ways to solve problems presented with division notation, and they consider ways to use multiplication to solve division problems.

Session 4: What Should We Do with the Extras? Students write problems to represent division situations. They solve their problems, considering the meaning of any remainders in a particular context.

Sessions 5 and 6: Relating Multiplication to Division Students find different ways to solve problems that can be modeled with multiplication. They discuss relationships between multiplication situations and division situations. They then write and solve problems that represent multiplication situations.

Session 7 (Excursion): Problems About Our School Students work on problems that involve real information gathered from places where large quantities of supplies are kept in the school, such as a supply closet or the cafeteria. After solving the problems, students go to see the actual objects and packages that their answers represent.

Mathematical Emphasis

- Developing, recording, and comparing strategies for solving multiplication and division problems
- Making sense of remainders
- Understanding relationships between multiplication and division
- Understanding how multiplication and division notation can represent a variety of situations
- Modeling situations with multiplication, division, and other operations

What to Plan Ahead of Time

Materials

- Multiple Tower for 21 from Investigation 1 (Sessions 1–2)
- Stick-on notes: 1 package for the class (Session 7, Excursion)
- Metersticks or rulers: 1 per pair (Session 7, Excursion)
- Samples and packages of items in your problem set (Session 7, Excursion). For more information, see the **Teacher Note,** Writing Problems About School Supplies (p. 70).
- Chart paper (Sessions 1–2, 4–6)
- Overhead projector (Sessions 3–6, optional)
- Bulletin board and tabletop surface (Session 7, Excursion)
- Calculator (Session 3, optional)

Other Preparation

- Duplicate student sheets and teaching resources (located at the end of this unit) in the following quantities. If you have Student Activity Booklets, no copying is needed.

  For Sessions 1–2
  Student Sheet 10, Ringles (p. 168): 1 per student
  Student Sheet 11, Boxes of Markers (p. 169): 1 per student
  Student Sheet 12, Zennies (p. 170): 1 per student (homework)

  Student Sheet 13, My Coin (p. 171): 1 per student (homework)
  300 Chart (p. 178): 1–2 per student (optional)

  For Session 3
  Student Sheet 14, A Division Problem (p. 172): 1 per student (homework)

  For Session 4
  Student Sheet 15, Division Situations (p. 173): 1 per student (homework)

  For Sessions 5–6
  Student Sheet 16, Milk Cartons (p. 174): 1 per student
  Student Sheet 17, Mimi's Mystery Multiple Tower (p. 175): 1 per student (homework)
  Student Sheet 18, Relating Multiplication and Division Situations (p. 176): 1 per student (homework)

  For Session 7
  Student Sheet 19, A Problem About Large Quantities (p. 177): 1 per student (homework)

- If you plan to do the Excursion, Session 7, you will need to write and duplicate sets of problems about supplies stored in quantities around the classroom or school, as described in the **Teacher Note,** Writing Problems About School Supplies (p. 70).

Sessions Within an investigation, the activities are organized by class session, a session being at least a one-hour math class. Sessions are numbered consecutively through an investigation. Often several sessions are grouped together, presenting a block of activities with a single major focus.

When you find a block of sessions presented together—for example, Sessions 1, 2, and 3—read through the entire block first to understand the overall flow and sequence of the activities. Make some preliminary decisions about how you will divide the activities into three sessions for your class, based on what you know about your students. You may need to modify your initial plans as you progress through the activities, and you may want to make notes in the margins of the pages as reminders for the next time you use the unit.

Be sure to read the Session Follow-Up section at the end of the session block to see what homework assignments and extensions are suggested as you make your initial plans.

While you may be used to a curriculum that tells you exactly what each class session should cover, we have found that the teacher is in a better position to make these decisions. Each unit is flexible and may be handled somewhat differently by every teacher. Although we provide guidance for how many sessions a particular group of activities is likely to need, we want you to be active in determining an appropriate pace and the best transition points for your class. It is not unusual for a teacher to spend more or less time than is proposed for the activities.

Ten-Minute Math At the beginning of some sessions, you will find Ten-Minute Math activities. These are designed to be used in tandem with the investigations, but not during the math hour. Rather, we hope you will do them whenever you have a spare 10 minutes—maybe before lunch or recess, or at the end of the day.

Ten-Minute Math offers practice in key concepts, but not always those being covered in the unit. For example, in a unit on using data, Ten-Minute Math might revisit geometric activities done earlier in the year. Complete directions for the suggested activities are included at the end of each unit.

Sessions 1 and 2

Multiplication and Division Strategies

Materials

- Student Sheet 10 (1 per student)
- Student Sheet 11 (1 per student)
- Student Sheet 12 (1 per student, homework)
- Student Sheet 13 (1 per student, homework)
- Chart paper (optional)
- Multiple Tower for 21 (from Investigation 1)
- 300 Chart (1–2 per student, optional)

What Happens

Students find different ways to solve problems that can be modeled with multiplication and division. They discuss how to think about remainders in a way that makes sense in the context of the problems. Student work focuses on:

- modeling situations with multiplication, division, and other operations
- developing, explaining, and comparing strategies for multiplication and division

Ten-Minute Math: What Is Likely? Continue to spend time on this activity in any 10-minute period you have outside of math class. Each time you do it, change the proportions of colors in your container. For more challenge, ask students to fill the container themselves in a way that is likely to yield a particular goal (for example, making it likely to draw more white than red). For full directions and variations, see p. 147.

Activity

The Ringle, an Imaginary Coin

Post where everyone can see it the Multiple Tower for multiples of 21 you made during Investigation 1. Distribute a copy of Student Sheet 10, Ringles, to each student. Ask students to name all the U.S. coins and their values.

Suppose our country decided to get rid of all these coins and make one new coin, worth 21 cents. It's called a ringle. No more dimes, or quarters, or pennies—just ringles. It would take us a while to get used to ringles. We'd want to compare the new coin to the money we are used to, and figure out how many ringles make a dollar, how many make 2 dollars, and so on.

The three problems on this sheet are all about the ringle. You can work on these problems alone or with a partner.

Students record their thinking, showing each step, so that someone looking at their papers could understand how they solved the problems. They may use 300 charts or they may refer to the Multiple Tower if they find it helpful, but they may not use calculators.

42 ■ *Investigation 2: Multiplication and Division Situations*

Activities The activities include pair and small-group work, individual tasks, and whole-class discussions. In any case, students are seated together, talking and sharing ideas during all work times. Students most often work cooperatively, although each student may record work individually.

Choice Time In some units, some sessions are structured with activity choices. In these cases, students may work simultaneously on different activities focused on the same mathematical ideas. Students choose which activities they want to do, and they cycle through them.

You will need to decide how to set up and introduce these activities and how to let students make their choices. Some teachers present them as station activities, in different parts of the room. Some list the choices on the board as reminders or have students keep their own lists.

Tips for the Linguistically Diverse Classroom At strategic points in each unit, you will find concrete suggestions for simple modifications of the teaching strategies to encourage the participation of all students. Many of these tips offer alternative ways to elicit critical thinking from students at varying levels of English proficiency, as well as from other students who find it difficult to verbalize their thinking.

The tips are supported by suggestions for specific vocabulary work to help ensure that all students can participate fully in the investigations. The Preview for the Linguistically Diverse Classroom lists important words that are assumed as part of the working vocabulary of the unit. Second-language learners will need to become familiar with these words in order to understand the problems and activities they will be doing. These terms can be incorporated into students' second-language work before or during the unit. Activities that can be used to present the words are found in the appendix, Vocabulary Support for Second-Language Learners. In addition, ideas for making connections to students' languages and cultures, included on the Preview page, help the class explore the unit's concepts from a multicultural perspective.

Session Follow-Up: Homework   In *Investigations,* homework is an extension of classroom work. Sometimes it offers review and practice of work done in class, sometimes preparation for upcoming activities, and sometimes numerical practice that revisits work in earlier units. Homework plays a role both in supporting students' learning and in helping inform families about the ways in which students in this curriculum work with mathematical ideas.

Depending on your school's homework policies and your own judgment, you may want to assign more homework than is suggested in the units. For this purpose you might use the practice pages, included as blackline masters at the end of this unit, to give students additional work with numbers.

For some homework assignments, you will want to adapt the activity to meet the needs of a variety of students in your class: those with special needs, those ready for more challenge, and second-language learners. You might change the numbers in a problem, make the activity more or less complex, or go through a sample activity with

those who need extra help. You can modify any student sheet for either homework or class use. In particular, making numbers in a problem smaller or larger can make the same basic activity appropriate for a wider range of students.

Another issue to consider is how to handle the homework that students bring back to class—how to recognize the work they have done at home without spending too much time on it. Some teachers hold a short group discussion of different approaches to the assignment; others ask students to share and discuss their work with a neighbor; still others post the homework around the room and give students time to tour it briefly. If you want to keep track of homework students bring in, be sure it ends up in a designated place.

Session Follow-Up: Extensions   Sometimes in Session Follow-Up, you will find suggested extension activities. These are opportunities for some or all students to explore a topic in greater depth or in a different context. They are not designed for "fast" students; mathematics is a multifaceted discipline, and different students will want to go further in different investigations. Look for and encourage the sparks of interest and enthusiasm you see in your students, and use the extensions to help them pursue these interests.

Excursions Some of the *Investigations* units include excursions—blocks of activities that could be omitted without harming the integrity of the unit. This is one way of dealing with the great depth and variety of elementary mathematics—much more than a class has time to explore in any one year. Excursions give you the flexibility to make different choices from year to year, doing the excursion in one unit this time, and next year trying another excursion.

Materials

A complete list of the materials needed for teaching this unit follows the unit overview. Some of these materials are available in kits for the *Investigations* curriculum. Individual items can also be purchased from school supply dealers.

Classroom Materials In an active mathematics classroom, certain basic materials should be available at all times: interlocking cubes, pencils, unlined paper, graph paper, calculators, things to count with, and measuring tools. Some activities in this curriculum require scissors and glue sticks or tape. Stick-on notes and large paper are also useful materials throughout.

So that students can independently get what they need at any time, they should know where these materials are kept, how they are stored, and how they are to be returned to the storage area. For example, interlocking cubes are best stored in towers of ten; then, whatever the activity, they should be returned to storage in groups of ten at the end of the hour. You'll find that establishing such routines at the beginning of the year is well worth the time and effort.

Student Sheets and Teaching Resources Student recording sheets and other teaching tools needed for both class and homework are provided as reproducible blackline masters at the end of each unit. We think it's important that students find their own ways of organizing and recording their work. They need to learn how to explain their thinking with both drawings and written words, and how to organize their results so someone else can understand them. For this reason, we deliberately do not provide student sheets for every activity. Regardless of the form in which students do their work, we recommend that they keep their

work in a mathematics folder, journal, or notebook so that it is always available to them for reference.

Student Activity Booklets These booklets contain all the sheets each student will need for individual work, freeing you from extensive copying (although you may need or want to copy the occasional teaching resource on transparency film or card stock, or make extra copies of a student sheet).

Calculators and Computers Calculators are used throughout *Investigations*. Many of the units recommend that you have at least one calculator for each pair. You will find calculator activities, plus Teacher Notes discussing this important mathematical tool, in an early unit at each grade level. It is assumed that calculators will be readily available for student use.

Computer activities are offered at all grade levels. How you use the computer activities depends on the number of computers you have available. Technology in the Curriculum discusses ways to incorporate the use of calculators and computers into classroom activities.

Name _____ Date _____

Student Sheet 20

Multiplication Cluster Problems

Solve each cluster of problems. Look for ways that the problems in each cluster are related.

10×123	20×123
2×123	22×123

10×18	5×18
50×18	2×18
20×18	40×18
45×18	47×18

400×9	500×9
90×9	8×9
2×9	498×9

2×72	10×72
5×72	20×72
200×72	210×72
215×72	

© Dale Seymour Publications®   **179**   *Investigation 3 • Sessions 1–3*
Building on Numbers You Know

Children's Literature   Each unit offers a list of related children's literature that can be used to support the mathematical ideas in the unit. Sometimes an activity is based on a specific children's book, with suggestions for substitutions where practical. While such activities can be adapted and taught without the book, the literature offers a rich introduction and should be used whenever possible.

Investigations **at Home**   It is a good idea to make your policy on homework explicit to both students and their families when you begin teaching with *Investigations*. How frequently will you be assigning homework? When do you expect homework to be completed and brought back to school? What are your goals in assigning homework? How independent should families expect their children to be? What should the parent's or guardian's role be? The more explicit you can be about your expectations, the better the homework experience will be for everyone.

Investigations at Home (a booklet available separately for each unit, to send home with students) gives you a way to communicate with families about the work students are doing in class. This booklet includes a brief description of every session, a list of the mathematics content emphasized in each investigation, and a discussion of each homework assignment to help families more effectively support their children. Whether or not you are using the *Investigations* at Home booklets, we expect you to make your own choices about homework assignments. Feel free to omit any and to add extra ones you think are appropriate.

Family Letter   A letter that you can send home to students' families is included with the blackline masters for each unit. Families need to be informed about the mathematics work in your classroom; they should be encouraged to participate in and support their children's work. A reminder to send home the letter for each unit appears in one of the early investigations. These letters are also available separately in Spanish, Vietnamese, Cantonese, Hmong, and Cambodian.

Help for You, the Teacher

Because we believe strongly that a new curriculum must help teachers think in new ways about mathematics and about their students' mathematical thinking processes, we have included a great deal of material to help you learn more about both.

About the Mathematics in This Unit   This introductory section summarizes the critical information about the mathematics you will be teaching. It describes the unit's central mathematical ideas and the ways students will encounter them through the unit's activities.

About the Assessment in this Unit   This introductory section highlights Teacher Checkpoints and assessment activities contained in the unit. It offers questions to stimulate your assessment as you observe the development of students' mathematical thinking and learning.

Teacher Notes   These reference notes provide practical information about the mathematics you are teaching and about our experience with how students learn. Many of the notes were written in response to actual questions from teachers or to discuss important things we saw happening in the

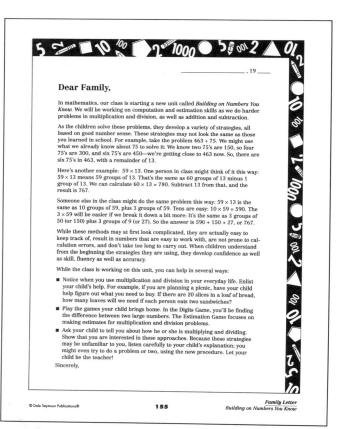

field-test classrooms. Some teachers like to read them all before starting the unit, then review them as they come up in particular investigations.

Dialogue Boxes Sample dialogues demonstrate how students typically express their mathematical ideas, what issues and confusions arise in their thinking, and how some teachers have guided class discussions.

These dialogues are based on the extensive classroom testing of this curriculum; many are word-for-word transcriptions of recorded class discussions. They are not always easy reading; sometimes it may take some effort to unravel what the students are trying to say. But this is the value

of these dialogues; they offer good clues to how your students may develop and express their approaches and strategies, helping you prepare for your own class discussions.

Where to Start You may not have time to read everything the first time you use this unit. As a first-time user, you will likely focus on understanding the activities and working them out with your students. Read completely through all the activities before starting to present them. Also read those sections listed in the Contents under the heading Where to Start.

Teacher Note *Remainders, Fractions, and Decimals*

Think about how you would solve the following problem and how you would write the answer:

> Four people want to share 13 apples. How many does each person get?

One way to solve the problem is to give each person three apples and put aside the one extra. We can write this answer as 3 R 1, or "3 apples and 1 extra."

Another way to solve this problem is to give each person three and a quarter apples. In this case, we can write the answer as 3¼ or 3.25. Since each person gets one-quarter of the extra apple, there is no remainder; nothing is left over.

It is important that students recognize both ways of thinking about the remainder: as an amount left over or extra, and as a fraction or part of the divisor. Many students are comfortable thinking about remainders as leftovers, but some have difficulty thinking about remainders as a fraction or part of the divisor. You can work on this with problems about things that can be subdivided, like pizza or apples or cookies. Start with a problem that uses small numbers, such as the apples problem above, then move to more difficult numbers. Ask students to talk about the meaning of the different ways of writing the answer.

How would we write the answer if we ended up with some left over? How would we write the answer if there was none left over after we shared all the apples? How many more apples would we need to give everyone another whole apple?

Throughout this unit, encourage students to find different ways to record the remainders and to think about when it is appropriate to use each different way. When solving purely numeric problems, such as 13 ÷ 4, students may record the leftovers in any format. When solving situational problems, they should express the remainder in a way that makes sense. If the problem is about sharing apples, for example, the remainder can be expressed either as a fraction or a decimal, or as an amount left over. If the problem is about sharing something that cannot be subdivided, such as pencils, the extras should be recorded as a remainder.

Watch to see that students, in expressing a remainder as a fraction, don't lose sense of what the numbers mean. In the apple problem above, using small numbers and a familiar context, the meaning of the ¼ may be clear to students: ¼ is a familiar fraction, and it is easy to visualize ¼ as a part of an apple. But the fractional parts in more complex problems may seem very mysterious. For example, if there are 692 people to be divided into groups of 25, we can make 27 groups, with 17 people left over:

$$682 \div 25 = 27 \text{ R } 17$$

or

$$682 \div 25 = 27\frac{17}{27}$$

What does the ¹⁷⁄₂₇ mean here? It is easy for students to write the fractional part of the answer without holding on to what that fraction means. In this problem, we might think of it as ¹⁷⁄₂₇ of a group, or 17 out of the next 27 people. It is as if we were in the process of forming a new group of 27, but ran out of people at 17. Where it makes sense to express the leftovers in a division problem as a fraction, discuss the meaning with students: What is this a fraction of? What does it tell you about the division situation?

D I A L O G U E B O X

Thinking About Remainders

To introduce the activity Looking at Division Clusters (p. 85), the teacher presents this cluster:

12 ÷ 12	120 ÷ 12
132 ÷ 12	133 ÷ 12

These students are talking about how they handled the remainder for the last problem in the cluster, 133 ÷ 12. Their discussion illustrates different ways they make sense of remainders: as a "leftover" (1 extra); as part of a group (1 of the next group of 12); and as a fraction (¹⁄₁₂ of a group). A common misconception also comes up: that the answer to a division problem is the sum of the quotient and the remainder.

Maricel: Well, 120 ÷ 12 is 10, and 12 ÷ 12 is 1. Put them together and get 132 ÷ 12 is 11. Between 132 and 133 there's only 1 difference. We're looking for 12 difference, so it's 11 R 1.

Julie: I got 12 for the answer. I know 132 ÷ 12 is 11, so 133 ÷ 12 would be 12. Just add the 1.

Sofia: No, it's one-twelfth of another group. It's 1 out of a group of 12, so ¹⁄₁₂.

Maricel: I think 133 ÷ 12 is the same as "How many 12's are in 133?" We know there's 11 of them in 132, and then you have 1 more left.

Noah: You can think of it like 132 ÷ 12 is 11, and then you need to do 1 ÷ 12 because there's 1 difference between 132 and 133. So it's 11 and ¹⁄₁₂. Anyway, it can't be 12, because 12 × 12 is 144 and we only want 133.

To present an easier problem with remainders, the teacher draws 5 circles on a piece of chart paper and writes 5 ÷ 2.

   5 ÷ 2

If I divided these 5 circles into two groups, how many are in each group? How many are left over?

A student comes to the board and circles two groups, and records the answer: 2 R 1.

⊙⊙o   5 ÷ 2 = 2 R 1

Julie: There's 1 left, because you can't take out any more groups of 2.

Sofia: But you don't have to have a remainder. You could divide that 1 into halves, so it would be 2½.

Maricel: That's how it is with 133 ÷ 12. You take out all the groups of 12 that you can and then there's 1 left.

Noah: Or ¹⁄₁₂ left. The ½ is like the ¹⁄₁₂. It's 1 out of 2, so it's ½, but we have 1 out of 12, so it's ¹⁄₁₂.

The *Investigations* curriculum incorporates the use of two forms of technology in the classroom: calculators and computers. Calculators are assumed to be standard classroom materials, available for student use in any unit. Computers are explicitly linked to one or more units at each grade level; they are used with the unit on 2-D geometry at each grade, as well as with some of the units on measuring, data, and changes.

Using Calculators

In this curriculum, calculators are considered tools for doing mathematics, similar to pattern blocks or interlocking cubes. Just as with other tools, students must learn both *how* to use calculators correctly and *when* they are appropriate to use. This knowledge is crucial for daily life, as calculators are now a standard way of handling numerical operations, both at work and at home.

Using a calculator correctly is not a simple task; it depends on a good knowledge of the four operations and of the number system, so that students can select suitable calculations and also determine what a reasonable result would be. These skills are the basis of any work with numbers, whether or not a calculator is involved.

Unfortunately, calculators are often seen as tools to check computations with, as if other methods are somehow more fallible. Students need to understand that any computational method can be used to check any other; it's just as easy to make a mistake on the calculator as it is to make a mistake on paper or with mental arithmetic. Throughout this curriculum, we encourage students to solve computation problems in more than one way in order to double-check their accuracy. We present mental arithmetic, paper-and-pencil computation, and calculators as three possible approaches.

In this curriculum we also recognize that, despite their importance, calculators are not always appropriate in mathematics instruction. Like any tools, calculators are useful for some tasks but not for others. You will need to make decisions about when to allow students access to calculators and when to ask that they solve problems without them so that they can concentrate on other tools and skills. At times when calculators are or are not appropriate for a particular activity, we make specific recommendations. Help your students develop their own sense of which problems they can tackle with their own reasoning and which ones might be better solved with a combination of their own reasoning and the calculator.

Managing calculators in your classroom so that they are a tool, and not a distraction, requires some planning. When calculators are first introduced, students often want to use them for everything, even problems that can be solved quite simply by other methods. However, once the novelty wears off, students are just as interested in developing their own strategies, especially when these strategies are emphasized and valued in the classroom. Over time, students will come to recognize the ease and value of solving problems mentally, with paper and pencil, or with manipulatives, while also understanding the power of the calculator to facilitate work with larger numbers.

Experience shows that if calculators are available only occasionally, students become excited and distracted when they are permitted to use them. They focus on the tool rather than on the mathematics. In order to learn when calculators are appropriate and when they are not, students must have easy access to them and use them routinely in their work.

If you have a calculator for each student, and if you think your students can accept the responsibility, you might allow them to keep their calculators with the rest of their individual materials, at least for the first few weeks of school. Alternatively, you might store them in boxes on a shelf, number each calculator, and assign a corresponding number to each student. This system can give students a sense of ownership while also helping you keep track of the calculators.

Using Computers

Students can use computers to approach and visualize mathematical situations in new ways. The computer allows students to construct and manipulate geometric shapes, see objects move according to rules they specify, and turn, flip, and repeat a pattern.

This curriculum calls for computers in units where they are a particularly effective tool for learning mathematics content. One unit on 2-D geometry at each of the grades 3–5 includes a core of activities that rely on access to computers, either in the classroom or in a lab. Other units on geometry, measuring, data, and changes include computer activities, but can be taught without them. In these units, however, students' experience is greatly enhanced by computer use.

The following list outlines the recommended use of computers in this curriculum:

Kindergarten
Unit: *Making Shapes and Building Blocks* (Exploring Geometry)
Software: *Shapes*
Source: provided with the unit

Grade 1
Unit: *Survey Questions and Secret Rules* (Collecting and Sorting Data)
Software: *Tabletop, Jr.*
Source: Broderbund

Unit: *Quilt Squares and Block Towns* (2-D and 3-D Geometry)
Software: *Shapes*
Source: provided with the unit

Grade 2
Unit: *Mathematical Thinking at Grade 2* (Introduction)
Software: *Shapes*
Source: provided with the unit

Unit: *Shapes, Halves, and Symmetry* (Geometry and Fractions)
Software: *Shapes*
Source: provided with the unit

Unit: *How Long? How Far?* (Measuring)
Software: *Geo-Logo*
Source: provided with the unit

Grade 3
Unit: *Flips, Turns, and Area* (2-D Geometry)
Software: *Tumbling Tetrominoes*
Source: provided with the unit

Unit: *Turtle Paths* (2-D Geometry)
Software: *Geo-Logo*
Source: provided with the unit

Grade 4
Unit: *Sunken Ships and Grid Patterns* (2-D Geometry)
Software: *Geo-Logo*
Source: provided with the unit

Grade 5
Unit: *Picturing Polygons* (2-D Geometry)
Software: *Geo-Logo*
Source: provided with the unit

Unit: *Patterns of Change* (Tables and Graphs)
Software: *Trips*
Source: provided with the unit

Unit: *Data: Kids, Cats, and Ads* (Statistics)
Software: *Tabletop, Sr.*
Source: Broderbund

The software provided with the *Investigations* units uses the power of the computer to help students explore mathematical ideas and relationships that cannot be explored in the same way with physical materials. With the *Shapes* (grades 1–2) and *Tumbling Tetrominoes* (grade 3) software, students explore symmetry, pattern, rotation and reflection, area, and characteristics of 2-D shapes. With the *Geo-Logo* software (grades 2–5), students investigate rotations and reflections, coordinate geometry, the properties of 2-D shapes, and angles. The *Trips* software (grade 5) is a mathematical exploration of motion in which students run experiments and interpret data presented in graphs and tables.

We suggest that students work in pairs on the computer; this not only maximizes computer resources but also encourages students to consult, monitor, and teach each other. Generally, more than two students at one computer find it difficult to share. Managing access to computers is an issue for every classroom. The curriculum gives you explicit support for setting up a system. The units are structured on the assumption that you have enough computers for half your students to work on the machines in pairs at one time. If you do not have access to that many computers, suggestions are made for structuring class time to use the unit with fewer than five.

Assessment plays a critical role in teaching and learning, and it is an integral part of the *Investigations* curriculum. For a teacher using these units, assessment is an ongoing process. You observe students' discussions and explanations of their strategies on a daily basis and examine their work as it evolves. While students are busy recording and representing their work, working on projects, sharing with partners, and playing mathematical games, you have many opportunities to observe their mathematical thinking. What you learn through observation guides your decisions about how to proceed. In any of the units, you will repeatedly consider questions like these:

- Do students come up with their own strategies for solving problems, or do they expect others to tell them what to do? What do their strategies reveal about their mathematical understanding?

- Do students understand that there are different strategies for solving problems? Do they articulate their strategies and try to understand other students' strategies?

- How effectively do students use materials as tools to help with their mathematical work?

- Do students have effective ideas for keeping track of and recording their work? Do keeping track of and recording their work seem difficult for them?

You will need to develop a comfortable and efficient system for recording and keeping track of your observations. Some teachers keep a clipboard handy and jot notes on a class list or on adhesive labels that are later transferred to student files. Others keep loose-leaf notebooks with a page for each student and make weekly notes about what they have observed in class.

Assessment Tools in the Unit

With the activities in each unit, you will find questions to guide your thinking while observing the students at work. You will also find two built-in assessment tools: Teacher Checkpoints and embedded Assessment activities.

Teacher Checkpoints   The designated Teacher Checkpoints in each unit offer a time to "check in" with individual students, watch them at work, and ask questions that illuminate how they are thinking.

At first it may be hard to know what to look for, hard to know what kinds of questions to ask. Students may be reluctant to talk; they may not be accustomed to having the teacher ask them about their work, or they may not know how to explain their thinking. Two important ingredients of this process are asking students open-ended questions about their work and showing genuine interest in how they are approaching the task. When students see that you are interested in their thinking and are counting on them to come up with their own ways of solving problems, they may surprise you with the depth of their understanding.

Teacher Checkpoints also give you the chance to pause in the teaching sequence and reflect on how your class is doing overall. Think about whether you need to adjust your pacing: Are most students fluent with strategies for solving a particular kind of problem? Are they just starting to formulate good strategies? Or are they still struggling with how to start? Depending on what you see as the students work, you may want to spend more time on similar problems, change some of the problems to use smaller numbers, move quickly to more-challenging material, modify subsequent activities for some students, work on particular ideas with a small group, or pair students who have good strategies with those who are having more difficulty.

Embedded Assessment Activities   Assessment activities embedded in each unit will help you examine specific pieces of student work, figure out what they mean, and provide feedback. From the students' point of view, these assessment activities are no different from any others. Each is a learning experience in and of itself, as well as an opportunity for you to gather evidence about students' mathematical understanding.

The embedded assessment activities sometimes involve writing and reflecting; at other times, a discussion or brief interaction between student and teacher; and in still other instances, the creation and explanation of a product. In most cases, the assessments require that students *show* what they did, *write* or *talk* about it, or do both. Having to explain how they worked through a problem helps students be more focused and clear in their mathematical thinking. It also helps them realize that doing mathematics is a process that may involve tentative starts, revising one's approach, taking different paths, and working through ideas.

Teachers often find the hardest part of assessment to be interpreting their students' work. We provide guidelines to help with that interpretation. If you have used a process approach to teaching writing, the assessment in *Investigations* will seem familiar. For many of the assessment activities, a Teacher Note provides examples of student work and a commentary on what it indicates about student thinking.

Documentation of Student Growth

To form an overall picture of mathematical progress, it is important to document each student's work. Many teachers have students keep their work in folders, notebooks, or journals, and some like to have students summarize their learning in journals at the end of each unit. It's important to document students' progress, and we recommend that you keep a portfolio of selected work for each student, unit by unit, for the entire year. The final activity in each *Investigations* unit, called Choosing Student Work to Save, helps you and the students select representative samples for a record of their work.

This kind of regular documentation helps you synthesize information about each student as a mathematical learner. From different pieces of evidence, you can put together the big picture. This synthesis will be invaluable in thinking about where to go next with a particular child, deciding where more work is needed, or explaining to parents (or other teachers) how a child is doing.

If you use portfolios, you need to collect a good balance of work, yet avoid being swamped with an overwhelming amount of paper. Following are some tips for effective portfolios:

- Collect a representative sample of work, including some pieces that students themselves select for inclusion in the portfolio. There should be just a few pieces for each unit, showing different kinds of work—some assignments that involve writing as well as some that do not.

- If students do not date their work, do so yourself so that you can reconstruct the order in which pieces were done.

- Include your reflections on the work. When you are looking back over the whole year, such comments are reminders of what seemed especially interesting about a particular piece; they can also be helpful to other teachers and to parents. Older students should be encouraged to write their own reflections about their work.

Assessment Overview

There are two places to turn for a preview of the assessment opportunities in each *Investigations* unit. The Assessment Resources column in the unit Overview Chart identifies the Teacher Checkpoints and Assessment activities embedded in each investigation, guidelines for observing the students that appear within classroom activities, and any Teacher Notes and Dialogue Boxes that explain what to look for and what types of student responses you might expect to see in your classroom. Additionally, the section About the Assessment in This Unit gives you a detailed list of questions for each investigation, keyed to the mathematical emphases, to help you observe student growth.

Depending on your situation, you may want to provide additional assessment opportunities. Most of the investigations lend themselves to more frequent assessment, simply by having students do more writing and recording while they are working.

Building on Numbers You Know

Content of This Unit Students explore a wide range of strategies for computation and estimation, especially with multiplication and division. They come to recognize that there are many ways to perform each operation: by reasoning about multiples, especially 10's; by skip counting; by approximating the numbers in a problem to nearby familiar numbers, and then adjusting; or by breaking problems into smaller, more manageable parts. The emphasis throughout is on using what they already know about number relationships and the meaning of the operations. Students also use estimation, both before calculating and after, to check the reasonableness of their results. In an Excursion, students get a sense of larger numbers as they "count" to 1 million by 5000's while putting together a display of a million dots.

Connections with Other Units If you are doing the full-year *Investigations* curriculum in the suggested sequence for grade 5, this is the fifth of nine units. Your class will have already had experience with skip counting, multiplication and division, and the composition of large numbers through their work in the unit *Mathematical Thinking at Grade 5*.

If your school is not using the full-year curriculum, this unit can also be used successfully at grade 6.

Investigations Curriculum ■ Suggested Grade 5 Sequence

Mathematical Thinking at Grade 5 (Introduction and Landmarks in the Number System)

Picturing Polygons (2-D Geometry)

Name That Portion (Fractions, Percents, and Decimals)

Between Never and Always (Probability)

▶ *Building on Numbers You Know* (Computation and Estimation Strategies)

Measurement Benchmarks (Estimating and Measuring)

Patterns of Change (Tables and Graphs)

Containers and Cubes (3-D Geometry: Volume)

Data: Kids, Cats, and Ads (Statistics)

Investigation 1 ■ Exploring Distance Between Numbers

Class Sessions	Activities	Pacing
Session 1 (p. 4) REASONING ABOUT MULTIPLES	Counting by Multiples of 100 Starting at Different Numbers Homework: How Many People Counted? Extension: Counting Backward to 0	minimum 1 hr
Session 2 (p. 12) COUNTING PUZZLES	What's the Counting Number? What's In Between? Homework: What's In Between? Extension: Make Your Own Puzzles Extension: Finding All the Counting Numbers	minimum 1 hr
Sessions 3 and 4 (p. 17) EXPLORING PATTERNS OF MULTIPLES	Sharing Puzzle Solutions Finding Multiples of 21 Making a Tower of Multiples of 21 Using Multiples to Solve Problems Homework: Different Ways to Count Homework: Using Multiples to Solve Problems	minimum 2 hr
Session 5 (p. 27) MULTIPLE TOWERS	Teacher Checkpoint: More Multiple Towers Homework: Multiple Towers	minimum 1 hr
Sessions 6 and 7 (p. 29) THE DIGITS GAME	Introducing the Digits Game Playing the Digits Game Homework: Playing the Digits Game Homework: Problems from the Digits Game	minimum 2 hr
Session 8 (p. 36) SUBTRACTION STRATEGIES	Strategies for Subtraction Teacher Checkpoint: Solving Subtraction Problems Homework: More Digits Game Practice	minimum 1 hr

◔ **Ten-Minute Math** ■ **What Is Likely?**

Mathematical Emphasis

- Skip counting by 2-, 3-, and 4-digit numbers between any two 4- or 5-digit numbers

- Relating repeated addition (or skip counting) to multiplication

- Using skip counting patterns to help solve multiplication and division problems

- Developing, explaining, and comparing strategies for subtracting 4- and 5-digit numbers

- Recording computation strategies using words, numbers, and arithmetic symbols

- Reading, writing, and sequencing 4- and 5-digit numbers

Assessment Resources

Recording Strategies (Teacher Note, p. 8)

What About Notation? (Teacher Note, p. 10)

Reasoning About Skip Counting (Dialogue Box, p. 11)

Counting the Number of Counting Numbers (Dialogue Box, p. 16)

Developing Computation Strategies That Make Sense (Teacher Note, p. 23)

11,000: Even or Odd? (Dialogue Box, p. 25)

How Many 21's Are in 945? (Dialogue Box, p. 26)

Teacher Checkpoint: More Multiple Towers (p. 27)

Observing the Students (p. 31)

Helping Students Think About Subtraction (Teacher Note, p. 34)

Strategies for Subtraction (Dialogue Box, p. 35)

Teacher Checkpoint: Solving Subtraction Problems (p. 37)

Materials

Stick-on notes

Adding machine tape

Tape

Envelopes or rubber bands

Overhead projector

Calculators

Student Sheets 1–9

Teaching resource sheets

Family letter

Investigation 2 ▪ Multiplication and Division Situations

Class Sessions	Activities	Pacing
Sessions 1 and 2 (p. 42) MULTIPLICATION AND DIVISION STRATEGIES	The Ringle, an Imaginary Coin Teacher Checkpoint: Boxes of Markers Homework: Zennies Homework: My Coin Extension: Ringles and Dollars Extension: International Currency	minimum 2 hr
Session 3 (p. 50) DIVISION STRATEGIES	Writing Division Equations Strategies for Division Homework: A Division Problem	minimum 1 hr
Session 4 (p. 57) WHAT SHOULD WE DO WITH THE EXTRAS?	Division Situations Homework: Division Situations	minimum 1 hr
Sessions 5 and 6 (p. 61) RELATING MULTIPLICATION TO DIVISION	Homework Review Multiplying with Cartons of Milk Dividing with Cartons of Milk Writing a Multiplication Situation Writing a Related Division Situation Homework: Mimi's Mystery Multiple Tower Homework: Relating Multiplication and Division Situations Extension: Making Sense of Division Situations	minimum 2 hr
Session 7 (Excursion)* (p. 66) PROBLEMS ABOUT OUR SCHOOL	Supplies for Our School Problems About Things in Our School Homework: A Problem About Large Quantities Extension: How Long Would Our Supplies Last? Extension: Package Sizes	minimum 1 hr

🕐 **Ten-Minute Math ▪ What Is Likely?**

* Excursions can be omitted without harming the integrity or continuity of the unit,
but offer good mathematical work if you have time to include them.

Mathematical Emphasis

- Developing, recording, and comparing strategies for solving multiplication and division problems

- Making sense of remainders

- Understanding relationships between multiplication and division

- Understanding how multiplication and division can represent a variety of situations

- Modeling situations with multiplication, division, and other operations

Assessment Resources

Teacher Checkpoint: Boxes of Markers (p. 44)

Observing the Students (p. 44)

Explaining and Comparing Procedures (Teacher Note, p. 47)

Strategies for Division: How Many Ringles? (Dialogue Box, p. 49)

Remainders, Fractions, and Decimals (Teacher Note, p. 54)

Creating Your Own Multiplication and Division Problems (Teacher Note, p. 55)

Helping Students Think About Operations (Teacher Note, p. 56)

What Should We Do with the Extras? (Teacher Note, p. 60)

Materials

Stick-on notes

Metersticks or rulers

Packages of school supplies

Chart paper

Overhead projector (opt.)

Bulletin board and tabletop surface

Calculators (opt.)

Student Sheets 10–19

Teaching resource sheets

Investigation 3 ■ Ways to Multiply and Divide

Class Sessions	Activities	Pacing
Sessions 1, 2, and 3 (p. 74) MULTIPLICATION CLUSTERS	Making Close Multiplication Estimates Reasoning About Estimates Multiplication Clusters Multiplication Cluster Strategies Making a Problem Cluster Homework: Writing About Multiplication Clusters Homework: Writing Multiplication and Division Situations	minimum 3 hr
Sessions 4, 5, and 6 (p. 83) DIVISION CLUSTERS	Making Close Division Estimates Reasoning About Division Estimates Teacher Checkpoint: Looking at Division Clusters Solving Division Clusters Making a Division Cluster Homework: Division Cluster Problems Homework: A Division Situation Homework: A Cluster of Problems	minimum 3 hr
Sessions 7, 8, and 9 (p. 91) HOW DID I SOLVE IT?	Practice with Estimating Solving a Problem with the First Step Given How Did I Solve It? Sharing Our Solution Strategies Homework: Two Ways Homework: My Own How Did I Solve It? Problem Homework: Another How Did I Solve It? Problem	minimum 3 hr
Session 10 (p. 100) WAYS TO MULTIPLY AND DIVIDE	Assessment: Ways to Multiply and Divide	minimum 1 hr

◔ Ten-Minute Math ■ Quick Images

Mathematical Emphasis

- Developing, explaining, and comparing strategies for estimating and finding exact answers to multiplication and division problems

- Recording strategies for solving multiplication and division problems

- Solving multiplication and division problems in more than one way

- Using relationships between multiplication and division to help solve problems

Assessment Resources

Observing the Students (p. 78)

Observing the Students (p. 79)

Estimation: Emphasizing Strategies (Teacher Note, p. 81)

About the Cluster Problems in This Unit (Teacher Note, p. 82)

Teacher Checkpoint: Looking at Division Clusters (p. 85)

Observing the Students (p. 86)

Thinking About Remainders (Dialogue Box, p. 90)

Choosing Strategies for Computation (Teacher Note, p. 97)

How Can 6×10 Help Us Solve $133 \div 6$? (Dialogue Box, p. 98)

Assessment: Ways to Multiply and Divide (p. 100)

Assessment: Ways to Multiply and Divide (Teacher Note, p. 102)

Materials

Stick-on notes

Overhead projector

Chart paper

Student Sheets 20–30

Teaching resource sheets

Investigation 4 ■ A Million Dots (Excursion)*

Class Sessions	Activities	Pacing
Session 1 (p. 108) ARRAYS OF DOTS	How Many Dots on a Page? Rectangles with 10,000 Dots How Many Dots in All? Homework: Counting Up and Down from 10,000 Extension: Counting to Say Large Numbers Extension: Counting to Say 0 Extension: Factor Pairs of 100,000	minimum 1 hr
Session 2 (p. 115) HOW BIG IS A MILLION?	How Big Is a Million? The Million Dots Display Are We Close to a Million? Homework: Our Million Dots Display Extension: How Long Would It Take to Count to a Million?	minimum 1 hr

* Excursions can be omitted without harming the integrity or continuity of the unit,
  but offer good mathematical work if you have time to include them.

Mathematical Emphasis

- Developing a sense of quantities in the thousands, ten thousands, and hundred thousands

- Using a rectangular array model to represent factor pairs of numbers 10,000 and larger

- Developing a sense of the size of 1,000,000

Assessment Resources

Have We Reached a Million Yet?
(Teacher Note, p. 119)

Materials

Scissors

Tape

Stick-on notes

Calculators

Chart paper (opt.)

Overhead projector

Overhead pens and blank
   transparencies (opt.)

Student Sheets 31–33

Teaching resource sheets

Investigation 5 ▪ Understanding Operations

Class Sessions	Activities	Pacing
Sessions 1 and 2 (p. 122) THE ESTIMATION GAME	Estimating Answers to Difficult Problems Introducing the Estimation Game Playing the Estimation Game Homework: The Estimation Game	minimum 2 hr
Session 3 (p. 128) SOLVING DIFFICULT PROBLEMS	Teacher Checkpoint: How Do We Solve Difficult Problems? Homework: Another Division Problem	minimum 1 hr
Sessions 4, 5, and 6 (p. 130) EXPLORING OPERATIONS	Choice Time: Exploring Operations Discussion: How Did I Solve It? Discussion: How Many Sheets of Paper? Homework: A Multiplication Problem Homework: How Can This Help? Homework: Different Paths to 10,000 Extension: Rewriting Multiplication Expressions Extension: How Many Factors? Extension: Multiplication and Division Practice	minimum 3 hr
Session 7 (p. 139) ASSESSING STUDENTS' UNDERSTANDING	Assessment: Solving Harder Problems How Far to a Million? Choosing Student Work to Save	minimum 1 hr

◑ **Ten-Minute Math** ▪ **Quick Images**

Mathematical Emphasis

- Applying computation strategies to more difficult problems, including both numeric and situational problems

- Developing strategies for estimating answers to difficult multiplication and division problems

- Reading, writing, and sequencing multiples of 5000 up to 1,000,000

- Developing a sense of the size of 1,000,000

- Understanding relationships among the four basic operations

Assessment Resources

Observing the Students (p. 127)

Teacher Checkpoint: How Do We Solve Difficult Problems? (p. 128)

Observing the Students (p. 134)

A Challenging Problem: 37×86 (Dialogue Box, p. 138)

Assessment: Solving Harder Problems (p. 139)

Choosing Student Work to Save (p. 140)

Assessment: Solving Harder Problems (Teacher Note, p. 141)

Materials

Class clock or watches with second hands

Overhead projector

Chart paper

Calculators

Student Sheets 34–41

Teaching resource sheets

Following are the basic materials needed for the activities in this unit. Many of the items can be purchased from the publisher, either individually or in the Teacher Resource Package and the Student Materials Kit for grade 5. Detailed information is available on the *Investigations* order form. To obtain this form, call toll-free 1-800-872-1100 and ask for a Dale Seymour customer service representative.

Calculators: at least 1 per pair

Adding machine tape (1 roll)

Envelopes or rubber bands

Metersticks or rulers: 1 per pair

Tape

Scissors: 1 per pair

Stick-on notes: 3 packages of 3-by-3-inch or larger notes

Overhead projector

Packages of supplies from around the school, in quantity, to use for real-world multiplication and division situations

Chart paper

Class clock or watches with second hands

Bulletin board and tabletop surface

The following materials are provided at the end of this unit as blackline masters. A Student Activity Booklet containing all student sheets and teaching resources needed for individual work is available.

Family Letter (p. 155)

Student Sheets 1–41 (p. 156)

Teaching Resources:

      Numeral Cards, pages 1–3 (p. 165)

      300 Chart (p. 178)

      How Many Dots? (p. 197)

      Million Dots Display Sheet (p. 198)

Practice Pages (p. 213)

Related Children's Literature

Chwast, Seymour, *The 12 Circus Rings*. San Diego: Harcourt Brace, 1993.

McKissak, Patricia C. *A Million Fish . . . More or Less*. New York: Knopf, 1992.

Schwartz, Amy. *Annabelle Swift, Kindergartner*. New York: Orchard, 1988.

Schwartz, David. *If You Made a Million*. New York: Lothrop, Lee and Shepard, 1989.

One emphasis of the *Investigations* curriculum is the development of good number sense. This unit continues that emphasis, focusing on computation and estimation skills—especially in multiplication and division, but also in subtraction and addition. As students solve both numeric and situational problems, they develop a wide range of strategies for both estimating and computing.

Through this unit, students come to see that there are many ways to perform each operation. They learn how these different strategies work; they explore relationships among them; they learn to use them flexibly, with a variety of problems; and they consider which strategies are most efficient for particular problems. Some students will develop many strategies; others just a few. The more strategies students come to understand well, the richer their sense of operations will be and the more choices they will have when solving problems.

As they develop their computation strategies, students find ways to use what they already know and understand well, such as familiar factor pairs, multiples of 10, skip-counting patterns, relationships among numbers, and problems they can solve easily. For example, to solve the problem $674 \div 32$, a student might use one of these strategies:

> *Strategy A:* Since $10 \times 32 = 320$, $20 \times 32 = 640$. Add another 32, and you get 672, so $21 \times 32 = 672$ and $672 \div 32 = 21$. Then 674 is 2 more, so $674 \div 32$ is 21 with 2 left over.

> *Strategy B:* You can break the problem into easier division problems. $320 \div 32 = 10$. Double that, and you get $640 \div 32$ equals 20. You're left with $34 \div 32$. You can think of that as $32 \div 32$ equals 1 and $2 \div 32$ equals $1/16$. Put them together and you get $21 1/16$.

> *Strategy C:* 32 plus 32 is 64. Since two 32's are 64, twenty 32's are 640. Twenty-one 32's are 672, and 674 is 2 more, so the answer is 21 R 2.

Some of the procedures students try will not be efficient at first, and like any algorithm will require practice before students achieve fluency. Part of your role is to evaluate students' procedures, help

them develop more efficient ones, and support them in practicing those procedures until they become fluent.

Students also develop a variety of ways to determine whether their solutions make sense. For example, students might solve a problem in more than one way and cross-check the answers. They might make up a situation using the numbers in the problem: "We have 674 pencils and want to share them equally among the 32 students in the class. How many will each student get? What will we do with the leftovers?" They might interpret the problem in words before solving it: "How many 32's are in 674?" Or they might make an estimate and see if their answer is in the ballpark.

With estimating, as with finding exact solutions, students develop a variety of strategies. One student might estimate the answer to $674 \div 32$ by rounding both numbers up:

> 32 is close to 35 and 674 is close to 700, and there are 20 35's in 700.

Another might arrive at the same answer by rounding both numbers down:

> 32 is close to 30 and 674 is a little more than 600, and there are 20 30's in 600.

A third might reason this way:

> There are twenty 32's in 640, so the answer to $674 \div 32$ is a little more than 20.

Much of students' initial work with multiplication and division in this unit involves problems with numbers such as 21, 36, 75, and 120—numbers that are familiar from earlier work with factors and multiples. When students work with numbers they understand well and know how to take apart and put together in different ways, they can concentrate on the *meaning* of operations and on finding strategies that make sense to them.

As the unit progresses and students' sense of multiplication and division grows, they apply their strategies to problems involving larger or less familiar numbers, such as 29, 89, 254, 767, and 1904. By the end of the unit, students have ways to solve a wide range of difficult computation problems. In an optional Excursion, students create a display of a million dots and develop a better sense of 6- and 7-digit numbers. This provides a foundation for computation with larger numbers.

The communication of students' thinking and reasoning plays a crucial role throughout this unit. Students learn to keep careful records of the steps they take in solving problems, and they learn to explain their strategies so that others can understand them. As students share their strategies verbally and in writing, they learn to clarify their thinking, to use mathematical notation correctly and unambiguously, to compare strategies and find relationships among them, and to listen to and learn from their peers.

One goal of this unit is that students develop both mental approaches and paper-and-pencil strategies they can rely on for solving problems they will encounter in daily life. A skill they will need is knowing how to break problems into parts, or into convenient subproblems that they can solve mentally or on paper. Therefore, many times in this unit students are asked to solve problems *without* calculators. At other times, in this unit and throughout the school year, students can be encouraged to use calculators as one of many problem-solving tools.

Keep in mind that in order to use calculators appropriately, students need a strong understanding of the four operations and of the number system, so that they can select suitable calculations and determine what a reasonable result might be. As students develop facility with a variety of strategies for computation, they will learn to move fluently between calculators and mental arithmetic and between mental arithmetic and paper-and-pencil methods as they choose approaches for solving problems.

At the beginning of each investigation, the Mathematical Emphasis section tells you what is most important for students to learn about during that investigation. Many of these understandings and processes are difficult and complex. Students gradually learn more and more about each idea over many years of schooling. Individual students will begin and end the unit with different levels of knowledge and skill, but all will gain a deeper understanding of the four basic operations and how to perform them.

Throughout the *Investigations* curriculum, there are many opportunities for ongoing daily assessment as you observe, listen to, and interact with students at work. In this unit, you will find five Teacher Checkpoints:

Investigation 1, Session 5:
More Multiple Towers (p. 27)

Investigation 1, Session 8:
Solving Subtraction Problems (p. 37)

Investigation 2, Sessions 1–2:
Boxes of Markers (p. 44)

Investigation 3, Sessions 4–6:
Looking at Division Clusters (p. 85)

Investigation 5, Session 3:
How Do We Solve Difficult Problems? (p. 128)

This unit also has two embedded assessment activities:

Investigation 3, Session 10:
Ways to Multiply and Divide (p. 100)

Investigation 5, Session 7:
Solving Harder Problems (p. 139)

In addition, you can use almost any activity in this unit to assess your students' needs and strengths. Listed below are questions to help you focus your observation in each investigation. You may want to keep track of your observations for each student to help you plan your curriculum and monitor students' growth. Suggestions for documenting student growth can be found in the section About Assessment.

Investigation 1: Exploring Distance Between Numbers

■ Are students able to skip count by 2-, 3-, and 4-digit numbers? How comfortable are they with skip counting between any two 4- and 5-digit numbers? How do they make predictions about counting sequences?

■ Do students relate skip counting and multiplication? Do they see multiplication as repeated addition?

■ Do students use skip-counting patterns to solve multiplication and division problems?

■ How do students solve subtraction problems with 4- and 5-digit numbers? Do they choose a

particular strategy depending on the problem? How do they record and explain their strategies? Do they compare their strategies with those of other students? Do they ever adopt another's strategy?

■ How do students record their strategies for solving computation problems? Do they use words? numbers? arithmetic symbols? some combination of these? Are they solving and recording problems in more than one way? Do they find some strategies to be easier than others?

■ How comfortable are students with reading, writing, and sequencing 4- and 5-digit numbers?

Investigation 2: Multiplication and Division Situations

■ What strategies are students developing for solving multiplication and division problems? Do they choose a particular strategy based on the problem? How do they record and compare their work? Do they ever adopt another's method?

■ How do students make sense of and deal with remainders? Do they describe the remainder in the context of the problem?

■ What relationships are students finding and using between multiplication and division? How comfortable are they using multiplication to solve a division situation or a problem presented in division notation?

■ Do students understand that multiplication and division notation can represent a variety of situations? Are they able to give examples of problems for which you would use multiplication, and others where division would be used?

■ How do students model situations with multiplication? division? other operations?

Investigation 3: Ways to Multiply and Divide

■ How do students make estimates to multiplication and division problems? On what do they base their estimates? Do they use landmarks or familiar numbers? Are their estimates reasonable? What strategies do they use to find exact answers to those problems? Can students refine their estimation strategy to solve a problem exactly? Are students able to explain their strategies? Are they comparing these strategies with other students'?

- How are students recording their strategies for solving multiplication and division problems? Can you follow students' strategies by looking at their work?

- Are students comfortable solving multiplication and division problems in more than one way? Are they keeping track of the steps used to solve the problems? How are they making sense of and recording remainders?

- Do students recognize relationships between multiplication and division? Do they use those relationships to solve problems?

Investigation 4: A Million Dots

- Are students developing a sense of the relative size of 1000, 10,000, and 100,000?

- How comfortable are students with a rectangular array model for representing factor pairs of numbers 10,000 and larger? What strategies did they use to make the rectangles?

- Are students beginning to develop a sense of the relative size of larger powers of 10? What strategies are they using to estimate how many rectangular arrays or sheets it will take to reach one million dots?

Investigation 5: Understanding Operations

- How do students solve more difficult numeric problems? Situational problems? Do they apply strategies they've developed over the course of the unit?

- What strategies are students developing for estimating answers to difficult multiplication and division problems? What information or familiar numbers do they use? Are their estimates reasonable?

- How comfortable are students reading, writing, and sequencing multiples of 5,000 up to 1,000,000?

- Are students developing a sense of the size of 1,000,000? What strategies are they using to estimate how many more dots it will take to reach one million?

- How flexibly do students use the four operations? How comfortably do they move among and relate the four operations?

In the *Investigations* curriculum, mathematical vocabulary is introduced naturally during the activities. We don't ask students to learn definitions of new terms; rather, they come to understand such words as *factor* or *area* or *symmetry* by hearing them used frequently in discussion as they investigate new concepts. This approach is compatible with current theories of second-language acquisition, which emphasize the use of new vocabulary in meaningful contexts while students are actively involved with objects, pictures, and physical movement.

Listed below are some key words used in this unit that will not be new to most English speakers at this age level, but may be unfamiliar to students with limited English proficiency. You will want to spend additional time working on these words with your students who are learning English. If your students are working with a second-language teacher, you might enlist your colleague's aid in familiarizing students with these words, before and during this unit. In the classroom, look for opportunities for students to hear and use these words. Activities you can use to present the words are given in the appendix, Vocabulary Support for Second-Language Learners (p. 151).

strategy, strategies   Throughout the unit, students are asked to share their own strategies—ideas and approaches—for solving computation problems. They discover that there are many different strategies, including ways of thinking that are quite different from conventional algorithms.

situation   Students relate multiplication and division problems to real-life situations with various objects. They discover that the type of division situation can affect what we do with the remainder.

imaginary, coin, dollar, worth   Students consider two imaginary coins, a ringle (worth 21 cents) and a zenny (worth 3 cents), and use multiplication and division to determine how many of each there are in a dollar.

share (divide) equally, extra   Division is related to situations in which we share things equally into a certain number of groups, and determine what to do with the extra (remainder).

Multicultural Extensions for All Students

Whenever possible, encourage students to share words, objects, customs, or any aspects of daily life from their own cultures and backgrounds that are relevant to the activities in this unit. For example, when students are making up problem situations that represent multiplication or division situations, encourage them to write problems that reflect their particular culture—foods, games, team sports, coin values, and so forth.

Investigations

Exploring Distance Between Numbers

What Happens

Session 1: Reasoning About Multiples Students begin this unit by skip counting by 25's, 50's, and 100's, recalling earlier experiences they may have had with multiples. They share and record strategies for making predictions about the numbers they will say when they count.

Session 2: Counting Puzzles Students solve two kinds of puzzles based on skip-counting sequences, What's the Counting Number? and What's In Between? They draw on their knowledge of factors and multiples as they find possible numbers to match each set of clues.

Sessions 3 and 4: Exploring Patterns of Multiples The class builds a Multiple Tower on a long strip of adding machine tape, listing multiples of 21 in order and looking for patterns in the sequence. They use the patterns they find to solve multiplication and division problems involving multiples of 21.

Session 5: Multiple Towers Students work in pairs to find the multiples of 2-, 3-, and 4-digit numbers. They record each sequence on a Multiple Tower and look for patterns.

Sessions 6 and 7: The Digits Game Students play the Digits Game, using randomly drawn digits to make numbers as close as possible to a target 4- or 5-digit number. Their score for each round is the difference between the number they make and the target. As they play, they develop strategies for finding the score without using a standard subtraction algorithm.

Session 8: Subtraction Strategies As a class, students share strategies for finding the difference between two 4- or 5-digit numbers. Then, they work individually to find and write about different ways to solve two subtraction problems.

Mathematical Emphasis

- Skip counting by 2-, 3-, and 4-digit numbers between any two 4- or 5-digit numbers
- Relating repeated addition (or skip counting) to multiplication
- Using skip-counting patterns to help solve multiplication and division problems
- Developing, explaining, and comparing strategies for subtracting 4- and 5-digit numbers
- Recording computation strategies using words, numbers, and arithmetic symbols
- Reading, writing, and sequencing 4- and 5-digit numbers

For multiples of 123, the pattern in the ones repeats after every ten 123's.

What to Plan Ahead of Time

Materials

- Stick-on notes: one 3-by-3-inch package for the class (Sessions 2–4)
- Adding machine tape: 1 roll (Sessions 3–5)
- Tape: 1–2 rolls to share (Session 5)
- Envelopes or rubber bands for storing Numeral Cards: 1 per pair, and 1 for transparent set (Sessions 6–7)
- Overhead projector (Sessions 6–8)
- Calculators: at least 1 per pair. **Note:** For certain activities in this unit, students are *not* to use calculators; these are clearly specified. For all other activities, it is assumed students will have calculators available to use as needed.
- Chart paper (Sessions 2–4; Session 8, optional)

Other Preparation

- Duplicate student sheets and teaching resources (located at the end of this unit) in the following quantities. If you have Student Activity Booklets, copy only those items marked with an asterisk.

For Session 1

Family letter* (p. 155): 1 per student. Sign and date before copying.

Student Sheet 1, How Many People Counted? (p. 156): 1 per student (homework)

For Session 2

Student Sheet 2, What's the Counting Number? (p. 157): 1 per student

Student Sheet 3, What's In Between? (p. 158): 1 per student

For Sessions 3 and 4

Student Sheet 4, Different Ways to Count (p. 159): 1 per student (homework)

Student Sheet 5, Using Multiples to Solve Problems (p. 160): 1 per student (homework)

For Session 5

Student Sheet 6, Multiple Towers (p. 161): 1 per student (homework)

For Sessions 6–7

Student Sheet 7, How to Play the Digits Game (p. 162): 1–2 per student (optional 1 for class, and 1 for homework)

Student Sheet 8, Digits Game Score Sheet (p. 163): 1–2 per student (1 for class, and optional 1 for homework) and 1 transparency*

Student Sheet 9, Problems from the Digits Game (p. 164): 1 per student (homework)

Numeral Cards (p. 165): 1 set per pair (if possible, duplicate on card stock), 1 transparency of each sheet,* and 1 set per student (homework, optional)

- For making Multiple Towers in Sessions 3–5, cut adding machine tape into strips at least 6 feet long to provide 1 strip per pair, plus a few extras.
- Cut apart the Numeral Cards and wrap each set with a rubber band or store it in an envelope. You might enlist student help outside of class. Also cut apart the transparent Numeral Cards to use for demonstration on the overhead. (Sessions 6–8)

Reasoning About Multiples

Materials

- Family letter (1 per student)
- Student Sheet 1 (1 per student, homework)

What Happens

Students begin this unit by skip counting by 25's, 50's, and 100's, recalling earlier experiences they may have had with multiples. They share and record strategies for making predictions about the numbers they will say when they count. Student work focuses on:

- skip counting by 2- and 3- digit numbers that are multiples of 25, 50, or 100
- reasoning about relationships among numbers
- recording computational strategies using words, numbers, and arithmetic symbols

Counting by Multiples of 100

If you are using the full-year *Investigations* curriculum for grade 5, students will be familiar with counting around the class, skip counting as they take turns saying the next number in the series. In *Mathematical Thinking at Grade 5,* the students counted around by 25's, 50's, and 100's. Review the process here, asking the class to count by 100's: the first person says "100," the second says "200," and so on. Rather than counting in a particular order, by seating, ask for volunteers to give the next number in the count. Stop the count at about 1200 to look back.

We're up to 1200 counting by 100. How many students have counted so far? How do you know?

Encourage the class to figure this out without actually counting heads. As students give their explanations, record their methods on the board. Label each strategy with a different letter so that, during discussion, students have an easy way to refer to them.

The **Teacher Note,** Recording Strategies (p. 8), discusses several possible strategies and the similarities students may notice among them. It also demonstrates how keeping a record of students' strategies can help them learn to communicate their ideas more clearly. Refer to another **Teacher Note,** What About Notation? (p. 10), for suggestions on varying the mathematical notation you use as you record students' ideas.

If we keep counting by 100's, what number will we end with if everyone in the class says one number in the count?

Again, encourage students to explain how they can find the answer without actually doing the counting; record their predictions and methods on the board.

Let's check your predictions. We'll count by 100's again, this time going in order around the class.

Explain the order in which students will count, so that everyone understands when his or her turn will be. As students count, write the first few numbers they say on the board. When everyone in the class has counted, ask students to compare their predictions to the actual ending number.

As students count, they may vary in the way they say 4-digit numbers: as hundreds (12 hundred), or as thousands and hundreds (1 thousand 2 hundred). Either way of saying the numbers is correct, although people do not usually say "10 hundred" for 1 thousand or "20 hundred" for 2 thousand. If the number names seem to confuse anyone, ask students to find different ways of saying the same number and to explain their reasoning.

Making Predictions About Counting Sequences Repeat this skip-counting activity with other numbers.

Now let's try counting by 200's. If everyone in class says just one number, what number will we end with?

As before, students make their predictions without actually doing the counting and describe their prediction strategies to the class. Encourage them to relate the strategies they are using to those already listed on the board (from counting by 100's).

Then, as students count around the class by 200's, stop one or more times partway through to look back on how many students have counted so far. As they finish, students compare the actual ending number with their predictions.

Continue the activity with numbers such as 50, 250, and 1000. Encourage students to use the ending number from an earlier count to help them predict the ending number of another count. For example, students might use the results of counting around the class by 200's and by 50's to predict the ending number for counting by 250's.

Starting at Different Numbers

So far, we've been starting our counts at 0. Suppose we started with a different number. What if we start at 1000 and count by 25's? What's the first number you would say? the next number?

Some students may think that the first number in the count will be 1000. Compare the process to counting from 0. When we begin counting at 0, the first person says 25; so when we begin at 1000, the first person says 1025. In the **Dialogue Box,** Reasoning About Skip Counting (p. 11), the students in one class talk about where to begin skip-counting sequences.

As students count around the class by 25's, beginning at 1000, record on the board the first few numbers they say. As before, stop partway through the count to ask how many students have counted so far and how they know. Ask students to relate their thinking to the strategies recorded on the board.

What if we start at 1000 and count backward by 25?

Students count around the class backward by 25's (starting at 1000), and by other numbers of their choosing. Recording the first few numbers they say will help establish the pattern.

To provide more practice with multiples and skip-counting patterns, plan a time in another math class (or outside of math) for students to count around the class both forward and backward, beginning at numbers other than 0. For example, they might count by 200's beginning at 500; count by 70's beginning at 1200; or count backward by 30's beginning at 1000.

Session 1 Follow-Up

How Many People Counted? Send home the family letter (p. 155) or the *Investigations* at Home booklet, along with Student Sheet 1, How Many People Counted? This sheet extends the class activity by presenting similar "counting around the class" situations. Students are to determine how many people have counted in each case without actually doing the counting themselves.

Homework

Counting Backward to 0 Once students have had some experience counting backward by different numbers, they choose their own starting number for their counts and find numbers that, counting backward, lead them exactly to 0. For example, suppose they pick the starting number 12,000. If they count backward by 600, they will land on 0, but if they count backward by 700, they will not. For any given starting number, how many different counting numbers can they find that will lead to 0?

Extension

Name _____ Date _____

Student Sheet 1

How Many People Counted?

Find your answers without counting.

1. Mr. Lu's class counted by 25's. The first person said 25, the second said 50, and the third said 75.

   How many people counted to get to 300? How do you know?

   The answer is 12 because there are 4 people in 100.
   $\overset{4}{100}\ \overset{8}{200}\ \overset{12}{300}$

2. Ms. Patterson's class counted by 20's. The first person said 20, the second said 40, and the third said 60.

   How many people counted to get to 300? How do you know?

   The answer is 15 because there are 5 people in each 100.
   $\overset{5}{100}\ \overset{10}{200}\ \overset{15}{300}$

3. Mrs. Gomez's class counted by 10's, starting at 100. The first person said 110, the second said 120, and the third said 130.

   How many people counted to get to 300? How do you know?

   20 counted because there are 10 people in each 100.
   $\overset{10}{200}\ \overset{20}{300}$

© Dale Seymour Publications®   156   *Investigation 1 • Session 1*
Building on Numbers You Know

As students explain their strategies for solving a problem, recording their approaches on the board can be a valuable teaching tool. The process helps students learn from one another as they clarify their thinking, compare strategies, make generalizations about strategies, and learn to record their strategies themselves. The examples from one teacher's experience illustrate the benefits of recording.

Explaining Their Ideas Clearly   The students in this class (there are 28) are counting by 100's. The teacher stops them in the middle of the count and asks them to predict the ending number of their count. As students give their predictions and explanations, the teacher records their ideas on the board, using a shorthand of numbers, arithmetic symbols, and words. Each strategy is labeled with a letter, so that students can refer to the strategies more easily as they discuss them. As the discussion unfolds, the teacher records five strategies as shown below.

Amy Lynn: We have seven tables of 4 people. Each table is 400, so I added up 400 seven times and got 2800.

The teacher records what she understands to be Amy Lynn's strategy and labels it A.

A. 400 at a table   7 tables
$$400+400+400...[7 \text{ times in all}]=2800$$

B. 400 at a table, count by 400
$$400, 800...[7 \text{ times in all}], 2800$$

C. 28 <u>ones</u> is 28, so 28 <u>hundreds</u> is 2800

D. $100 \times 28 = 2800$

E. $100+100+100 [28 \text{ times in all}]=2800$

Is this what you did? Did I get your strategy down?

Amy Lynn: Sort of, but I didn't really add the 400's like that.

How did you get up to 2800?

Amy Lynn: I went, 400, 800... Oh, I mean I counted by 400—like I added it up each time, not all at the end.

The teacher records what she now understands to be Amy Lynn's strategy, and labels it B.

Amy Lynn: That's what I did—that's how I thought of it.

Would that other way work?

Amy Lynn: Yes, that's like what I did, except the first way you don't add it up until the end.

As happened with Amy Lynn, recording what students say can show them the importance of expressing their ideas carefully and unambiguously, so that others don't interpret their words in a way that was not intended.

Comparing Strategies   After the teacher records three more strategies, she asks students to look at the list and talk about any similarities they notice among the strategies.

Toshi: In A and E, you're adding all those things up, but A is easier because you already added them into 4's.

Antonio: B is like A, except you're adding as you go along.

Corey: In D and E, you're going one hundred 28 times, either way.

Any time several strategies have been recorded, students should begin comparing them. Which strategies accomplish the same thing in a different number of steps? Which are easier to use? Which use different operations to do the same thing? These questions can help students select the strategies that work best for them.

Continued on next page

Making Generalizations After students finish counting by 100's, the teacher asks them to predict what number they would end up on if they count by 200's.

Sofia: Instead of 400 per table, it's 800. It's the same number of people at each table as last time, but they say double what they said before, so it's 5600—twice what we got last time.

Is that like any of the methods on the board already?

Sofia: It's like B and A— you can just think of how many at a table instead of adding up each number people say. Like you're making groups first. The first time the groups were 400. This time, the groups are 800.

Here, the list of strategies for solving one problem helped solve another problem. Finding relationships among strategies used to solve different problems can help students think of strategies as general approaches, rather than just ways to solve a single problem.

Using Mathematical Notation When you record students' strategies, you are modeling correct mathematical writing: writing equations, using a variety of notations for the same operation, and using both horizontal and vertical formats for presenting problems. As students become more comfortable recording their own strategies, invite them to do so at the board. This gives you the chance to see how students interpret one another's mathematical writing and whether they recognize appropriate ways of writing mathematical expressions. For example, are the expressions on each side of an equals sign really equivalent?

Consider the following example: The teacher has just asked students to predict the ending number if they counted around the class by 250's. Trevor comes to the board to explain and record his approach.

Trevor: Since 5×50 is 250, you can multiply 1400—that's the number we got when we counted by 50's—by 5.

$$50 \times 5 = 250$$
$$50 \times 28 = 1400 \times 5 = 7000$$

What do you think? Can someone put Trevor's strategy into their own words?

Kevin: You can times 1400 by 5 because 50×5 is 250.

Jasmine: Since 250 is 5 times 50, the answer is 5 times more than 1400. Wait... Don't you need to go 250×28 instead of 50×28? There's 28 in the class and we're counting by 250, not 50.

Trevor: That shows how we got 1400. We did 50×28 equals 1400, and then we multiplied by 5 and that equals 7000.

Let's look carefully at how we can record that. What does it mean when you use an equals sign?

Jasmine: All the parts need to equal up to the same thing. You can't put 50×28 in there. It's not the same as 7000 and 1400×5.

How else could we show that?

Mei-Ling: You can break it up. First do 50 times 28 equals 1400. Then you do 1400 times 5 is 7000. And that equals 250×28.

Mei-Ling goes to the board and records the strategy this way:

$$50 \times 28 = 1400$$
$$1400 \times 5 = 7000 = 250 \times 28$$

It is important that your students learn to recognize, interpret, and use the standard forms and symbols for addition, subtraction, multiplication, and division, both on paper and on the calculator. These include:

$$497 + 548 \qquad \begin{array}{r} 497 \\ + 548 \\ \hline \end{array}$$

$$2015 - 598 \qquad \begin{array}{r} 2015 \\ - 598 \\ \hline \end{array}$$

$$\begin{array}{r} 32 \\ \times 18 \\ \hline \end{array} \qquad 32 \times 18$$

$$242 \div 12 \qquad 12\,)\overline{\,242\,} \qquad \frac{242}{12}$$

What does each form mean? Students must first understand *what is being asked* in a problem that is written in standard notation. They can then devise their own way to find an answer. Notation is an efficient way to record a problem and its answer. It is *not* a directive to carry out a particular procedure, or a signal to forget everything you ever knew about the relationships between the numbers in the problem.

Your students may come to you already believing that when they see a problem written in the traditional, vertical subtraction format, they must carry out the borrowing algorithm. Instead, we want students to recognize that they can use what they know about the two numbers in order to solve the problem. Here are two examples of reasoning based on good number sense:

$$\begin{array}{r} 2015 \\ - 598 \\ \hline \end{array}$$

Student 1:
I found the answer [1417] by adding 2 + 400 + 1000 + 15. I added 2 to 598 to get 600. Then I added 400 to get 1000. Then 1000 to get 2000. Then the last 15.

Student 2:
I found the answer [1417] by adding 1000 + 100 + 100 + 100 + 100 + 10 + 7. Start with 598. Add 1000 to get 1598. Add 100 to get to 1698. Keep adding 100's to get to 1998. Then add 10 to get to 2008. Then add 7 more.

Similarly, when students see a division problem like $12\,)\overline{\,242\,}$ they may try to carry out a standard long division algorithm, rather than reasoning about relationships between 12 and 242. We want students to look at the whole problem and to recognize that they can find the answer by using what they already know. For example:

Student 1:
I know that 10×12 is 120. So, 20×12 is 240, and $240 \div 12$ is 20. 242 is 2 more, so $242 \div 12$ is 20, with 2 left over.

Student 2:
$12 \times 2 = 24$, so 12×20 is 240 and $240 \div 12$ is 20. $241 \div 12$ is 20 with 1 left over, and $242 \div 12$ is 20 with 2 left over.

Throughout this unit, while you help students read and use standard notation, keep the emphasis on understanding the problem and using good number sense to find the answer.

Reasoning About Skip Counting

Students are counting around the class by 100's. When the count reaches 1300, the teacher stops the class and asks how they can find out how many people have counted.

Amir: Ten times 100 is 1000, and 1300 is 300 more, so 3 more. That's 13 in all.

Cara: I did 1300 divided by 100 is 13.

Leon: I'm not sure if you can just divide it like that. Did we start counting at 0 or 100?

Good question. Did we start out at 0 or 100?

Mei-Ling: We started at 100. We went 100, 200, 300, up to 1300.

What would be different if we started at 0?

Leon: Then 14 people would have counted, because the first person would say 0, and then you'd need 13 people more to get up to 1300.

Do you think we should start at 0 when we count around the class?

Sofia: No, you start at 100. Say we had 100 dollar bills and we were handing them out to everyone in the class. The first person would get 100 dollars, and they say 100 because they *have* 100 dollars. Then the second person would get another 100 dollars and that person would say 200. And it would keep going up by 100 dollars. You'd only have 0 before you started and you wouldn't be saying any numbers then, so 100 is the first you say.

Leon: You sort of start at 0. You start with a clean slate. No one has anything. But you don't say it. That's before you started counting.

Cara: I think it can go either way. It depends. When you count real things, you start counting when you have something. But when you're counting numbers maybe it's different.

Leon: I'm not sure. When you count by 2's, you go 2, 4, 6, 8... You don't say 0.

Sofia: It's the same with numbers and real things. Say you're counting by 2's. *[She goes to the board and draws six lines.]* You'd go 1, 2 *[she circles the first two lines].*

That's your first 2. If you're counting by 2's, you don't say anything until you have your first 2. Here's your second 2 *[circling the second pair].* So that's 2, 4. And here's your third 2 *[circling the last pair].* That's 2, 4, 6. You're building up groups of 2 things. You say a number once you have a group.

Zach: It's the multiples of 2. Like when you're counting by 2's, the first person is 1×2, or 2. The next person is 2×2, or 4. The next person is 3×2, or 6. The number of people that count are the number of multiples.

Leon: If you said 0 like I thought you did, the first person says 0, the second person says 2, and the third person says 4. It would push the numbers up. You'd say 2 less than you need to.

How does this help us think about our original question? When we count by 100's, do we start at 0 or 100?

Trevor: You can be counting by 2's or 100's or anything. You don't say where you start. You say what you have after you get your first thing, like your first 2 or your first 100.

Sofia: If you're regular counting, you say 100 first, because that's your first 100. If you say 0, it's like you're starting at negative 100. Then you'll be up to 0 when you get your first 100.

Cara: If you start at 200, you say 300 first because that's what you have when you get your first 100. If you start at 1000, you'd say 1100 first because that's what you'd have after you get 100.

Leon: I have a way you could start at 0 and say 0 first. You can count by 0. And the next number would be 0, too.

Counting Puzzles

Materials

- Student Sheet 2 (1 per student)
- Student Sheet 3 (1 per student)
- Stick-on notes
- Chart paper

What Happens

Students solve two kinds of puzzles based on skip-counting sequences, What's the Counting Number? and What's In Between? They draw on their knowledge of factors and multiples as they find possible numbers to match each set of clues. Student work focuses on:

- approximating 4- and 5-digit numbers to the nearest multiple of 100 or 1000
- developing strategies for determining and comparing distance between numbers (such as skip counting, mental arithmetic, reasoning about number size)
- skip counting between any two 4- or 5-digit numbers
- finding and ordering numbers in between two other numbers

Activity

What's the Counting Number?

Distribute Student Sheet 2, What's the Counting Number? Students may work in pairs but complete their own sheet. Each puzzle has several answers. Without actually doing the counting, students are to find three numbers that will work for each puzzle.

❖ **Tip for the Linguistically Diverse Classroom** Pair second-language learners with English-proficient students who can read aloud the puzzles. They might add simple pictures and symbols over words like these: *started, stopped, between, more than, fewer than*. For example, students familiar with the alphabet might use *A* for *started, Z* for *stopped*, and *M* for *between*, with the mathematical signs > for *more than* and < for *fewer than*.

As you observe students working on this activity, consider the following questions:

- What strategies do they have for finding numbers without actually doing the counting?
- Do they draw on their knowledge of factors and multiples?
- If the count does not start at 0, do they find the difference between the start and finish number? What strategies do they use to do this?

■ Do they recognize that as the size of the counting number increases, the number of times they say a number decreases? For example, counting by 1's from 0 to 100, we say 100 numbers, but counting by 25's, we say only 4 numbers.

For students who are having difficulty, suggest they think of a way to use what they know about *factors* and *multiples* to help them solve the puzzles. (The counting numbers are factors of the difference between the starting number and the ending number.)

As students finish the five puzzles, they compare their answers with another pair. Those who want a further challenge can find *all* the answers to each problem, or they can figure out *how many* answers each puzzle has.

Sharing Solutions As students are working on this activity, post a sheet of chart paper divided into five sections, one for each puzzle. Each pair chooses a puzzle and records one or two answers on this sheet. Students also check the other answers classmates have written on the sheet. If they disagree with any, they post a stick-on note with a question mark and a brief indication of why they disagree. Bring the class together to discuss any disagreement. The **Dialogue Box,** Counting the Number of Counting Numbers (p. 16), shows how sharing their answers to these puzzles helped students in one class better understand the relationship between the *size* of the counting number and the number of numbers said during a count.

What's In Between?

Give each student a copy of Student Sheet 3, What's In Between? Each of the six puzzles here has at least three answers. Students may work alone or with a partner.

❖ **Tip for the Linguistically Diverse Classroom** Take the same approach suggested for Student Sheet 2. Students may want to add rebuses for the words *odd* (perhaps 1, 3, 5, 7...) and *even* (2, 4, 6, 8...). Students might underline or circle the number in each choice that is closer to the mystery number:

This number is closer to 2000 than it is to 1000.

As students begin work on the first puzzle, circulate quickly to observe how they are finding numbers. Students who are having no difficulty may continue working on the puzzles in class and finish them for homework.

Practice with Finding Numbers In Between If some students are having difficulty with the first puzzle, call them together to review reading, writing, and ordering 4- and 5-digit numbers. For example, ask students to name a few numbers between 4000 and 6000. Record four or five responses on the board. Encourage some responses that are not multiples of 100, such as 4957.

Students then put these numbers in order, from smallest to largest. When everyone agrees on the order, record it in sequence. For example:

4000　　4200　　4957　　5073　　5999　　**6000**

Ask students to explain how they know which of the numbers in the sequence are closer to 4000 than to 6000, and which are closer to 6000. Possible responses might include these:

- 5000 is halfway between 4000 and 6000, so anything more than 5000 is closer to 6000.
- 6000 and 4000 are 2000 apart. Half of that is 1000. 4200 and 4957 are less than 1000 away from 4000, so they're closer to 4000. The other numbers are more than 1000 away from 4000, so they're closer to 6000.

You might also ask students to find and order numbers between two multiples of 10,000 (such as 20,000 and 30,000); between two 4-digit multiples of 50 (such as 4950 and 5150); or between two 5-digit multiples of 100 (such as 12,500 and 12,600).

What's In Between?   Students complete the puzzles they began in class on Student Sheet 3, What's In Between? Students who are ready for more challenge can try to find *how many* answers each puzzle has.

Make Your Own Puzzles   Students make up their own What's In Between? puzzles to trade with each other. Specify one answer:

> One answer to your puzzle is 5000. Your puzzle must have at least two other answers.

If you think it is necessary, you might provide a template like this for students to complete:

> This number is between _____ and _____.
>
> You say this number if you start at _____ and count by _____.
>
> This number is closer to _____ than to _____ .

Students find at least three answers to their puzzle, and they write about how they created it. They trade puzzles with a partner, each finding three answers and explaining his or her solution process. After students have shared in pairs, you might record all their clues on chart paper. This can help students recognize the wide variety of clues that can be used to create a puzzle that has 5000 as one answer.

> In Between Puzzle
>
> This number is between 4000 and 6500.
> You say this number if you start at 4100 and count by 150.
> This number is closer to 4000 than to 6500.
> This number is a multiple of 100.

Finding All the Counting Numbers   Challenge students to find all the ways to count between two given numbers. You might present starting and ending numbers like these:

0 to 2000	0 to 60,000	500 to 1000	9900 to 10,000
1000 to 47,000	9288 to 9488	2637 to 9375	

Counting the Number of Counting Numbers

Solving the puzzles on Student Sheet 2, What's the Counting Number? and sharing solution strategies can help students explore connections between skip counting and factor pairs. In the following discussion, students explain their strategies for solving puzzle 1. They draw on their understanding of factor pairs as they reason about relationships between the counting numbers and the number of numbers in a skip-counting sequence. The clues to puzzle 1 are: "I started counting at 0. I stopped counting at 180. I said fewer than 12 numbers when I counted."

Students have recorded their answers on a piece of chart paper.

There are a couple of question marks on the answers to puzzle 1. Let's hear from someone who had a question.

Julie: Well, 165 is listed, but 165 × 1 doesn't work, and 165 × 2 is way over.

Tai: Neither does 150 or 120. There's nothing over 90 except 180.

Desiree: Corey and I wrote down those numbers. First we did 12 goes into 180, because the question is fewer than 12 numbers. That goes in 15 times. So we needed numbers bigger than 15, so we did 15 × 2 is 30, that's one of the answers, then 15 × 3 is 45, and then we kept going on that way.

Antonio: The only way to get factors is to get something smaller than that number that goes into it. Like 90 is smaller than 180, and it goes into it. And 105 is smaller, but it doesn't go into it.

Julie: We started from 180. We did divide 180 by 1 is 1, you count one time. That's not above 12. Divide by 2, 90. Divide by 3, 60, and keep going on. We tried 1, 2, 3, 4, 5, 6, 7, 8, 9, 10, 11 and found which ones go into 180.

Marcus: You start with anything that's a factor of 180, and then if it goes in less than 12 times, you can use it. First we tried 6 to see how many times it went in, and it was too high. So then we tried bigger numbers. We couldn't do any smaller numbers because you'd count too many numbers.

Rachel: We started like Desiree. First we thought that any multiple of 15 would work. We listed them all, and then we found that only some of them do.

Corey: Oh, I see what happened. First we found a number that would go in 12 times, and that was 15, but we couldn't do 15. We knew it would have to be a bigger number than that. Then we tried 15 × 2, and 30 goes in 6 times. You say 30, 60, 90, 120, 150, and 180. Then we tried 45, and it goes in 4 times— 45, 90, 135, 180, and then we just wrote down the rest. We thought those bigger numbers go in fewer times, but now I see they don't all hit 180. You need to see what goes into 180, too.

Julie: There's a way you can check. When you find a number that goes 4 times [in this case, 45], you can't have more than 3 larger counting numbers. There might be one number that goes in 3 times [60], one that goes in 2 times [90], and then 180, but you can't have more than that.

Exploring Patterns of Multiples

What Happens

The class builds a Multiple Tower on a long strip of adding machine tape, listing multiples of 21 in order and looking for patterns in the sequence. They use the patterns they find to solve multiplication and division problems involving multiples of 21. Student work focuses on:

- finding patterns in sequences of multiples

- relating repeated addition (or skip counting) to multiplication

- using skip-counting patterns to help solve multiplication and division problems

Materials

- Students' completed Student Sheet 3

- Adding machine tape cut into 6-foot strip

- Stick-on notes

- Student Sheet 4 (1 per student, homework)

- Student Sheet 5 (1 per student, homework)

- Calculators

- Chart paper

Activity

Sharing Puzzle Solutions

In pairs, students compare their answers to Student Sheet 3, What's In Between? As you did for the What's the Counting Number? puzzles, post a chart, divided into six sections, where pairs record one or two answers to one of the puzzles. As students check each other's answers, they post stick-on notes to indicate any disagreement. Use these as a basis for class discussion.

Some puzzles have so many answers, it is unlikely students will list them all. In these cases, encourage students to characterize the answers and to estimate how many there are in all.

Do you think we have listed all the answers to puzzle 6? How do you know? If I gave you a number, could you tell me if it is an answer? About how many answers do you think there are in all? about 10? about 100? What's the largest number that's an answer?

The **Dialogue Box,** 11,000: Even or Odd? (p. 25), shows how sharing solutions to puzzle 4 helped students in one class develop their understanding of what makes a number even or odd.

Finding Multiples of 21

Note: If you have done the *Investigations* unit *Mathematical Thinking at Grade 5,* students will be familiar with the terms *factor* and *multiple.* Review their meanings as needed.

When we skip count by a certain number, we are finding the *multiples* of that number. What are some multiples of 21? See how many you can find.

Write *Multiples of 21* on the board and list the first three or four multiples as students say them. Student pairs then work together, listing multiples of 21. They may use calculators for this activity.

After about 5 minutes, ask students to report briefly on how they found multiples of 21. Record each strategy they suggest. Typical strategies include these:

- Using a calculator to repeatedly add 21 to itself.
- Using patterns that involve thinking of 21 as 20 and 1. For example: "I found multiples of 20 and then added on a number 1 larger each time. So 20 is the first one, and add 1. Then 40, add 2. Then 60, add 3."
- Using patterns involving the amount the digits increase with each count. For example: "The ones digit goes up by 1 with each number. The rest of the number goes up by 2, except when the ones digit goes from 9 to 0. Then it goes up by 3, because adding 1 more to the 9 makes an extra 10."

If students do not mention using patterns, list multiples of 21 on the board in order as students count around the class by 21. During the count, ask students if they see any patterns that could help them predict what number comes next.

Students take about 5 more minutes to continue finding multiples of 21. You might challenge students to use patterns, rather than calculators, to find more multiples. Bring the class together again, and ask students to share any new patterns they discovered.

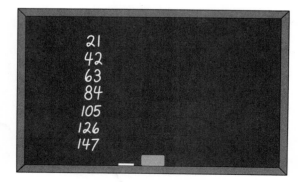

Making a Tower of Multiples of 21

Tape a 6-foot strip of adding machine tape to the wall (vertically). Explain that this is for a Multiple Tower. Ask for a volunteer to record multiples of 21 on the tower, as students call them out, in order. The multiples should be written in large print (about an inch high), starting from the floor.

Exploring Multiples of 10   After 210 but before the class gets to 420, stop to draw attention to patterns involving multiples of 10.

How many multiples of 21 does it take to get to 210? Can you tell me how you know without counting?

Record students' strategies on the board. Some might reason that there are ten multiples because $21 \times 10 = 210$; some might notice that every tenth number is a multiple of 10 (or ends in "0"); others might recognize that 210 is the same as ten 20's and ten 1's. If some students say that 210 is ten 21's because you just add a 0, ask them to explain why that is so.

Write on the board:

____ $\times$ 21 = 210   210 $\div$ 21 = ____

We found that there are ten 21's in 210. How does that help us solve these two problems? How could we complete these expressions? Which one is a way of saying there are ten 21's in 210? (Both are.)

Redirect attention to the Multiple Tower.

After 210, what's the next multiple of 21 that ends in 0? How do you know?

When the class has agreed that the next number to end in 0 will be 420, ask students if they can predict, without actually doing the counting, how many multiples of 21 it will take to get to 420. Again, as students give their reasoning, record their strategies on the board. Encourage students to explain any similarities they notice among the strategies.

Ask how knowing that there are twenty 21's in 420 can help solve these problems:

___ $\times$ 21 = 420   420 $\div$ 21 = ____

336
315
294
273
252
231
210 ◄
189
168
147
126
105
84
63
42
21

As the class continues filling the Multiple Tower for 21, stop once or twice more to draw attention to patterns involving multiples of 10. For example, you might stop again after 630 but before 840. Ask students to explain how many multiples of 21 it takes to get to 630, and to predict what the next two or three multiples of 21 that end in 0 will be. Continue to write the corresponding multiplication and division problems on the board, and ask students how they can use what they know about multiples of 21 to find the answers.

Note: To help students avoid making an incorrect generalization about multiples of 10, you might point out that for some counting numbers, multiples of 10 (numbers that end in 0) appear more frequently than once every ten numbers. Challenge students to find these. For example:

For what counting number is every *fifth* multiple also a multiple of 10? (2, 4, 14, or other multiples of 2) **For what counting number is *every other multiple* a multiple of 10? (5, 15, 35, or other multiples of 5) For what counting number is *every multiple* of this number also a multiple of 10?** (20, 100, 130, or other multiples of 10)

Making Predictions About the Tower As the tower grows, encourage students to use patterns in the list of multiples as a way of predicting what number will come next. You might periodically ask students to predict what multiples will correspond to various heights. What do they estimate the highest number in the tower will be when the tower reaches your elbows? your shoulders? your head?

Continue the tower until it is as tall as you are. Then ask students to determine the total number of multiples in the tower.

We found multiples of 21, and the highest number in the tower is [945]. Can you figure out how many multiples are in the tower— that is, how many 21's are in [945]—without counting?

Again, write the corresponding multiplication and division problems—both a way of asking the question, "How many 21's are in [for example, 945]?" As students explain their strategies, record them on the board. See the **Dialogue Box,** How Many 21's Are in 945? (p. 26), for the strategies one class used.

If some students find the answer using a standard algorithm, acknowledge that this is one way to solve the problem, and ask them to use what they know about multiples of 21 to find the answer in a different way:

How many 21's in 210? in 420? in 840? Can you use the fact that there are forty 21's in 840 to help you find the answer?

945
924
903
882
861
840 ◄
819
798
777
756
735
714
693
672
651
630 ◄
609
588
567
546
525
504
483
462
441
420 ◄
399
378
357
336
315
294
273
252
231
210 ◄
189
168
147
126
105
84
63
42
21

See the **Teacher Note,** Developing Computation Strategies That Make Sense (p. 23), for a discussion of the value of developing a variety of strategies for computation.

Leave the list of students' strategies on the board for reference during the next activity.

Using Multiples to Solve Problems

Write several multiplication and division problems involving multiples of 21 on the board. For example:

$\_\_\_ \times 21 = 987$ $903 \div 21 = \_\_\_$ $21 \times \_\_\_ = 1260$

$1239 \div 21 = \_\_\_$ $\_\_\_ \times 21 = 1344$ $1890 \div 21 = \_\_\_$

Students work alone or in pairs, using what they know about multiples of 21 to find the answer to one problem. As they work, circulate to observe their solution strategies. Ask any students using a standard algorithm to find the answer in a different way as well.

Students who are having difficulty might look at the list of strategies from the previous activity. The **Dialogue Box,** How Many 21's Are in 945? (p. 26), offers another possibility for helping students: Present one of those strategies (A–C), ask students to explain why it works, and suggest they use the same strategy to solve one of the problems on the board.

When students finish, they share solution strategies with a partner. Pairs that finish early might find other ways to solve the problem, or they might choose a different problem to solve.

What are some other multiplication and division problems you could solve by using what you know about multiples of 21?

A few volunteers suggest problems and explain how they would use what they know about multiples of 21 to find the answer. Record the problems they suggest on the board. Each student chooses one of these (or another problem you wrote on the board for this activity) to solve for homework.

Sessions 3 and 4 Follow-Up

Different Ways to Count   After Session 3, send home Student Sheet 4, Different Ways to Count. In Part 1, students find numbers they can count by to get from one number to another (such as from 1100 to 1200). In Part 2, they find numbers they could *not* count by to get from one number to another, and they write about how they know their answers are correct.

❖ **Tip for the Linguistically Diverse Classroom**   Students who are not comfortable writing in English can demonstrate with numbers, symbols, and diagrams how they found their answers.

Some students may need to spend two nights on this homework. If time permits, spend a few minutes at the end of Session 4 sharing students' answers on Student Sheet 4, perhaps with a class solution chart.

Part 2

For each question below, find a counting number and write about how you found it.

■ If you start at 0 and count by this number, you never say 10,000.

3. I found this answer by thinking what are the factors of 10,000. Once I thought what most of those were I just picked a non-factor. I also knew 3 wasn't a factor because it doesn't go into 10 or 100.

■ If you start at 1000 and count backward by this number, you never say 0.

7. I knew this because seven doesn't go into 10 or 100 evenly. I know 1,000 is a multiple of 10 and 100. So when I count backwards I will go right past 0. Also the only odd number that could be a factor of 1,000 is a number with five at the end.

Using Multiples to Solve Problems   After Session 4, students choose a problem involving 21. They record the problem they choose on Student Sheet 5, Using Multiples to Solve Problems. Students work *without* using a standard algorithm or a calculator. They record their work so that someone looking at it could understand how they solved the problem. These papers can give you a sense of students' solution strategies and show you how they record their thinking.

Developing Computation Strategies That Make Sense

There are many different ways to solve computation problems. In this unit, students develop a variety of procedures, building on numbers and relationships they know to devise strategies appropriate to particular problems.

The procedures that adults are generally most familiar with—what we sometimes call "standard" algorithms—are those that have been historically taught in American schools: the carrying and borrowing algorithms for addition and subtraction, the right-to-left algorithm for multidigit multiplication, and the long division algorithm. They were extremely valuable in the days when all computation was done by hand. Imagine what it was like to keep the records for a small business entirely by hand—not only without calculators and computers, but even without adding machines. People who did repetitive calculations wanted as many pencil-and-paper shortcuts as possible. (Which of these shortcuts were chosen to be taught in public schools is, in part, a matter of historical accident. At other times in our history and in other countries, the schools have taught algorithms different from those currently considered "standard" in American education.)

Throughout the *Investigations* curriculum, we encourage students to find and use computation strategies that grow out of their developing number sense. Some students will have learned the standard algorithms; it is important that they learn other strategies as well. This is because the traditional algorithms have a serious drawback: They lead students away from thinking about the meaning of the problem and the relationships between the numbers in it. In their focus on the manipulation of individual digits, the students too often lose sight of the numbers as whole quantities.

There are many approaches to computation that keep more visible the connections between the numbers and the problem situation. Let's look at a specific example: 59×13.

Rachel, a fifth grade student, approaches this computation by thinking of 59×13 as 50 groups of 13 plus 9 groups of 13. She doesn't yet feel confident multiplying 50 by 13 directly, so she breaks that part of the problem into tens:

$50 \times 13 = (10 \times 13) + (10 \times 13) + (10 \times 13) + (10 \times 13) + (10 \times 13)$

Rachel also needs to calculate 9×13, which she breaks into 9×10 and 9×3. Her partial solution then looks like this:

$130 + 130 + 130 + 130 + 130 + 90 + 27 =$

By grouping 100's and multiples of 10, Rachel quickly condenses this sum as follows:

$500 + 150 + 100 + 17 = 767$

This is her procedure: First, she groups the five 100's from the 130's to make 500, then the five 30's from the 130's to make 150, then makes another 100 with the 90 and 10 from the 27, which leaves 17 from the 27. These parts are then easily added.

While Rachel's method may look more cumbersome at first glance than the historically taught multidigit multiplication algorithm, it is actually easy to keep track of, results in numbers that are easy to work with, is not prone to calculation errors, and, for someone fluent with the relationships in the problem, can be carried out fairly quickly. The approach can be generalized to any multiplication problem. And it is built solidly on the student's mental model of the meaning of multiplication.

Not all the procedures that students try will be equally manageable. For example, Kevin's strategy for multiplying 59×13 might be to add up thirteen 59's. He *has* developed a mental model of the meaning of 59×13; his method, if carried out accurately, will give a correct solution. However, adding 59 thirteen times is tedious and error-prone—it is not very manageable. Kevin needs to develop, over time, a more efficient strategy, still based on his understanding of the

Continued on next page

numbers and the operation, but easier to carry out. A next step for Kevin is to learn to break up a multiplication problem into smaller problems, as Rachel does.

A next step for Rachel, who is using her approach confidently and fluently, is to gain more skill in operating with multiples of 10. This would enable her, for example, to break up 50×13 into $(50 \times 10) + (50 \times 3)$. As she gains experience and confidence with multiples of 10, she can develop increasingly efficient approaches to multidigit multiplication—like another student, who thought about 59×13 as 60 thirteens minus 1 thirteen, and worked it out this way:

$60 \times 13 = (60 \times 10) + (60 \times 3) =$
$600 + 180 = 780$, then $780 - 13 = 767$

Watch and listen carefully as your students develop their procedures. Find out what makes sense to them. To understand a student's procedures better, try to do a problem or two yourself using the student's approach. Don't assume that what seems easy and efficient to you is necessarily the best or most efficient approach. Most of us learned certain algorithms in school that we have been using for 20 or 30 or 40 years. It is not surprising that something we have used for so long feels familiar and "easy" to us.

Many of the procedures students develop are based on sound knowledge of operations, are efficient, and, once mastered, are also easy to use. When students develop their own procedures for addition or multiplication, for example, they tend to move from left to right in the problem, focusing on the largest part of the number first, rather than moving from right to left as in the historically taught procedure. Using this approach, many students might approach a problem like $1342 + 3295$ by adding thousands, then hundreds, then tens, then ones: $1342 + 3295 = 4000 + 500 + 130 + 7 = 4637$. Focusing on the largest part of the numbers helps them maintain a sense of the size of the quantities involved.

Learn to judge students' efficiency by watching them at work. We are not aiming for students to solve problems as quickly as possible—there is no particular virtue in solving a problem in 10 seconds rather than 30 seconds. No one does a timed page of multiplication or division problems in real life. But students do need to develop strategies that allow them to solve computation problems in ways that are manageable and fluent.

If students have procedures that they can apply easily and accurately, that do not bog them down in calculations that are too difficult, and that they know how to apply to a variety of problems of a particular type, then they have the tools they need to solve virtually any problem that they would need to do by hand in daily life. If, on the other hand, students lose track of their own procedures, make many errors, or end up with calculations that are very difficult, they need to become more proficient at decomposing their problems into manageable parts in order to develop strategies that both make sense to them and are easy to carry out.

Keep in mind reasonable goals for doing computation by hand. In the real world, no one who does complex calculations regularly relies on doing them by hand. In fact, an employer would be quite concerned if an employee responsible for totaling receipts, determining inventory quantities, or keeping track of a budget did not use technological aids such as a calculator or a computer spreadsheet. That employer would also be quite concerned if the employee did not bring good skills of estimation to the work in order to continually evaluate the reasonableness of the results obtained with technology. Those situations that we do commonly encounter in daily life—balancing a checkbook, estimating what we are about to spend in a store, adding up prices on a mail-order form, figuring out how many miles per gallon our car is getting—will be handled easily by students who have learned to do the kind of numerical reasoning that is emphasized in this unit.

11,000: Even or Odd?

The following dialogue shows how a discussion of solutions to puzzle 4 on Student Sheet 3, What's In Between? deepens students' understanding of what makes a number even or odd. The puzzle has three clues: The number is between 11,000 and 12,000; it is even; and it is closer to 11,000 than to 12,000. In trying to "prove" that 11,000 is even, students begin thinking about why numbers with 0, 2, 4, 6, or 8 in the ones place are even. They develop several ways of understanding what "being an even number" means: We can construct even numbers if we count by 2's beginning at 0. We know a number is even if we can divide it by 2 with no remainder. If we know a number is even, we know that a multiple of that number is even.

Kevin and Leon listed 11,002, 11,004, and 11,006 for their answers to puzzle 4. Do their answers fit the clues?

Katrina: No! They're not even numbers because of the 11—11,000 is not even.

Desiree: No, it ends in 0, so it is even.

How could you prove to me it's odd or even?

Desiree: You could clear the calculator and then do + 2 = = = = ... all the way to 11,000, and if it lands there, you know it's even.

If it gets there by 2's, will you believe that as proof?

Christine and Katrina agree and begin skip counting on the calculator, using Desiree's method.

Shakita: If 1 is an odd number, everyone knows 1 is odd ... then the numbers that come before and after are even [0 and 2], because it goes every other. So if 0 is even, and 11,000 ends in 0, it's even.

Yu-Wei: Zero makes odd numbers even. Like 30.

Becky: It's like going by 10's. All the numbers when you count by 10's are even because of 0 at the end.

How about 12? Is it even? How do you know?

Katrina: I just know it. I've known that since first grade.

Robby: If it ends in 0, 2, 4, 6, and 8, it's even. Same with the big numbers like 11,000.

Noah: You can also divide by 2. Like, 24 divided by 2 is 12. You know it's even. 25 divided by 2 doesn't work, so it's odd.

Do we agree that dividing by 2 will prove if a number is even? *[Most agree.]* **OK, someone take a calculator and divide 11,000 by 2.**

Katrina: OK, 11,000 divided by 2 *[she presses keys on the calculator]* ... is 5500, and that divided by 2 is 2750. And that divided by 2 is 1375. And that divided by 2 is 687.5. And if it's a decimal, it doesn't work, so it must be odd.

Danny: But you can only divide the first number by 2. *That's* the one you want to know if it's even or not. Those other ones you did, you were finding out if *they* were odd or even.

The class goes on to discuss other work. After 10 minutes, Katrina raises her hand excitedly.

Katrina: We got to 9000! If you keep doing + 2 = you get there.

You did? What did you start at? What number were you counting by?

Christine: We started at 0, and we counted by 2. And we landed on 7000 and 5000, too. So it must be the same for 11,000. I think we were wrong, Katrina. It's even.

Shakita: You know how we could have done it? Remember early in the year when we did that thing about what can you count by, and if you count by 100 you get to 1000. And if you do it with 2, you get to 100. So if it worked for 100, that's even, and if it worked for 100 it works for 1000, so that's even. If it worked for 1000, it makes sense that it would work for 11,000 because 11,000 is just a whole bunch of 1000's put together.

▭D▭I▭A▭L▭O▭G▭U▭E▭ ▭B▭O▭X▭

How Many 21's Are in 945?

The students in this class have just built a Tower of Multiples, showing the multiples of 21. The highest number in the tower is 945. Students are sharing strategies for finding out how many 21's are in the tower. Some of the strategies they suggest involve reasoning about multiples of 21; others involve breaking the problem into smaller parts and drawing on their knowledge of factors and multiples.

Heather: I knew that 210 is ten 21's, 420 is 20, and 630 is 30, 840 is 40. Then I knew there were 5 more 21's, because of the patterns in the ones column.

Can you tell me more about the patterns in the ones column?

Heather: When you count by 21's, the ones column goes up by 1. The first 21 after a multiple of 10 ends in 1, and the second ends in 2, and the fifth number ends in 5. So it's 45. *[The teacher records her strategy and labels it A.]*

Manuel: I didn't use 21's. I started with a number I knew better. I thought that plain 20, not 21, goes into 800 forty times. Then add 5 more, because 20 goes into 100 five times. Put them together and there's forty-five 20's in 900. Then 21 would be another 45.

How did you know that 21 would be another 45?

Manuel: Because 21 is one more than 20, so you add a one 45 times. You add 1 for every 20. *[The teacher records his strategy and labels it B.]*

Lindsay: I did 21 into 84 is 4, so it's 40, because it's 10 times more. Then, I did 945 minus 840 equals 105. So, I needed to find how many 21's are in 105. Everybody knows that 20 goes into 100 five times. Add the 100 to the 840 and you get 940. And then since it's 21, you need to do 5 times 1 is 5. Add 5 to 940 and you get 945. So, 21 goes into 945 exactly 45 times—40 for 840, and then the 5. *[The teacher records this as strategy C.]*

A $210 = 10 \times 21 \dots 840 = 40 \times 21$
+5 more 21's because of ones digit.

B $20 \times 40 = 800$ $20 \times 5 = 100$
$20 \times 45 = 900$
$1 \times 45 = 45$
$21 \times 45 = 945$

C $21 \times 4 = 84$
$21 \times 40 = 840$
$945 - 840 = 105$
$20 \times 5 = 100$
$1 \times 5 = 5$
$21 \times 5 = 105$
$40 + 5 = 45$

945
924
903
882
861
840.
819
798
777
756
73
714
69
67
6
6

Multiple Towers

What Happens

Materials

- Adding machine tape, cut into 6-foot strips (1 strip per pair)
- Tape (1 or 2 rolls to share)
- Calculators (1 per pair)
- Student Sheet 6 (1 per student, homework)

Students work in pairs to find the multiples of 2-, 3-, and 4-digit numbers. They record each sequence on a Multiple Tower and look for patterns. Student work focuses on:

- finding multiples of (or skip counting by) 2-, 3-, and 4-digit numbers

Ten-Minute Math: What Is Likely?   Once or twice during Investigation 1 and again during Investigation 2, present the Ten-Minute Math activity, What Is Likely? Like other Ten-Minute Math activities, this one is intended for any spare 10 minutes you have outside of math class—at the beginning of the day or just before lunch, for example.

You will need a clear container (a fish bowl or a large jar) filled with cubes, beads, or beans in two colors. At first, be sure there is much more of one color than the other (say, a 9:1 ratio). Mix the objects well.

Students predict what will happen if they draw ten objects out of the container: How many of each color will they get? Record their predictions. Then, with eyes closed, draw ten objects from the container, replacing after each draw. Record the results with tallies.

Compare the actual results with students' predictions. Discuss what happened, focusing on likely and unlikely results. Then draw another ten objects and compare the two results.

For full instructions and variations on this activity, see p. 148.

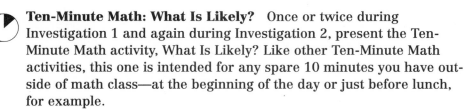

Activity

Teacher Checkpoint

More Multiple Towers

List the following numbers on the board:

26, 32, 37, 49, 72, 91, 105, 123, 201, 403, 925, 1007, 1011

Distribute calculators and a strip of adding machine tape to each pair. The students will be making Multiple Towers that are at least as high as one of the partners can reach. For each tower, they choose one number from the list and write its multiples, in order, working from the bottom of the strip upward.

You might want to designate a particular space in the classroom for building the Multiple Towers. Provide tape so that students can fasten their strips to the wall, the bottom of the strip flush with the floor.

Observing the Students   As students work, circulate to observe how they are finding, saying, and recording the multiples.

- How are students finding what number comes next in the sequence? Are they looking for number patterns to help them?
- How are students writing the numbers? Do they use repeated addition on the calculator to check how to write the numbers?
- How are students saying the numbers they write? Do they recognize that a number such as "1 thousand 2 hundred and 9" is the same as "12 hundred and 9"?

Students who finish early can extend their Multiple Towers. Choose a landmark in the room (perhaps the top of a window, or the ceiling) and challenge students to make towers reaching that high.

Five to 10 minutes before the end of the session, distribute Student Sheet 6, Multiple Towers, to each student. In the strip at one side, students record the numbers they have written on their own classroom tower. They will answer the questions for homework.

Save all the Multiple Towers for use again in Investigations 2 and 3.

Session 5 Follow-Up

 **Homework**

Multiple Towers   Students take home Student Sheet 6, Multiple Towers, with the sequence of numbers on their own Multiple Tower filled in. They may use the back of the sheet or notebook paper if they need more room to answer the questions.

❖   **Tip for the Linguistically Diverse Classroom**   Read each question aloud. Have students write their own rebuses for key words, to help them understand each question when they are at home.

Review students' work to get a sense of their strategies for using skip-counting patterns and multiples to help solve multiplication and division problems.

The Digits Game

What Happens

Students play the Digits Game, using randomly drawn digits to make numbers as close as possible to a target 4- or 5-digit number. Their score for each round is the difference between the number they make and the target. As they play, they develop strategies for finding the score without using a standard subtraction algorithm. Student work focuses on:

■ developing, explaining, and comparing strategies for subtracting 4- and 5-digit numbers

■ using a random set of digits to approximate a 4- or 5-digit number

Materials

■ Numeral Cards (1 deck per pair; 1 per student, homework, optional)

■ Transparencies of Numeral Cards and Student Sheet 8

■ Student Sheet 7 (1–2 per student, homework)

■ Student Sheet 8 (1–2 per student, homework)

■ Student Sheet 9 (1 per student, homework)

■ Overhead projector

Activity

Introducing the Digits Game

Display the following five transparent Numeral Cards on the overhead, or draw the cards on the board:

| 1 | 7 | 4 | 5 | 8 |

What are some numbers we can make with any four of these digits?

As students call out numbers, record them on the board or overhead. Then ask students for some numbers they can make with all five of the digits and record their suggestions.

We're going to be playing a game called the Digits Game. You'll be dealt five Numeral Cards, and you'll need to arrange the digits to make a number as close as possible to the target number.

Write the following on the board:

    Target number   5000

For this round, your target number is 5000. (There will be a different target for each round of the game.) You can use as many of the digits as you want. The number you make can be _over_ or _under_ 5000. To find your score, figure out how far your number is from 5000—how much below, or how much above. No one uses calculators.

Using the digits 1, 7, 4, 5, and 8 (shown on the overhead or the board), student pairs make a number as close as possible to the target and determine its distance from 5000. They may use paper and pencil to record the number they make. Circulate and talk to them about their strategies. Encourage them to find the difference between 5000 and the numbers they make in a way that does not use a standard subtraction algorithm.

If any students need help getting started, give them an example:

One student made the number 4571. Another made the number 5714. Which is closer to 5000? Can you arrange four of these digits to make a number that is even closer?

Ask a few volunteers to tell what numbers they made and to explain the strategies they used to find the difference between their numbers and 5000. Record each example on the board as a subtraction expression, written horizontally rather than vertically to help students focus on the numbers as whole quantities. For example:

$$5000 - 4875 = 125$$

Use the transparency of Student Sheet 8, Digits Game Score Sheet, to explain how to score the game. Demonstrate with numbers students made, showing how to score with numbers both above and below the target.

Suppose you made 5147. How far apart are 5147 and 5000? (147) Your score would be 147.

Suppose you made 4875. How far apart are 5000 and 4875? (125) Your score is 125. Your goal in this game is to get the lowest score, so 125 is better than 147.

If you think some students need more practice before playing on their own, play again with the class, choosing a target that includes one or two nonzero digits, such as 9500 or 3044.

Activity

Playing the Digits Game

Distribute a deck of Numeral Cards to each pair. For this game, students remove the four Wild Cards from the deck. Each student also needs a copy of Student Sheet 8, Digits Game Score Sheet. Students can use this sheet as a model to make additional score sheets as needed.

On the board or overhead, list the targets for each of the first three games as shown on the next page. Students use the same target for each round in the game. If necessary, adjust the difficulty level of the targets for your students.

You might list three of the following targets:

	Targets	
5000	2300	9975
4180	3251	6029

Students play at least one more game with targets they choose themselves. As students become more experienced with the game, ask them to play with larger targets such as 50,000; 24,500; and 70,103.

The game rules are given on Student Sheet 7, How to Play the Digits Game. Because the game is relatively simple, you may decide not to distribute this sheet except as homework, to help students teach the game to their families. Whether or not you hand out the page for class use, go over the rules as a group.

Three rounds make up a game. For each round, the dealer lays out one set of Numeral Cards that both players use, dealing one more card than there are digits in the target. Each player records the target, the closest number he or she made, and the difference between the two numbers on the Digits Game Score Sheet.

If you prefer a cooperative game, players can use a single score sheet and work together to make the number closest to the target.

Observing the Students As students begin, circulate quickly to make sure everyone understands how to play. Also observe what strategies students are using to make their numbers and to determine how close they are to the target.

Some students may work almost randomly at first, making several numbers and then finding how far away each is from the target. A more efficient approach involves making just two numbers—the closest number above the target and the closest below—and then finding which of those two numbers is closer. Encourage students to determine which is closer without actually finding the difference between each number and the target. For example, suppose the target is 6029, the available Numeral Cards are 2, 8, 5, 6, and 3, and a player has identified 6235 and 5863 as the closest numbers. Students might determine which one is closer in one of these ways:

■ Reasoning about the general distance between each number and the target: "I know 6235 is more than 200 away from 6029, so 5863 is closer because it's less than 200 away (100 more is 5963, and another 100 more is 6063)."

■ Approximating numbers to multiples of 25, 50, or 100: "Round 5863 to 5850 and 6029 to 6025. Then it would be 50 more to get to 5900, then 100 more, then 25, or 175 to the target, but it's really less because it's 5863. If you round 6235 to 6229, it would be 200 to the target, but really it's even more."

- Expressing the distance between each number and the target as a sum of familiar numbers: "I know 6235 and 6029 are 1 + 70 + 100 + 35 apart. I added 1 to get from 6029 to 6030, then 70 to get to 6100, then 100, then 35. For the other pair, 5863 and 6029 are 7 + 30 + 100 + 29 apart. I started at 5863 and added 7 to get to 5870, then 30 to get to 5900, then 100 then 29. I know 5863 is closer because I know it's going to add up to less."

To determine their scores, students need to find the actual difference between the closest number and the target. See the **Teacher Note,** Helping Students Think About Subtraction (p. 34), for tips to give students for this step. The **Dialogue Box,** Strategies for Subtraction (p. 35), demonstrates some student thinking. You may want to work with students in smaller groups to share strategies.

After the first three games, students play additional games with targets of their own choice. Some may need guidance in choosing targets.

If they seem to need more practice, suggest that they choose 4-digit targets that are multiples of 1000 or 100, such as 4000 or 2400. For additional practice outside the regular game format, they could find the largest and smallest numbers that can be made with each set of Numeral Cards dealt.

Students who are ready for more challenge can choose 5- or 6-digit targets that have mostly nonzero digits. Students comfortable with decimal numbers could use a 1-digit target, such as 1 or 3. They deal three Numeral Cards and make numbers with two decimal places. For example, a player with a target of 1 deals 0, 2, and 7. To get a number close to 1, the player might make 0.72 or 2.07.

Save the sets of Numeral Cards for use in the Estimation Game in Investigation 5.

Reserve a few minutes at the end of Session 7 to review one of the problems on Student Sheet 9, Problems from the Digits Game (homework after Session 7). Choose one of the problems and ask students to share their strategies for finding the score.

Sessions 6 and 7 Follow-Up

Homework

Playing the Digits Game   After Session 6, students play the Digits Game with family members or a small group of friends. Each student will need Student Sheet 7, How to Play the Digits Game, and Student Sheet 8, Digits Game Score Sheet (or, students can make their own score sheets on notebook paper). They will also need a set of Numeral Cards. Simple cards can be made by writing numbers on small squares of paper. Or, they might use another method to generate random digits for the game, such as repeatedly opening a large book at random and using the tens digit of the page number.

If students make their own cards, encourage them to find a safe place to keep them at home as they will be used again for playing the Estimation Game with family members during Investigation 5.

Problems from the Digits Game   After Session 7, students complete Student Sheet 9, Problems from the Digits Game.

Helping Students Think About Subtraction

Some students find it difficult to think about the difference between two numbers without writing one above the other and performing a standard algorithm. However, a standard algorithm is just one of many ways to find the difference between two numbers. Students need to understand a variety of methods for subtraction; they need to have a sense of what it means to subtract so they can determine if their answers are correct; and they need to be able to use their methods flexibly, with different types of problems.

Students who understand several subtraction methods can choose the one that is most appropriate for a given problem. For example, many students find it particularly difficult to carry out a standard algorithm when the minuend (the number that is subtracted from) has 0's in it. Solving a problem such as 10,102 – 3997 with a standard algorithm involves a complex series of borrowings, complete with crossing out numbers and writing in new ones.

By contrast, another student might think of the problem as "How far apart are 3997 and 10,102?" This student might reason: "I need to add 3 to 3997 to get 4000. Then I add 6000 more to go from 4000 to 10,000. Then from 10,000 to 10,102 is 102. So they are 3 + 6000 + 102 apart... that's 6105."

Knowing several solution methods also gives students a variety of ways to determine if their answers are correct. For example, before solving the problem 10,102 – 3997, suppose you estimate that the answer is about 6000 (10,102 is close to 10,000; 3997 is close to 4000; and 10,000 and 4000 are 6000 apart). Adding on from 3997, you calculate an exact answer of 6105. From your original estimate of 6000, you know that this answer is in the ballpark; you can then use a different method to check that the answer is correct.

Following are some ways you can help students become familiar with a wider range of subtraction strategies and make choices among them.

■ Write subtraction problems both horizontally and vertically, and remind students that they can use the same strategies to solve problems written in either format.

■ Help students see that we can think of subtraction in different ways: finding the difference between two numbers; finding how far apart two numbers are; finding how much you have to "add on" to get from the smaller number to the larger number.

■ Encourage students to make an estimate before finding the exact answer. Estimates are useful for checking to see if an answer is approximately correct. Sharing strategies for making estimates can help students think of new ways they might find the exact answer.

■ Remind students of the different strategies they have used to find their scores for the Digits Game. You might also present one of the strategies from the **Dialogue Box,** Strategies for Subtraction (p. 35), and ask students to use it to solve a problem.

■ Ask students to explain why their strategies work. Suppose that, to solve a problem such as 3251 – 2876, a student begins by adding 100's to 2876 to get as close as possible to 3251 without going over. You might ask this student to explain why *adding* can help us find an answer to a subtraction problem.

Or, suppose another student writes one number above the other and tells you, "I need to borrow 1 from the 5 because I can't take 6 away from 1." You might then ask: "If you are taking away 1 from the 5 and adding it to the 1, why doesn't 1 become 2 instead of 11? If you change the first number by borrowing from one place to another, are you still solving the same subtraction problem?"

■ Ask students to solve problems in more than one way. This can help them recognize that some strategies may be easier than others for a given problem. It also brings to light similarities and differences among strategies, and helps students develop a deeper sense of what it means to subtract.

Strategies for Subtraction

As this class plays the Digits Game in small groups, the teacher observes one group at a time. As they play, the teacher records their strategies for finding the score on a piece of chart paper, labeling each strategy with a letter for ease in discussing them.

These students are sharing their strategies for finding the score when the target is 6029 and the closest number is 4873.

Remember, I'm not interested in hearing just the answer right now. You could use a calculator if you wanted just the answer. I want to hear how you're thinking about the problem.

Leon: First I did 4873 plus 7 equals 4880. Then 20 more equals 4900, and 100 more is 5000. Then 1000 more, then 29 [Strategy A].

Greg: I started with numbers that were easy to add. 4873 plus 1000 is 5873. You can't add another 1000 so add 100. That's 5973. And then from there start adding 10's up to 6023. You need five 10's. Then add 6 to get to 6029 [Strategy B].

Natalie: I did it sort of opposite what Greg did. I started with 6029 and took away 1000 and got 5029. Then I took away 100 and got 4929. Then I took away 29 to get 4900, then 25… that's 4875, then 2, that's 4873. When I had to add them all up, I thought that 29 is like 25 and 4, so I put the two 25's together, and then the 4 and 2 makes 6, gives you 56 [Strategy C].

Alani: I rounded off. I said 6000 minus 5000 equals 1000 and then I added 29 and 127. You add them together and you get 156. 127 and 30 would be 157 and 29 is 1 less so it's 156 [Strategy D].

Where did you get the 127?

Alani: I got 127 because its 2 more to 875 and 875 is 125 away from 1000.

Becky: I did it like Alani, but first I thought you had to subtract the 127. Then I looked at the numbers and saw that it won't work because the

answer has to be at least 1000. Then I thought you have to do *plus* 127 because you need to add in how far it is from 5000 to 4873.

Leon: I didn't do it this way, but you could do it by subtracting if you round the 4873 down. First you make 4873 into 4000 and 6029 into 6000. Then find the difference between 6000 and 4000 and that equals 2000. And you have to add 29 because the problem is 6029. Then you minus the 873 because 4873 is more than 4000 [Strategy E].

Becky: That seems hard. How do you remember if you need to add the 873 or subtract it?

Leon: It would be hard to do for this problem, but sometimes the numbers could make it easier to do it that way.

$$6029 - 4873 = ?$$

Strategies:

(A) $7 + 20 + 100 + 1000 + 29$

(B) $1000 + 100 + 10 + 10 + 10 + 10 \quad 10 + 6$

(C) $1000 + 100 + 29 + 25 + 2$
$1000 + 100 + 25 + 4 + 25 + 2$
$100 + 100 + 50 + 6$

(D) $1000 + 127 + 29$

(E) $2000 + 29 - 873$

Subtraction Strategies

Materials

- Transparent set of Numeral Cards
- Overhead projector
- Chart paper (optional)

What Happens

As a class, students share strategies for finding the difference between two 4- or 5-digit numbers. Then, they work individually to find and write about different ways to solve two subtraction problems. Student work focuses on:

- explaining thinking and reasoning about subtraction in writing

---

Activity

Strategies for Subtraction

Display the following five transparent Numeral Cards on the overhead, or draw them on the board:

| 9 | 2 | 0 | 3 | 4 |

Imagine you are playing the Digits Game and you are dealt these cards. Your target is 7974. Find the closest number you can make to 7974, and figure what your score would be with that answer.

Write the target on the board. Students work alone to find the answer; they may *not* use calculators or standard algorithms.

What is the closest number you can make? (9023) How did you figure out your score? Did anyone do it a different way?

As students explain their strategies for finding the score, record them on chart paper or the board (or invite students to record their strategies themselves). Encourage students to think of as many different ways of solving the problem as they can and to explain any similarities they can find among the strategies.

Write another subtraction problem on the board:

6021 – 3550

Challenge the class to see how many *different* ways they can find to do this subtraction problem. Suggest that students record their work clearly, showing each step, so that someone else looking at it could understand how they solved the problem. As they work, circulate to observe what strategies they are using and to remind them to keep a careful record of their solution process. For students having difficulty, encourage them to first estimate about how far apart the two numbers are. They might look at the solution methods for the previous problem (on chart paper or the board) for ideas.

As students finish, they join with a partner. Each reads what the other has written and tries to explain how his or her partner solved the problem. If the explanation is not clear, the two work together to find a way of explaining the solution strategy in writing more clearly. Pairs that finish early can try to solve the problem in a different way.

In class discussion, students explain *their partner's strategy,* rather than their own. Record the strategies on the board.

Repeat this activity with one or two more subtraction problems. Include at least one problem written in vertical format. For example:

$$5402 - 3189 \qquad 12{,}100 - 5010 \qquad 54{,}103 - 25{,}867 \qquad \begin{array}{r} 8012 \\ -\,3738 \\ \hline \end{array}$$

The vertical format tends to trigger use of the traditional algorithm, and you may need to remind students that they can use the strategies for subtraction that they have been discussing, even though the numbers are on top of one another. Some students may recognize that problems with 0's in the minuend (the number that is subtracted from) can be easier to solve with strategies they develop themselves.

Activity

Teacher Checkpoint

Solving Subtraction Problems

Write the following two problems on the board:

$$7{,}504 - 1{,}886 \qquad\qquad 30{,}017 - 18{,}520$$

Explain that students are to work individually to solve each problem without using calculators or standard algorithms. In addition to finding the answer, they must communicate how they solved the problem by using equations or words.

Observing the Students   As you observe students working and later, as you read what they have written, think about the following:

- What types of strategies did students use to solve the problem? Did they break the problem into smaller problems? use their knowledge of multiples of 10, 25, 50, and 100? add to get from one number to the other?
- Do the students think about *the distance between two numbers* as a way of subtracting?

If some students finish early, encourage them to find another way to solve each problem.

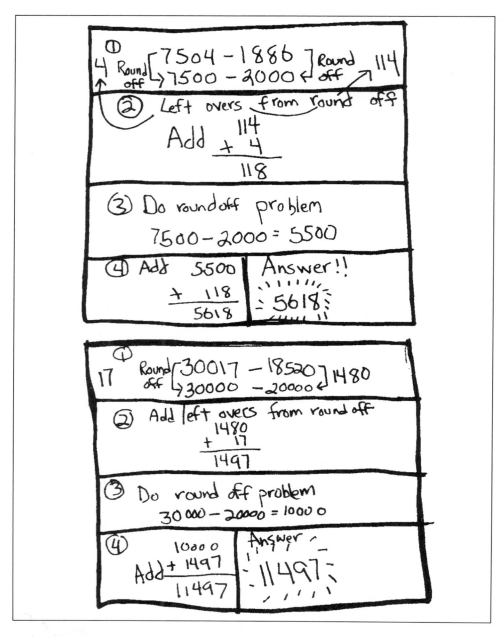

In the checkpoint activity, this student used rounding and then adjusted for "leftovers."

$$7,504 - 1,886 =$$

$$1886 + 14 = 1900$$

$$14$$
$$5,000$$
$$100$$
$$504$$

$$1900 + 5,000 = 6,900$$
$$6,900 + 100 = 7,000$$
$$7,000 + 504 = 7,504$$

$$14 + 5,000 + 100 + 504$$

$$5,100$$

$$\boxed{5,618} \qquad 5,604$$

$$30,017 - 18,520 =$$

$$18,520 + 80 = 18,600$$
$$18,600 + 400 = 19,000$$
$$19,000 + 11,000 = 30,000$$
$$30,000 + 17 = 30,017$$

$$80$$
$$400$$
$$11,000$$
$$17$$

$$11,400$$
$$97 \qquad \boxed{11,497}$$

This student used an "adding-on" strategy to find the difference between the two numbers.

Session 8 Follow-Up

More Digits Game Practice At home or outside of class, students continue playing the Digits Game, which offers good practice with choosing subtraction strategies for different problems.

 **Homework**

Multiplication and Division Situations

What Happens

Sessions 1 and 2: Multiplication and Division Strategies   Students find different ways to solve problems that can be modeled with multiplication and division. They discuss how to think about remainders in a way that makes sense in the context of the problems.

Session 3: Division Strategies   Students share what they know about notation for recording division equations and remainders, and they discuss relationships between multiplication and division. They find different ways to solve problems presented with division notation, and they consider ways to use multiplication to solve division problems.

Session 4: What Should We Do with the Extras?   Students write problems to represent division situations. They solve their problems, considering the meaning of any remainders in a particular context.

Sessions 5 and 6: Relating Multiplication to Division   Students find different ways to solve problems that can be modeled with multiplication. They discuss relationships between multiplication situations and division situations. They then write and solve problems that represent multiplication situations.

Session 7 (Excursion): Problems About Our School   Students work on problems that involve real information gathered from places where large quantities of supplies are kept in the school, such as a supply closet or the cafeteria. After solving the problems, students go to see the actual objects and packages that their answers represent.

Mathematical Emphasis

■ Developing, recording, and comparing strategies for solving multiplication and division problems

■ Making sense of remainders

■ Understanding relationships between multiplication and division

■ Understanding how multiplication and division notation can represent a variety of situations

■ Modeling situations with multiplication, division, and other operations

What to Plan Ahead of Time

Materials

- Multiple Tower for 21 from Investigation 1 (Sessions 1–2)
- Stick-on notes: 1 package for the class (Session 7, Excursion)
- Metersticks or rulers: 1 per pair (Session 7, Excursion)
- Samples and packages of items in your problem set (Session 7, Excursion). For more information, see the **Teacher Note,** Writing Problems About School Supplies (p. 70).
- Chart paper (Sessions 1–2, 4–6)
- Overhead projector (Sessions 3–6, optional)
- Bulletin board and tabletop surface (Session 7, Excursion)
- Calculator (Session 3, optional)

Other Preparation

- Duplicate student sheets and teaching resources (located at the end of this unit) in the following quantities. If you have Student Activity Booklets, no copying is needed.

For Sessions 1–2

Student Sheet 10, Ringles (p. 168): 1 per student

Student Sheet 11, Boxes of Markers (p. 169): 1 per student

Student Sheet 12, Zennies (p. 170): 1 per student (homework)

Student Sheet 13, My Coin (p. 171): 1 per student (homework)

300 Chart (p. 178): 1–2 per student (optional)

For Session 3

Student Sheet 14, A Division Problem (p. 172): 1 per student (homework)

For Session 4

Student Sheet 15, Division Situations (p. 173): 1 per student (homework)

For Sessions 5–6

Student Sheet 16, Milk Cartons (p. 174): 1 per student

Student Sheet 17, Mimi's Mystery Multiple Tower (p. 175): 1 per student (homework)

Student Sheet 18, Relating Multiplication and Division Situations (p. 176): 1 per student (homework)

For Session 7

Student Sheet 19, A Problem About Large Quantities (p. 177): 1 per student (homework)

- If you plan to do the Excursion, Session 7, you will need to write and duplicate sets of problems about supplies stored in quantities around the classroom or school, as described in the **Teacher Note,** Writing Problems About School Supplies (p. 70).

Multiplication and Division Strategies

Materials

- Student Sheet 10 (1 per student)
- Student Sheet 11 (1 per student)
- Student Sheet 12 (1 per student, homework)
- Student Sheet 13 (1 per student, homework)
- Chart paper (optional)
- Multiple Tower for 21 (from Investigation 1)
- 300 Chart (1–2 per student, optional)

What Happens

Students find different ways to solve problems that can be modeled with multiplication and division. They discuss how to think about remainders in a way that makes sense in the context of the problems. Student work focuses on:

- modeling situations with multiplication, division, and other operations
- developing, explaining, and comparing strategies for multiplication and division

◗ **Ten-Minute Math: What Is Likely?** Continue to spend time on this activity in any 10-minute period you have outside of math class. Each time you do it, change the proportions of colors in your container. For more challenge, ask students to fill the container themselves in a way that is likely to yield a particular goal (for example, making it likely to draw more white than red). For full directions and variations, see p. 147.

Activity

The Ringle, an Imaginary Coin

Post where everyone can see it the Multiple Tower for multiples of 21 you made during Investigation 1. Distribute a copy of Student Sheet 10, Ringles, to each student. Ask students to name all the U.S. coins and their values.

Suppose our country decided to get rid of all these coins and make one new coin, worth 21 cents. It's called a ringle. No more dimes, or quarters, or pennies—just ringles. It would take us a while to get used to ringles. We'd want to compare the new coin to the money we are used to, and figure out how many ringles make a dollar, how many make 2 dollars, and so on.

The three problems on this sheet are all about the ringle. You can work on these problems alone or with a partner.

Students record their thinking, showing each step, so that someone looking at their papers could understand how they solved the problems. They may use 300 charts or they may refer to the Multiple Tower if they find it helpful, but they may not use calculators.

As students work, circulate to observe how they are solving the problems and making sense of the remainders, and to remind them to keep a careful record of their solution processes. If some students use standard algorithms, continue to acknowledge that this is one way to find the answers, but ask them to solve the problems in another way as well.

Students having difficulty may find it helpful to first estimate about how many ringles are in the given dollar amount, by using relationships among familiar coin values. For example, you might ask them how many quarters are in a dollar (or, how many 20's are in 100), and then suggest they try to use that result to determine how many ringles are in a dollar.

Students who finish early can figure out how many ringles are in $10, in a mixed dollars-and-cents amount such as $7.40, or in an amount of money they choose themselves.

Communicating Our Strategies   When everyone has finished at least the first two ringles problems, ask students to share their solution strategies. Start a list on chart paper or on a part of the board you will not need to erase for a couple of days. Head the list *Strategies,* and record students' ideas for solving each problem. See the **Dialogue Box,** Strategies for Division: How Many Ringles? (p. 49), for examples of strategies developed by students in one class, and some connections they noticed among their strategies.

If no one suggests a strategy using 10×21, write $10 \times 21 = 210$ on the board. Ask students if they can find a way to use this equation to help find the number of ringles in 2 dollars. Then, ask if they can use this equation to help find the number of ringles in 5 dollars.

Note: If some students used a standard algorithm as one of the ways they solved the problems, you might ask them to record what they did on the class list of strategies and to explain why their algorithms work. For example, if a student writes $21 \overline{)500}$ and explains that you put a 2 above the leftmost 0 in 500 because there are two 21's in 50, ask for an explanation:

If you are trying to find out how many 21's in 500, why do you need to start with how many 21's are in 50? What does the leftover 8 represent?

Encourage students to find connections between standard algorithms and other strategies. The **Teacher Note,** Explaining and Comparing Procedures (p. 47), provides more information on this.

Shakita started out by thinking about multiples of 21. She said that since 2 times 21 is 42, 20 times 21 is 420. How is that like what Jeff did when he said "I knew there are two 21's in 50"?

Note: Some teachers find they need a full session for completing and discussing the ringles problems; other classes will take less time. Generally, plan to spend most of Session 1 on ringles and most of Session 2 on the following checkpoint activity.

Teacher Checkpoint

Boxes of Markers

Leave the *Strategies* list from the ringles activity where students can see it. Distribute a copy of Student Sheet 11, Boxes of Markers, to each student.

When the school buys classroom supplies, like erasers or colored markers, we don't buy them one at a time; we buy them by the box. A box will have a certain number of items inside—maybe 10, or a dozen, or 25, or 50. When I order things for the classroom, I must decide how many we need, and then how many boxes I should order. The three problems on this sheet ask about boxes of markers we might order for our class.

❖ **Tip for the Linguistically Diverse Classroom**   Read each problem aloud, showing an actual box of markers. As a reminder of the meaning of shared equally, students might make a simple sketch:

shared equally   • • | • •
                        • • | • •

Observing the Students   Students work alone or in pairs on Student Sheet 11. Remind them to record their thinking so that someone else could understand how they solved each problem. As you observe students working, and when you later read what they have written, consider the following:

■ What types of strategies did students use to solve the problem? Look for these: using familiar multiplication pairs; reasoning about multiples of 10 times the number of students in the class; breaking the problem into smaller components; reasoning about multiples of 70; adding or subtracting.

■ How do students keep track of the steps in each problem?

■ How do students use arithmetic notation to record their work?

■ Do students deal with remainders sensibly?

Ask any students who are using standard algorithms to find the answer in another way as well.

Students who finish early can find another way to solve each problem. You might also challenge them with problems involving larger numbers of markers: How many boxes would we need for each student to get 25 markers?

When everyone has finished at least the first two problems, bring the class together to share the solution strategies they used. Record students' ideas on the board or chart paper. If no one suggests using 10 times the number of students in the class to help solve the third problem, bring it up yourself.

Encourage students to explain any similarities they notice between these strategies and those already on the class *Strategies* list. Continue to keep this list posted for reference through the next session.

Name Noah   Date Feb. 7

Boxes of Markers

For each problem, show how you found your solution.

Number of students in your class: ___27___

Suppose that markers come in boxes of 70.

1. Suppose your class has 1 box of markers. How many would each person get if the markers were shared equally among the students in your class?

$$\begin{array}{r} 27 \\ +27 \\ \hline 54 \end{array} \qquad \begin{array}{r} 54 \\ +27 \\ \hline 81 \end{array}$$

(2 markers) if add 1 more 27 it would be 81 which is over 70.

(5 markers)

2. Suppose your class has 2 boxes of markers. How many would each person get if the markers were shared equally among the students in your class?

140 markers

$27 \times 10 = 270$ too much $27 \times 6 = 162$ too much

$27 \times 5 = 135$ — only 5 less $27 \times 4 = 108$ can get closer

$$\begin{array}{r} 135 \\ +27 \\ \hline 162 \end{array}$$

I tried different numbers times 27 and when I came close to 140 I stopped.

3. Suppose your class has 5 boxes of markers. How many would each person get if the markers were shared equally among the students in your class?

(12 markers)

$$\begin{array}{r} 70 \\ \times 5 \\ \hline 350 \end{array}$$

$27 \times 10 = 270$
$27 \times 20 = 540$ double
$27 \times 15 = 405$ +135 (27×5)
$27 \times 12 = 324$ +54 (27×2)

© Dale Seymour Publications®   **169**

Investigation 2 • Sessions 1–2
Building on Numbers You Know

Sessions 1 and 2 Follow-Up

Homework

Zennies   After Session 1, students complete Student Sheet 12, Zennies. Remind them to record their thinking so that someone reading their papers would understand how they solved each problem.

My Coin   After Session 2, students make up a value and name for a new coin on Student Sheet 13, My Coin. They determine how many of their invented coins there would be in 1 dollar, 2 dollars, 5 dollars, and 10 dollars.

Extensions

Ringles and Dollars   Students find the smallest whole-dollar amount that they can make exactly with ringles. They write about how they know their answer is correct.

International Currency   Check the foreign exchange tables in a newspaper to determine how much the standard unit of currency in another country is worth in U.S. dollars. Students then find out how many there are in $5, $10, $50, and $100.

Explaining and Comparing Procedures

When students use the standard algorithms, often they are performing the steps by rote and cannot explain how their notation relates to their understanding of the problem. When this happens, you need to work with them on developing procedures they can explain.

In one fifth grade class, two students regularly used more traditional algorithms. Both had solved the problem $159 \div 13$ by long division. The teacher sat down with each of them to find out how much they understood about this procedure. In each case, the teacher asked the student to relate that procedure to what the student had previously explained about the meaning of the problem. Following are excerpts from each conversation as the teacher asked them why they used a 1 as the first digit in the dividend.

$$
\begin{array}{r}
12 \text{ R}3 \\
13\overline{)159} \\
\underline{13} \\
29 \\
\underline{26} \\
3
\end{array}
$$

So explain to me why you put a 1 here.

Matt: Because 13 doesn't go into 1, so you have to do 13 goes into 15, and it goes once.

Uh-huh. So you're figuring out how many 13's are in 15?

Matt: Yup. There's only one, because two would be 26 and that's too much.

OK. But you told me before that this problem is about finding out how many 13's are in 159. Why do you want to know how many 13's are in just 15?

Matt: Because that's how you do it. You do 13 goes into 1, but you can't do that, because no 13's will fit, so you have to go 13 into 15, and that's 1.

Matt could only reiterate the steps that he had used. He did not have a sense of what the individual digits he wrote down represented or how they related to his model of the problem, finding out how many 13's are in 159. He simply knew that this procedure worked. The teacher asked Matt to put this method aside for a while and to develop other strategies that he can justify and explain.

Here is how a similar conversation with Noah went:

Explain to me why you put a 1 here.

Noah: Because 1 is too small, so you have to move over and take 13 into 15, and that's 1.

You mean you're figuring out how many 13's are in 15?

Noah: Yeah, you say how many 13's are in 15, and you know there's only 1 because it's just a little bit under 15.

Earlier you told me that this problem is about how many 13's you can take out of 159. How does what you're doing here help you find that out?

Noah: Well, it's like how many 13's in 15—see, it's like this is really 150, so how many 13's in 150, would be 1.

You can only take one 13 out of 150?

Noah: No, I mean, that's actually 10, I think, because ten 13's is kind of close to 150.

Noah showed some understanding of what the numbers in his work meant. Because he was at least beginning to interpret his procedure meaningfully—seeing that the 15 represents 150 and the 1 in the dividend represents 10—the teacher probed further to see if he could explain all the parts of his work. At the same time, she still insisted that Noah develop some other approaches, to give him a flexible repertoire of strategies to use for a variety of problems.

Continued on next page

All students can be helped to better understand the meaning of their procedures by explaining and comparing their strategies. Some time after her conversations with Matt and Noah, when students were sharing their approaches in a whole-class discussion, this teacher pointed out the connection between two student methods for dividing 159 by 13.

Antonio's method   Matt's method

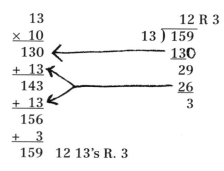

The teacher helped the class think about how the 1 in the 12 in Matt's solution actually represents the 10 in the 13 × 10. As she talked about Antonio's 13 × 10, she wrote in the 0 to make the 13 into the 130 that it actually represents in Matt's work. She also pointed out how the 26 from Matt's two 13's also shows up as two 13's in Antonio's work.

It is important that students who know the historically taught algorithms learn other strategies as well. All students need to develop more than one approach for solving any problem, so that they can choose among approaches for a particular problem and can use one approach to double-check another.

Strategies for Division: How Many Ringles?

Students are sharing their strategies for solving the problems on Student Sheet 10, Ringles. Each took a different approach.

Matt used multiples of 21 and 210. He relates his strategy to his earlier work with Multiple Towers:

Matt: For number 1, I got 4 ringles. Because of the whole 21 thing we did with the tower, I knew the first five multiples of 21, so I knew 21 times 5 is 105, and that was too high. So I figured 1 below that, so 4. For number 2, I used problem 1. I did 84 times 2 and got 168. I knew 84 had a big remainder so double that would have more, so it's more than 8. I tried 10 times 21 equals 210, but that was too big, so I figured it had to be 9. For number 3 I did 21 times 20 equals 420, and I added 105 because I knew that's 21 times 5 and that's 525. And I figured 1 below is 504, so it would be another 1 below that, or 23 ringles.

Christine solved the problems by finding multiples of 21 and then multiplying by 21:

Christine: I did it sort of like Matt, except I went by 21's instead of 210. For $5, I thought the first multiple of 21 after 21 is 42. Next is 63. If you multiply them by 10, it's like $4.20 and $6.30. $4.20 is the closest one less than $5.00, so then I counted up by multiples of 21 three times from $4.20.

Heather counted by 21's for problem 1; then, to solve problems 2 and 3, repeatedly added her answer to problem 1:

Heather: For the first [problem] we counted by 21's and counted how many 21's that was. How many to 100 was 4 and 16 left over. So there are 4 ringles in a dollar because if you did 5 you would have 105 and that's too much. The second [problem] we doubled the answer for the first one, because if you double 100 it equals 200. We doubled 4 and got 8. Then we doubled the remainder 16 and got 32. Then we minused 21 from 32 because we can get another ringle from 32 cents and added 1 more ringle to the answer. The third [problem] we added the amounts for

100, 200, and 200. We added 9 and 9 and 4 and got 22. Then we added the remainders 11, 11, and 16 and got 38. We minused 21 from 38 and got 17. So we added another ringle to 22, and we got 23 ringles.

Greg solved one of the problems by subtracting 21's from the dollar amount, rather than adding up:

Greg: We did it like Heather except for the first [problem], we did minus 21's. We did 100 minus 21, and that was 79 and then we did 79 minus 21— 58 left, then 37, then 16. You can't take another 21 away, so we knew there are four 21's and 16 left, and then we used that to do the other problems.

Maricel found the solutions for a coin worth 20 cents and then adjusted her answers to account for the missing cent:

Maricel: Instead of doing it by 21's, it was easier to do it by 20's. We found out how many 20's go into each number. Like, 500... or $5... and that was 25. We knew that we had 21 as our number and we knew 21 was greater than 20 so 25 could not be the answer to the problem or anything higher than 25. So we went to the next lower, 24, and did 24 times 20 and that's 480, and we added on 1 twenty-four times because our number is 20 and you have to do the extra 1. That's 504, so we had to go to the next lower, 23.

Tai found the solutions for a quarter (25 cents) and then adjusted his answers to account for the extra 4 cents:

Tai: I used 25¢, the quarter. I took the quarter and since I know there's 4 quarters in a dollar I subtracted 4 from 25 four times because the ringle is 21¢ and got 16¢ left over. So, 4 ringles. For 2 dollars, I know there's 8 quarters, and I took away 4 eight times and got 32¢, and then you can take another ringle from that, so 9. For 5 dollars I did 4 quarters in a dollar and 5 dollars is 20 quarters, take away 4 times 20 is 80. There are 3 ringles in 80¢ because 21, 42, 63, so 23 ringles.

Session 3

Division Strategies

Materials

- Class *Strategies* list (from Sessions 1–2)
- Student Sheet 14 (1 per student, homework)
- Overhead projector (optional)
- Calculator (optional)

What Happens

Students share what they know about notation for recording division equations and remainders, and they discuss relationships between multiplication and division. They find different ways to solve problems presented with division notation, and they consider ways to use multiplication to solve division problems. Student work focuses on:

- developing, explaining, and comparing strategies for solving division problems
- relating multiplication and division equations
- recording division equations and remainders using different types of notation

Activity

Writing Division Equations

Write the following question on the board or overhead:

> How many 21's are in 100?

You answered this question when you solved the problem, "How many ringles are in 1 dollar?" What are some different ways we can write this as a division problem?

Record students' suggestions on the board. Look for these three forms, suggesting any yourself as necessary:

$$\frac{100}{21} \qquad 21\,)\,\overline{100} \qquad 100 \div 21$$

Remind students that when they found how many ringles are in a dollar, they came up with many different strategies for solving these problems. The long division format is just one way of writing a division problem. Students need to understand that when they see a problem in long division format, they don't need to go through a long division algorithm, but can use a wide range of strategies to solve it, just as they did with the ringles.

Give students a minute or two to solve the problem and record their answer. You might ask a few students to solve $100 \div 21$ on a calculator to find a way to write the answer to the problem with decimals.

50 ■ *Investigation 2: Multiplication and Division Situations*

How did you write the answer to this problem?

Spend a few minutes reviewing how to read each form of notation.

$$\frac{100}{21} = 4\frac{16}{21} \qquad 21\overline{)\,100}^{\,4\,R\,16} \qquad 100 \div 21 = 4.76 \text{ (approximately)}$$

If no one has written the remainder as a fraction, ask if anyone can. See the **Teacher Note,** Remainders, Fractions, and Decimals (p. 54), for some suggestions on ways to help students think about remainders as fractions.

Is there a way to write this problem using multiplication? (21 × ? = 100) **How would we write the answer?**

Some students will recognize that we can record the solution as 4.76 × 21 = 100, and a few may know that we can also record it as 21 × (4¹⁶/21) = 100. However, it is possible that no one will know how to write this form as a multiplication expression:

$$21\overline{)\,100}^{\,4\,R\,16}$$

If that is the case, remind the class of ways they found how many ringles are in a dollar with multiplication, and show how these strategies can be recorded with multiplication notation. For example, a student might have determined that there are 4 ringles in a dollar with 16 cents left over by multiplying 4 × 21, and then adding on 16 to get to 100. The problem would then be recorded as 21 × 4 + 16 = 100.

Strategies for Division

Note: In this activity and throughout the unit, you may need to adjust the numbers in problems to make them easier or more difficult. At the outset, students should be working with numbers they are quite comfortable with. That way, they can focus on the *meaning* of the operations and on developing strategies that make sense. As students gain a deeper sense of operations and become more confident in their strategies, you can begin to increase the size and difficulty of the numbers in the problems. The **Teacher Note,** Creating Your Own Multiplication and Division Problems (p. 55), discusses choosing numbers at the appropriate level of difficulty.

When we solved the problems about ringles and the boxes of markers, you came up with a lot of different ways to divide. Let's see how many different ways you can find to solve another division problem.

Write this problem on the board:

$$136 \div 11$$

Give students a few minutes to work individually to solve the problem without using standard algorithms or calculators. Since the problem is not about a particular situation, students may record remainders in any format they choose (probably 12$\frac{4}{11}$ or 12 R 4).

As students work, circulate to observe their approaches. Remind them to keep a careful record of their solution process. As needed, refer students to the class *Strategies* list for ideas. Have they considered using multiplication to solve this division problem? Students having difficulty may also find it helpful to make an estimate of the answer first: Do they think the answer is about 5? about 10? about 20? about 100? How do they know?

If students use standard algorithms, acknowledge that this is one way to find the answer and ask them to find another way. The **Teacher Note**, Helping Students Think About Operations (p. 56), offers guidelines for helping students develop their own strategies for division and other operations.

Note: As students work on multiplication and division problems throughout the unit, observe whether any students are having difficulty with factor pairs. If they are, suggest that they keep a list of troublesome factor pairs and work with a partner to list strategies for remembering them. They can return periodically to their lists of difficult factor pairs, cross off those that no longer seem difficult, and (with a partner) brainstorm and list more strategies for any pairs they still find difficult.

When students finish solving $136 \div 11$, they trade papers with another student. If anyone cannot understand what his or her partner has written, the pair works together to rewrite the solution strategy more clearly. Pairs that finish early find yet another way to solve the problem.

Bring the class together to pool their strategies. Record them on the board and look for similarities among the strategies. If no one has suggested a strategy involving multiples of 10, ask how the answer to 10×11 might help them.

Repeat this activity with division problems written in different formats. For example:

$$\frac{103}{8} \qquad 19\,\overline{)\,120} \qquad 159 \div 13$$

As necessary, remind students to try the strategies for division that they have been discussing, including those that involve multiplication.

Session 3 Follow-Up

A Division Problem   After Session 3, send home Student Sheet 14, A Division Problem. Students solve one of the following problems without using standard algorithms or calculators:

$67 \div 7$	$98 \div 12$	$175 \div 15$
$245 \div 8$	$363 \div 24$	$477 \div 21$

You might let students choose, or you might assign different problems to different students, according to the appropriate level of difficulty. Remind them to record their work so that anyone could follow their thinking. Collect students' work to get a sense of the strategies they are using and how they are recording their work.

Think about how you would solve the following problem and how you would write the answer:

> Four people want to share 13 apples. How many does each person get?

One way to solve the problem is to give each person three apples and put aside the one extra. We can write this answer as 3 R 1, or "3 apples and 1 extra."

Another way to solve this problem is to give each person three and a quarter apples. In this case, we can write the answer as 3¼ or 3.25. Since each person gets one-quarter of the extra apple, there is no remainder; nothing is left over.

It is important that students recognize both ways of thinking about the remainder: as an amount left over or extra, and as a fraction or part of the divisor. Many students are comfortable thinking about remainders as leftovers, but some have difficulty thinking about remainders as a fraction or part of the divisor. You can work on this with problems about things that can be subdivided, like pizza or apples or cookies. Start with a problem that uses small numbers, such as the apples problem above, then move to more difficult numbers. Ask students to talk about the meaning of the different ways of writing the answer.

How would we write the answer if we ended up with some left over? How would we write the answer if there was none left over after we shared all the apples? How many more apples would we need to give everyone another whole apple?

Throughout this unit, encourage students to find different ways to record the remainders and to think about when it is appropriate to use each different way. When solving purely numeric problems, such as 13 ÷ 4, students may record the leftovers in any format. When solving situational problems, they should express the remainder in a way that makes sense. If the problem is about sharing apples, for example, the remainder can be expressed either as a fraction or a decimal, or as an amount left over. If the problem is about sharing something that cannot be subdivided, such as pencils, the extras should be recorded as a remainder.

Watch to see that students, in expressing a remainder as a fraction, don't lose sense of what the numbers mean. In the apple problem above, using small numbers and a familiar context, the meaning of the ¼ may be clear to students: ¼ is a familiar fraction, and it is easy to visualize ¼ as a part of an apple. But the fractional parts in more complex problems may seem very mysterious. For example, if there are 692 people to be divided into groups of 25, we can make 27 groups, with 17 people left over:

$$682 \div 25 = 27 \text{ R } 17$$

or

$$682 \div 25 = 27\tfrac{17}{27}$$

What does the 17/27 mean here? It is easy for students to write the fractional part of the answer without holding on to what that fraction means. In this problem, we might think of it as 17/27 of a group, or 17 out of the next 27 people. It is as if we were in the process of forming a new group of 27, but ran out of people at 17. Where it makes sense to express the leftovers in a division problem as a fraction, discuss the meaning with students: What is this a fraction of? What does it tell you about the division situation?

Creating Your Own Multiplication and Division Problems

In this unit, the students solve many multiplication and division problems. If the problems in the text are either too difficult or too easy for your students, change the numbers in the problems accordingly. Following are some things to keep in mind as you decide if and how to adjust the numbers and as you help students choose problems at the appropriate level of challenge.

How difficult are the numbers to manipulate mentally? Many of the strategies that students develop for multiplication and division involve finding multiples of one of the numbers in the problem. This is easiest when they can do it mentally or with relatively little paper-and-pencil computation. For example, 378×19 can be quite difficult, since solving it may involve finding and adding multiples of 378 or 19. Students who are working out their own strategies for multiplying may be side-tracked by the amount of computation and recordkeeping needed. The problem 902×31 may be more appropriate, even though the numbers are larger, since multiples of 902 and 31 are easier to find mentally.

What numbers are your students most familiar with? Your students will have had a great deal of experience with particular numbers. For example, they are likely to have encountered 12, 21, and 60 many times as they worked with multiplication tables, explored factors and multiples, and practiced skip counting. They are also likely to be quite familiar with multiples of 25, 50, and 100. Most students are less comfortable with numbers like 19, 46, and 117. Their factors and multiples are less familiar, so problems with these numbers will be more challenging.

How large are the numbers your students are comfortable with? Some of your students may be comfortable with a wide range of numbers under 300. They may have a sense of how large these numbers are, recognize some skip-counting patterns up to 300, and be able to relate a less familiar number, such as 219, to more familiar ones, such as 200, 220, or 225. Other students may need to work first with smaller

numbers, such as 31, 57, or 101, that they can more easily visualize or model with concrete objects (paper clips, counters).

How complex is the problem? Some problems may be difficult because of the relationships among the numbers. For example, students often use a division strategy that involves finding multiples of the divisor. For $501 \div 28$, this will take quite a few steps:

> There are ten 28's in 280. $501 - 280$ is 221, so the answer is 10 plus the answer to $221 \div 28$. Since 10×28 is 280, 5×28 is half of that, or 140. Then 1 more 28 is 168, that's 6 28's; 1 more after that is 196, that's 7 28's; and there's 25 left over. The answer is 7 with 25 left over, plus 10, or 17 with 25 left over.

The problem $826 \div 41$ is much easier because the dividend is much closer to a multiple of 10 times the divisor:

> There are ten 41's in 410, and $826 - 410$ is 416. Take away another ten 41's ($416 - 410$), and there's 6 left over, so the answer is 20 with 6 left over.

If you are unsure of the complexity of a problem, try it yourself before assigning it, using strategies your students are likely to use.

How can I help students choose problems at an appropriate level of difficulty? Encourage them to choose problems that are just a little difficult: not so easy that they don't have to think, but not so hard that they seem out of reach. Explain that different numbers will be challenging for different students, and help them to think about their own "right" level of challenge. For example, a student who has difficulty remembering factor pairs that include the numbers 8 and 7 may find the problem 38×17 challenging, but may solve 416×35 with relative ease; on the other hand, a student who needs more practice making sense of larger numbers may find 416×35 quite difficult.

Some students equate division (or multiplication, or subtraction, or addition) with the standard algorithms they have been taught. They need to recognize that there are many other ways to perform each operation: by reasoning about multiples, by skip counting, by approximating to nearby familiar numbers and then adjusting, or by breaking problems into smaller, more familiar components.

The more strategies students understand well, the deeper their sense of operations will be. Following are some questions you might ask students throughout the unit to help them gain a better sense of operations.

How else can we write this problem?
Encourage students to write problems in a variety of formats, and remind them that they can use the same strategies to solve problems written in different ways. For example, students can use exactly the same strategies to solve these six problems:

How many ringles are in $5.00?

$500 \div 21$

$21 \overline{) 500}$

$\frac{500}{21}$

$21 \times ? = 500$

I want to share $500 among 21 people. How much money does each get?

Students develop their own strategies for division as they solve situational problems at the beginning of Investigation 2. When they later encounter numeric problems presented with division notation, some students believe that they must use a standard algorithm. Help them see that they can use the same strategies that worked for the situational problems.

Why does your strategy work? Ask students to explain why each step is needed. For example, in solving $19 \overline{) 409}$, Robby wrote 2 above the 0 in 409 and explained that he did this because there are two 19's in 40. Ask him to talk about why he needs to find how many 19's in 40 in order to find the number of 19's in 409. Can he explain why the fact that there are two 19's in 40 means that there are twenty 19's in 400? Can he explain what happens to the extra 20 (when 380, or 20×19, is subtracted from 400)? What happens to the extra 9 (the difference between 400 and 409)?

How are these strategies similar? Encourage students to look for ways that different strategies are alike. For example, Toshi started out solving $409 \div 19$ by adding 19×10 and 19×10. Jeff began by adding 19 and 19 to get 38, and then multiplying by 10. How are those two approaches alike? How are they like what Robby, who was using a standard algorithm, did when he explained that 19 goes into 40 two times?

Why does your answer make sense? Students might show that their answer makes sense by making an estimate before or after they solve the problem, by solving the problem in a different way, or by making up a situation to match the numbers.

How else can we solve this problem? After students have shared their strategies with partners or with the class, challenge them to find still other ways to solve the problem. Some students find that sharing strategies for making estimates helps them think of new ways to find the exact answer. By solving problems in different ways, they discover that some strategies may be easier than others to use for a given problem. It can also help them to appreciate that they can use mathematics creatively, as they develop their own ways of carrying out each operation.

What Should We Do with the Extras?

What Happens

Students write problems to represent division situations. They solve their problems, considering the meaning of any remainders in a particular context. Student work focuses on:

- making sense of remainders
- understanding how division notation can represent a variety of division situations

Materials

- Student Sheet 15 (1 per student, homework)
- Overhead projector (optional)
- Chart paper

Division Situations

Earlier you worked on two situations in which you could use division to find the answer: How many ringles are in a certain amount of money, and how many markers everyone gets when you share boxes of markers. Now take a look at this division problem.

Write 94 ÷ 4 on the board or overhead.

Let's make up a situation for this problem. Think of a situation in which you (or someone else) might need to solve this problem. What could the situation be? What could the problem be about? What will you do if the numbers do not divide evenly?

Students take a few minutes to talk in pairs about problems based on 94 ÷ 4. You might remind them of two ways to think about 94 ÷ 4:

1. How many 4's are in 94?
2. If I divide 94 into 4 groups, how big is each group?

After some discussion with their partner, students write their own problem about a situation that uses 94 ÷ 4. They then solve their own problem without using calculators or standard algorithms, and write about what they did with the extras.

❖ **Tip for the Linguistically Diverse Classroom** Students who are not writing comfortably in English might work with partners; they can relate their problem through pictures and a few words, and can illustrate what they did with the extras.

What About the Extras?   A few volunteers share the division problems they wrote. Ask them to talk about what they would do with the extras. See the **Teacher Note,** What Should We Do with the Extras? (p. 60), for examples of division situations in which remainders are handled in different ways.

To help students to recognize that depending on the situation or context of the problems, remainders are handled differently, post three sheets of chart paper:

Round answer to next largest number	Round answer to next smallest number	Include remainder in answer

Students post their problems on the appropriate chart. You might need a fourth chart for problems that handle remainders in yet another way, such as the final "divide 94 students into teams of 4" problem described in the **Teacher Note,** What Should We Do with the Extras? (p. 60)

As students circulate to read the posted problems, encourage them to note the wide range of situations that handle remainders in the same way.

There were 4 Kids and 94 chocolate bars. How many would each Kid get?

23 ½ pieces

Seasoned surfboards produces 94 each month in the mid-summer. They send a quiver of 4 boards to each shop that orders boards. They make both long and short boards, also customs. How many surfshops receive a quiver of boards in the mid-summer?

Answer: 23 shops got a quiver, and the extra went 1 to the shaper, 1 to the glosser.

There were 94 pounds of water melons
there were 4 groups of people
How many pounds of watermelon did
each group of people get?

Answer: each group of people get

23 water melons and 2 groups
      get 24.

Note: There are two division concepts that you may see reflected in students' problems. Some problems will reflect a "sharing" situation, in which division is used to separate an amount into equal-sized groups ("I need to pack 94 cookies into 4 boxes. How many should I put in each box?"). Other problems will reflect a "grouping" situation, in which division is used to find how many groups will make up a total amount ("I want to get 94 cookies. They come in boxes of 4. How many boxes should I get?"). Talking about this can help students recognize the variety of situations a division equation can represent.

If time permits or if you think students need more practice, they might write a situation based on one of the following division problems:

$$139 \div 9 \qquad 160 \div 14 \qquad 246 \div 12 \qquad 227 \div 16$$

On a separate sheet of paper, they solve the problem without using calculators or standard algorithms, and they write about what they did with the extras. As students work, circulate to observe how they are solving their problems and how they are making sense of the remainders. They then trade problems, solving their partner's problem and explaining what to do with the extras.

Session 4 Follow-Up

Division Situations Students complete Student Sheet 15, Division Situations. They show how they solved the problems and write about what they would do with the extras. Remind students to bring this sheet back to class for review in the next session.

 **Homework**

❖ **Tip for the Linguistically Diverse Classroom** Read each problem aloud, clarifying unfamiliar vocabulary with pictures and pantomime. Students may add simple sketches and rebus drawings to the sheet to help them understand the problems when they are working at home.

What Should We Do with the Extras?

Different division situations call for handling remainders in different ways. In some problems, the answer is "rounded down" and the remainder is ignored.

> There are 94 pencils and 4 students. The teacher wants to give the same number to each student. How many does each student get?

If 4 people share 94 pencils equally, each person gets 23 pencils. The remaining 2 pencils cannot be distributed evenly among the 4 people.

In other problems, the answer must be "rounded up":

> I need to put 94 pencils in boxes. I can fit 4 pencils in a box. How many boxes do I need?

If 94 pencils are to be put in boxes that hold 4, you would need 24 boxes; 23 of the boxes would be full, and the other box would hold just 2 pencils.

In still other problems, remainders are an important part of the answer:

> I won 94 dollars in a raffle and decided to share it with my family. There are 4 of us. How much do we each get?

When 4 people are sharing 94 dollars instead of 94 pencils, the remaining 2 dollars can be further divided so that each person gets 23 dollars and 50 cents.

Students may come up with still other ways of handling remainders that do not necessarily involve dividing into equal-size groups, but that make sense given the problem context.

> There were 94 students in the fifth grade and we wanted to put them in teams of 4 for the field day. How many teams were there?

The student who created this problem explained his thinking about the remainders:

> We could have done 23 teams of 4 and a team of 2, but they wouldn't win anything. We thought about having floaters who would fill in for kids absent that day, but we decide to have 22 teams of 4 and a team of 6. That team is for kids who don't want to do every event. Some people can sit out while the other people in their team take their turns. If it's money, you can split up the extra money. You can't split the kids or send them home. You have to do something with them.

As students in your class share their division situations, ask them to explain how they would handle the leftovers. By describing the remainder in the context of the problem and not just writing R 2, they are solving the problem more completely and in a way that they can follow and make sense of. They are also deepening their understanding of what it means to divide.

Sessions 5 and 6

Relating Multiplication to Division

What Happens

Students find different ways to solve problems that can be modeled with multiplication. They discuss relationships between multiplication situations and division situations. They then write and solve problems that represent multiplication situations. Student work focuses on:

■ understanding how multiplication notation can represent a variety of multiplication situations

■ finding relationships between multiplication and division situations

Materials

■ Students' completed Student Sheet 15

■ Student Sheet 16 (1 per student)

■ Student Sheet 17 (1 per student, homework)

■ Student Sheet 18 (1 per student, homework)

■ Chart paper (optional)

■ Overhead projector (optional)

Activity

Homework Review

Take about 10 minutes to review the homework (Student Sheet 15, Division Situations). Ask a few volunteers to share their strategies for solving each of the problems and to explain how they decided what to do with the remainders. Some students may have recognized that each of the problems can be represented by 171 ÷ 5 and thus done only one calculation. Others may have used different strategies for different problems. Record students' strategies on the board or on chart paper or invite them to come up and record their own.

Activity

Multiplying with Cartons of Milk

Distribute a copy of Student Sheet 16, Milk Cartons, to each student.

A few days ago we talked about classroom supplies that come in boxes, things like erasers and markers. Cafeteria supplies, like milk, straws, and napkins, also come in boxes and packages. To order supplies for the cafeteria, we need to think about how many boxes or packages we need for lunches every day. This sheet has three problems about the milk we might need to order.

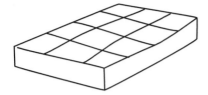

❖ **Tip for the Linguistically Diverse Classroom** To help students understand the basic premise, sketch a one-layer box with 12 divisions on the board. As you read aloud the problems on Student Sheet 16, refer to your sketch.

Students work individually or in pairs, without calculators or standard algorithms, carefully recording all the steps of their thinking. Circulate to observe. If students are having difficulty working without standard algorithms, ask how they might use multiples of 12 or multiples of 15. You might also ask them to make an estimate of the answer first:

Do you think it is about 50? about 100? about 400? How do you know?

Students who finish early can write about how long they think the total number of milk cartons in each problem would last. Would there be enough for one day of lunches? two days? a week? How much milk do the students drink? Does everyone drink one carton of milk? Do some people drink more than one? none?

When everyone has finished at least the first two problems, bring the class together to share solution strategies. If no one suggests a strategy involving 12×10 or 15×10, ask if anyone can tell you how one of those expressions could help.

Activity

Dividing with Cartons of Milk

On the board or chart paper, write a multiplication problem that corresponds to the first milk carton problem. Write it horizontally and vertically to illustrate both multiplication notations.

$$12 \times 15 = ? \qquad \begin{array}{r} 15 \\ \times\, 12 \\ \hline ? \end{array}$$

You solved this multiplication problem when you figured out how many cartons of milk are in 15 boxes. What are some ways we could write this as a division problem?

Possibilities include these:

$$\frac{?}{15} = 12 \qquad ? \div 12 = 15 \qquad ? \div 15 = 12 \qquad 15\overline{)\,?}^{\,12}$$

You are going to write two problem situations based on these division expressions and the same boxes of 12 milk cartons. First make up a situation, about milk cartons, that involves dividing 180 by 12. Then make up another situation about boxes of milk cartons that involves dividing 180 by 15.

Students may work alone or with a partner.

As a few volunteers share their division situations with the class, point out examples of different ways to use division. For example, we can use division to find out the number of boxes:

If we have 180 cartons of milk and want to pack them into boxes that hold 12, how many boxes will we need?

We can also use division to find out how many are in each box:

We ordered 180 cartons of milk. When they arrived, they were packed in 15 boxes. How many cartons were in each box?

Writing a Multiplication Situation

Write 13×32 on the board or overhead.

Think of a situation in which you or someone else might need to solve this problem. What could the situation be? What could the problem be about?

Students take a few minutes to talk in pairs about situations that use 13×32. Then, each student writes a problem in words and shows how he or she solved it without standard algorithms or calculators. As students work, circulate to observe their solution strategies. Students who finish early find another way to solve the problem.

Ask a few volunteers to share their multiplication situations with the class. Point out that some problems may be about 13 groups of 32 (There are 32 students in a class, and 13 classes. How many students in all?), while others may be about 32 groups of 13 (A baker packed muffins in boxes of 13. How many muffins are in 32 boxes?).

Take about 5 minutes for students to share a couple of their strategies for solving 13×32. If no one suggests using 13×10 or 32×10, ask students how one of those expressions might be useful in thinking about the problem.

Writing a Related Division Situation

Students now write a division situation that corresponds to their multiplication situation for 13×32. They also write the corresponding equation with division notation. For example, suppose a student wrote:

> There are 32 students in a class and 13 classes. How many in all?

That student might now write:

> There are 416 students in our school, and 13 classes. There are the same number of students in each class. How many students are in each class?
>
> $416 \div 13 = 32$

As students work, circulate to observe how they are recording division equations and to read the situations they are writing.

For More Challenge   Ask students to write a situation for a division problem that involves remainders, such as $101 \div 4$, $150 \div 7$, $162 \div 12$, $205 \div 9$, or $306 \div 15$. They solve the problem, they write a multiplication situation that corresponds to their division situation, and they write the corresponding equation with multiplication notation.

Sessions 5 and 6 Follow-Up

Homework

Mimi's Mystery Multiple Tower   After Session 5, students do Student Sheet 17, Mimi's Mystery Multiple Tower. The top portion of a multiple tower is shown. Students answer questions that involve the numbers in the tower (including the smaller numbers not shown), and they use the multiples in the tower to help solve multiplication and division problems. Students work *without* calculators.

❖   **Tip for the Linguistically Diverse Classroom**   Read each problem aloud, helping with any unfamiliar vocabulary. Encourage students to add rebus pictures and symbols over key words to help them at home.

Reserve about 5 to 10 minutes during Session 6 for a few students to share with the class the multiplication and division problems they wrote for problems 4 and 5. How did they use what they knew about the multiples in Mimi's tower to solve the problems?

Collect their work to get a sense of how they use reasoning about multiples to solve computation problems.

Relating Multiplication and Division Situations   After Session 6, students write a multiplication situation about one of the following problems on Student Sheet 18, Relating Multiplication and Division Situations.

$$21 \times 14 \quad 51 \times 23 \quad 125 \times 36 \quad 144 \times 25 \quad 212 \times 9 \quad 21 \times 288$$

You might let students choose, or you might assign problems to students, according to the appropriate level of difficulty. Students solve the problem without using a standard algorithm or calculator, and they show how they found the answer. Then they write a division situation that corresponds to their multiplication situation, and they write the corresponding equation with division notation.

Students might copy either their division or multiplication situation on a separate piece of paper and challenge an adult to solve the problem without using a standard algorithm or calculator. Then they show the adult *their* way to solve the problem.

Extension

Making Sense of Division Situations   Students write four division situations for the problem $112 \div 5$. Each situation requires handling the remainder in a different way:

■ In one situation, the answer is 22 R 2.
■ In another situation, the answer is 22⅖.
■ In a third situation, the answer is 22.
■ In a fourth situation, the answer is 23.

Problems About Our School

Materials

- Sheets of problems you have prepared (1 per student)
- Samples and packages of items in your problem set
- Stick-on notes (1 package per class)
- Metersticks or rulers (1 per pair)
- Student Sheet 19 (1 per student, homework)
- Bulletin board and tabletop surface

What Happens

Students work on problems that involve real information gathered from places where large quantities of supplies are kept in the school, such as a supply closet or the cafeteria. After solving the problems, students go to see the actual objects and packages that their answers represent. Student work focuses on:

- developing real-life meaning for quantities in the thousands, ten thousands, and hundred thousands
- modeling situations with multiplication and other operations

Activity

Supplies for Our School

Briefly show the kinds of supplies available in your school, especially those you have used in the problems you wrote. Discuss where these things are stored and how they are distributed. Then present an introductory problem set, as described in the **Teacher Note,** Writing Problems About School Supplies (p. 70). Begin with a "how many in all?" problem. The discussion that follows is based on boxes of erasers; adjust the questions to fit your particular problem set.

Problem About Quantity   Hold up a new eraser.

Erasers are stored in the supply closet. Does anyone have an idea of about how many there might be there? about 10? 100? 1000? 10,000? more than 10,000?

Gather a few guesses and record them on the board. Then, hold up a *package* of erasers.

When I went to the supply closet yesterday, I got this package of erasers. How many erasers do you think are in it?

Gather a few guesses, then tell students how many are in the package. Next, pose a "how many in all?" problem:

There are 144 erasers in a box. Yesterday, there were 24 boxes of erasers in the supply closet. How many erasers were there in all?

Students find the answer without standard algorithms or calculators, then share their strategies.

Problem About Measurement   Next present a problem about the same supply that involves measurement.

The boxes of erasers in the supply closet are arranged in two equal stacks. How could we figure out about how high each stack is?

If you have several boxes of erasers, pass them around the classroom. Make rulers or metersticks available so that students can measure the height of a box, or ask students to make an estimate. If you have only one box available, hold it up and ask students to estimate its height. You might then call on a pair of students to measure the box.

Students work alone or in pairs to determine the height of each stack of erasers. As they work, write one or more further problems on the board. Students can work on these if they finish early.

- What do you see in the classroom that is about as high as a stack of 12 boxes of erasers?
- How many erasers are in one of the stacks?
- Could we arrange the boxes in four equal stacks? How many erasers would be in each stack?
- Could we arrange the boxes in five equal stacks? How many erasers would be in each stack?

Encourage students to approximate measurements and make size estimates. Do not be overly concerned if you see some measurement errors. If time permits, you may want to discuss measurement techniques. However, students will have many opportunities to practice taking exact measurements and to develop their measurement estimation skills in the *Investigations* grade 5 unit, *Measurement Benchmarks*.

Problems About Things in Our School

Distribute to each pair:

- a set of problems to solve (each student needs his or her own copy)
- a container or package of items in the problem set
- at least one of the items (for example, a pencil eraser, a paper clip, a milk carton)
- at least one meterstick or ruler, if students are to measure

You might assign problems to pairs or let them choose from several problem sets. Two pairs working on the same problem may share materials.

If you have included any problems about items packaged in groups of 144 or 288, students may be interested to know that 144 (12 dozen) is *one gross,* so 288 is *two gross.*

Remind students to record their solution strategies clearly and completely. Those who finish early can trade materials with another pair; they will need new copies of the corresponding problem sets.

Sharing Completed Problem Sets Make available a bulletin board and a surface where students can post their completed problem sets and display the supplies with which they worked. Allow time for students to circulate to read their classmates' answers. If they have any questions, they post a stick-on note with a question mark and a brief note about what they do not understand or agree with. Take a few minutes to discuss these questions as a whole class. You might also call on a few pairs to present their solution strategies.

At the end of the session or outside of math time, take the class to visit the area where supplies are kept. Students should bring their work with them so they can relate their answers to the real-life quantities.

Session 7 Follow-Up

🏠 **Homework**

A Problem About Large Quantities After Session 7, send home Student Sheet 19, A Problem About Large Quantities. Students look at home or in a store for items that are packaged in groups. For example, some small cereal boxes come in packages of 6 or 12; some crayons, markers, and other art supplies come in boxes of 48 or 50; some paper tissues and napkins come in packages of 100, 144, or 500. Students make up and solve a "how many in all?" problem that includes the number of items in the package and the total number of packages found at home or in the store. For example:

> Boxes of tissues contain 144 sheets each. We have 3 full boxes. How many tissues are there in all?

Students then ask someone at home to solve it. For items found around the home, students might first ask for an estimate of the number of items on hand before presenting the problem:

> About how many tissues do you think we have? about 100? about 250? about 500? about 1000?

❖ **Tip for the Linguistically Diverse Classroom** Students can present their problems through a combination of pictures and words. They might present the problem to family members in their primary language.

How Long Would Our Supplies Last?   Students choose one of the supplies they explored in Session 7. Working alone, in pairs, or in small groups, they estimate how long it would take for their class (or the whole school) to use up the supplies. For example:

How long would the yellow lined paper in the supply closet last our class (or our school)? Is it enough for a month? three months? a year? two years? Are there ways in which we could cut down on our paper use?

Students begin by planning how they will solve the problem. They will need to gather data and then use their data as a basis for making a series of estimates. That is, they might record the amount of paper they use in a week, and then use that as a basis for estimating how much they would use in a month. They might estimate how much paper students in other grades are likely to use in a week by gathering more data or by adjusting their own estimates. Would students in second grade use more paper than we do because they write larger or make more mistakes, or would they use less paper because they do less writing?

Students might approach the problem in a variety of ways. Once students develop their plans, they gather the information they need, make their calculations, and then write about how they arrived at their answers.

Package Sizes   Create a class chart on which students record the items and package sizes they found for the problems they wrote for homework, as well as other packaged items that they find at home, around school, or in stores. You might title this chart *How Many in a Package?* and label columns *About 10, About 50, About 100, About 500,* and *More than 500.*

Once students have recorded their information in the appropriate columns, discuss the information on the chart.

What kinds of items are stored in packages of about 50? What kinds in packages of about 500? Can we find something that comes in packages of about 1000?

In the Excursion Session 7, students solve sets of problems that you have written about real items stored in large quantities around your school, including questions about quantities, groupings, and how much space these items take up.

For each problem set, plan to write 4 to 6 problems about a particular item. You will need to gather information for several problem sets: one introductory problem set for group discussion (see eraser example, p. 66), and additional sets for students to solve in pairs. (More than one pair may work on the same problem set.)

The problems you write will depend on what you find. In the supply closet, look for packages of pens, pencils, paper, stick-on notes, file folders, push pins, staples, and paper clips. If your school has a cafeteria, you might be able to gather information about cartons of milk or juice, loaves of bread, fruit, canned goods, paper napkins, paper towels, sponges, and other cleaning supplies. You might also gather information at the school library or art room.

Take along a notepad and a meterstick or ruler so that you can jot down both quantities (number in each box or package, and number of boxes or packages) and sizes. As you choose items for your problem sets, consider the following:

■ **Will the items be available in approximately the same quantities in the near future?** Once students have solved your problems, they will visit the area where the items are stored to get a sense of the real-life quantities and sizes that correspond to their answers. Check with the person responsible for supplies to find out if the same quantities will be there when students arrive to visit.

■ **How large are the numbers that the problems will involve? Will students be able to work without calculators?** Many items are packaged in multiples of 12, 25, or 100. Problems about these probably can be solved without calculators, even if the total numbers are large. Look for information that you can use to construct problems at different levels of challenge: some with small familiar numbers, such as 25, 50, or 100; some with larger familiar numbers, such as 500 or 1000; some with familiar numbers such as 12, 24, 48, and 144; and some with numbers that students may find more challenging, such as 288, 375, and 512 (for these, you may decide to permit calculator use). You might also look for information that you can use to write two-step problems:

Pads of paper contain 50 sheets each. This package contains 12 pads of paper. There are 15 of these packages on a shelf. How many pads are there? How many sheets of paper in all?

■ **Will you be able to borrow a box or package to take to your classroom?** If at all possible, you'll want to borrow a box or package of *each* item you're writing about. If you cannot borrow a full package, try an empty one. For example, if you are writing problems about milk cartons stored in milk crates, you might bring to class an empty milk carton and an empty milk crate. If you think a particular item would make a good problem but you are unable to take a box or package to the classroom, jot down its dimensions. Then find something that is about the same size as the items in the problems.

■ **Will you need an appointment to take your class to visit the place the items are stored?** If so, arrange for a time when you can return with your students, after they have completed the activity.

Continued on next page

Use the information you have gathered to write problem sets, each set on a separate sheet of paper. Following are some types of problems you might include.

- **How many in all?** Provide information about the number of items in each package or container and the number of packages. Students determine how many items in all.

- **How many in each stack or row?** Provide information about how the packages are arranged (for example, in two equal stacks or in four equal rows). Students use their answers to the "how many in all?" questions to determine the number of items in each stack or pile.

- **How much space?** Provide information about how the packages are arranged. If students will be unable to take measurements or make estimates of height, length, or width themselves, you will also need to provide the approximate dimensions. Students determine the total height, length, or width of the stored packages. They also find something in the classroom about that size.

- **How else could we arrange them?** Students find other ways that the packages could be arranged, and they determine how many items would be in each row or stack.

For your introductory problem set, choose one that can be solved without calculators. Be sure you can take a sample of the item and its package. Write an opening "how many in all?" question and at least two others. You will not need to make duplicates of this problem set.

Make several copies of the other problem sets, so that each student has a copy of one set. Keep in mind that some pairs may have time to solve more than one problem set.

Ways to Multiply and Divide

What Happens

Sessions 1, 2, and 3: Multiplication Clusters
Students reason about estimating the answers to multiplication problems, considering which strategies give the closest estimates. Then they solve multiplication clusters that offer practice splitting multiplication problems into components that are easier to solve with particular emphasis on the use of multiples of 10 and 100—that is, seeing 24×31 as $(24 \times 10) + (24 \times 10) + (24 \times 10) + 24$. Students also write and solve their own multiplication cluster problems.

Sessions 4, 5, and 6: Division Clusters
Students explore strategies for making close estimates in division. Then they solve division clusters that emphasize using multiplication to solve division problems and making use of multiples of 10 and 100. They also write and solve their own division cluster problems.

Sessions 7, 8, and 9: How Did I Solve It? The emphasis on multiplication and division continues in a new kind of problem, called How Did I Solve It? Students are challenged to complete partial solutions, each of which reflects a different solution strategy. They work in pairs on How Did I Solve It? problems, and they create their own How Did I Solve It? problems for homework.

Session 10: Ways to Multiply and Divide As an assessment, students show the strategies they use to solve one multiplication problem and one division problem, without standard algorithms or calculators.

Mathematical Emphasis

- Developing, explaining, and comparing strategies for estimating and finding exact answers to multiplication and division problems
- Recording strategies for solving multiplication and division problems
- Solving multiplication and division problems in more than one way
- Using relationships between multiplication and division to help solve problems

For 39 x 22 you could estimate 40 x 22 or 39 x 20. I think 40 x 22 would be closer because plus two 39's is further off than minus one 22.

What to Plan Ahead of Time

Materials

- Students' Multiple Towers from Investigation 1 (Sessions 1–9)
- Stick-on notes: 1 package (Sessions 1–9)
- Overhead projector (Sessions 1–6, optional)
- Chart paper (Sessions 1–9, optional)

Other Preparation

- Duplicate student sheets and teaching resources (located at the end of this unit) in the following quantities. If you have Student Activity Booklets, no copying is needed.

For Sessions 1–3

Student Sheet 20, Multiplication Cluster Problems (p. 179): 1 per student

Student Sheet 21, Writing About Multiplication Clusters (p. 180): 1 per student (homework)

Student Sheet 22, Writing Multiplication and Division Situations (p. 181): 2 per student (homework)

For Sessions 4–6

Student Sheet 23, Division Cluster Problems (p. 182): 1 per student (homework)

Student Sheet 24, Thinking About Division (p. 183): 1 per student (optional)

Student Sheet 25, A Division Situation (p. 184): 1 per student (homework)

Student Sheet 26, A Cluster of Problems (p. 185): 1 per student (homework)

For Sessions 7–9

Student Sheet 27, How Did I Solve It? (p. 186): 1 per student

Student Sheet 28, Different Strategies (p. 189): 1 per student (optional)

Student Sheet 29, Two Ways (p. 191): 1 per student (homework)

Student Sheet 30, My Own How Did I Solve It? Problem (p. 192): 1 per student (homework)

Multiplication Clusters

Materials

- Student Sheet 20 (1 per student)
- Student Sheet 21 (1 per student, homework)
- Student Sheet 22 (2 per student, homework)
- Students' Multiple Towers (from Investigation 1)
- Stick-on notes
- Chart paper (optional)
- Overhead projector (optional)

What Happens

Students reason about estimating the answers to multiplication problems, considering which strategies give the closest estimates. Then they solve multiplication clusters that offer practice splitting multiplication problems into components that are easier to solve, with particular emphasis on the use of multiples of 10 and 100—that is, seeing 24×31 as $(24 \times 10) + (24 \times 10) + (24 \times 10) + 24$. Students also write and solve their own multiplication cluster problems. Student work focuses on:

- using familiar multiplication problems to estimate answers to unfamiliar multiplication problems
- using familiar multiplication problems (especially those involving multiples of 10) to solve unfamiliar multiplication problems
- splitting multiplication problems involving 2- and 3-digit numbers into more manageable components

 **Ten-Minute Math: Quick Images** The Quick Images activity provides valuable practice in spatial concepts. Two or three times during this investigation, outside of math time, use the overhead to present a geometric design. Use three or four Power Polygons, pattern blocks, or other regular polygons, leaving small spaces between the polygons so that students can identify the individual shapes. For example:

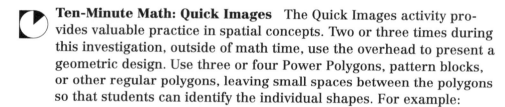

Flash the pattern for 3 seconds and then cover it while students try to recreate the design themselves. They might use their own set of shapes, or draw what they saw. Flash the design for another 3 seconds and let students revise their work. When most students have finished, show the design again and leave it visible for further revision. If students are having difficulty, suggest that they try to find the familiar shapes that make up the figure.

After students finish a design, encourage them to talk about what they saw in successive flashes. You may hear comments such as "I saw a long box with wings." During this discussion, introduce correct terminology for the shapes (*parallelograms, octagons, trapezoids,* and so forth). As you use the terms naturally, students will begin to recognize and use the terms themselves.

For variations on the Quick Images activity, see p. 149.

**Making Close
Multiplication
Estimates**

Write the problem 27 × 8 on the board.

When we solve a problem like this one, we can make a close estimate as a way of beginning. How would you estimate the answer to this problem? Would the answer be more than 100? more than 200? more than 300? What helps you make an estimate?

As students share their strategies for estimating, record them on the board. Strategies may fall into these categories:

- Using familiar multiplication pairs:

  Half of 8 is 4 and there are 4 25's in 100. If you double that you get 200. So, it's about 200.

  The answer is a little less than 240 because 27 is a little less than 30, and 30 × 8 is 240.

  It's between 200 and 240 because you can round 27 off to 25 or 30. If it's 25 then it multiplies out to 200, and if it's 30, it's 240.

- Using multiples of 10:

  I know 27 × 10 is 270, so the answer is a little less than 270.

  It's about 200 because 10 × 8 is 80, and double it is 160, and then you have to add on the 7 × 8.

- Breaking the problem into more familiar components:

  I know 12 × 8, so I said it's close to 12 × 8 + 12 × 8 because 12 and 12 is 24. That's 196.

Students with limited estimating experience may think that estimating is the same as "rounding off." That is, they may try to find the exact answer first, then approximate it to a round number. The **Teacher Note**, Estimation: Emphasizing Strategies (p. 81), suggests ways to help students approach estimation more meaningfully.

After they have discussed their estimates, students find the exact answer to 27 × 8 (without standard algorithms or calculators), then share solution strategies.

Repeat the activity with 27 × 13. If students are having difficulty making estimates, offer them familiar round numbers to think about, as you did in the previous problem:

Is it more than 100? more than 500?

You might also ask if the answer to the previous problem could help them estimate the answer to 27 × 13.

Reasoning About Estimates

I'm going to give you a multiplication problem and two possible ways to estimate the answer. Talk with a partner about which way would give a closer estimate. See if you can decide *without doing any calculations*, even in your head.

Write the following on the board or chart paper:

Problem: 47×32 Estimates: 40×32 50×32

As students talk in pairs, circulate to remind them to decide which estimate is closer *without* doing any calculations; that is, without finding the answers to 40×32 or 50×32. Ask a few volunteers to share their thinking with the class. For example:

50×32 is a closer estimate because it is three 32's away from the answer, and 40×32 is seven 32's away.

50 is closer to 47 than 40 is, so 50×32 is a closer estimate.

I would round to 50 if the number was more than 45, and 40 if it was less than 45.

If you think your students need more practice, repeat the activity with another problem and two estimates that involve changing only one of the numbers in the problem. For example:

Problem: 22×17 Estimates: 20×17 25×17

More Challenging Problems Next present a problem and two estimates, each of which involves changing a *different* number in the problem. For example:

Problem: 39×22 Estimates: 40×22 39×20

Again, students determine which estimate is closer to the exact answer without doing any calculations. Encourage them to think about how many more or less than the exact answer the estimates are.

Is 40×22 larger or smaller than 39×22? How many more 22's larger? Is 39×20 larger or smaller? How many more 39's smaller?

Continue to repeat the activity, asking questions as needed to encourage the same kind of thinking.

Problem: 312×9 Estimates: 312×10 300×9
Problem: 123×38 Estimates: 123×40 120×38

Multiplication Clusters

Before starting this activity, have the Multiple Towers from Investigation 1 posted where students can see them. Some of the problems in this activity (and throughout the rest of this investigation) involve numbers for which students built towers. Students may always refer to the Multiple Towers if it helps them to solve those problems.

Introducing Cluster Problems Write the following cluster of problems on the board. Students with previous experience in the unit *Mathematical Thinking at Grade 5* or in the *Investigations* grade 4 curriculum will be familiar with cluster problems. See the **Teacher Note,** About the Cluster Problems in This Unit (p. 82), for background information.

10×32 5×32

20×32 30×32

    35×32

This is a cluster of multiplication problems. In a cluster, you can use relationships among the problems to help you find the answers. For example, the first four problems here can help you find an answer to the last one (35×32). Try it. If you think another problem will help you solve 35×32, add it to the cluster.

Working with a partner, students first make an estimate for 35×32, then solve all the problems. They may refer to the Multiple Towers, but they may not use standard algorithms or calculators.

Circulate as students work. Encourage them to think about which multiplication pairs they "just know," and when they need to apply a strategy to find the answer. After students have been working for several minutes, call the class together to talk about relationships among the problems in the cluster.

How can knowing $10 \times 32 = 320$ help you to solve 5×32? How can knowing 10×32 help you to solve 20×32? Which of the problems in this cluster helped you to figure out the answer to 35×32? Are there other problems not in this cluster that might have helped you?

Add 36×32 to the cluster. Ask students to explain how the answer to 35×32 can help them with 36×32.

Working on Multiplication Clusters Give each student a copy of Student Sheet 20, Multiplication Cluster Problems. Students may work alone or in pairs. Remind them to use relationships among the problems to solve the *last* problem in the cluster. Students may refer to the Multiple Towers, but may not use standard algorithms or calculators.

Observing the Students While students are working, observe what strategies they have for relating known factor pairs to new multiplication problems. Remind students to add to the cluster any other problems that help them solve the last problem in the cluster.

■ Do they use multiplication by multiples of 10 to solve problems? For example, do they solve 47×18 by thinking $(10 \times 18) + (10 \times 18) + (10 \times 18) + (10 \times 18) + (7 \times 18)$? Can they relate 2×72 to 20×72?

■ Do they use doubling and halving to find solutions? For example, to solve 5×18, do they use $10 \times 18 = 180$, then halve 180? Or do they think of 20×18 as double 10×18?

■ Can they put together answers to two or more easier problems to solve a more difficult one? (40×18 is 720, and 5×18 is 90, so 45×18 is 810). Do they see how to use subtraction as well as addition to solve multiplication problems, for example, thinking of 498×9 as $(500 \times 9) - (2 \times 9)$?

■ Do they have strategies for determining whether an answer makes sense? Do they use estimation? Do they try solving the problem in a different way? Do they make up a multiplication situation to fit the problem?

■ What factor pairs do they know by heart?

If some students are having difficulty solving cluster problems, you might want to work with them in a small group. Encourage these students to talk about how they can use what they know to solve more difficult problems. Students may find it helpful to make an estimate of the answer to the final problem in the cluster, or another problem in the cluster they find difficult. As students make an estimate using multiplication pairs they are familiar with, they may begin to see ways that they can use what they know to solve more difficult problems.

If you feel that some students are ready for harder problems, or conversely that the problems on Student Sheet 20 are too difficult for some students, adjust the numbers.

Students who finish early can find a different way to solve the final problem in each cluster, or they can build a Multiple Tower for a number no one has explored yet (perhaps 29, 68, 77, 85, 154, 281, 326, 543, or 1233).

Activity

Multiplication Cluster Strategies

Write the second cluster from Student Sheet 20 on the board.

10×18	5×18
50×18	2×18
20×18	40×18
45×18	47×18

Ask students to describe ways they used the problems in the cluster to find the answer to 47×18. What other problems *not* in this cluster might have helped them?

Following are some possible strategies for solving 47×18:

■ Breaking the problem into 40×18 and 7×18, and adding the two results. Students might solve 7×18 by breaking it into 5×18 and 2×18, or by counting up by 18's from 5×18.

■ Finding the result of 50×18 and counting down by 18's.

■ Recognizing that 45×18 is 9 times 5×18. Students multiply the result of 5×18 by 9, and then add on 2×18.

As students explain their strategies, draw their attention to examples that involve multiplying by 10, doubling, and partitioning larger numbers into smaller or more familiar components. Many students will see a pattern when a number is multiplied by 10. They may notice that you always add a zero and be unable to explain why. Encourage students to doublecheck their work using other strategies. They should be able to estimate that their answer is a reasonable one. For example, if a student solves 20×18 by saying that "It's like 2×18, but it's 20, not 2, so you add 0 and get 360," you might ask "And how do you know 360 is a reasonable answer? Is there another way you can prove it? How do you know it's not 3600?"

Making a Problem Cluster

Allow at least 30 minutes at the end of Session 3 for this activity. Write on the board or overhead:

26×31

Students work with a partner to create their own cluster of several problems that would help them find the answer to 26×31 without using algorithms or calculators. They solve all the problems in their cluster.

If students are having difficulty getting started, ask two or three volunteers to suggest a problem that might help them think about how to solve 26×31. Record these ideas as the students briefly explain how each problem might help. The clusters that student pairs write may include some or all of the problems on the board.

Observing the Students   As students work, circulate to observe what strategies they are using. Are they beginning with familiar factor pairs? reasoning about multiples of 26 or 31? skip counting? using relationships among factor pairs? partitioning numbers into two or more components? Encourage any students having difficulty to use strategies that involve multiplying one of the factors by 10.

As pairs finish, they write their clusters on the board or post them on a bulletin board. Set aside about 5 minutes for students to look at each other's sets, to see if they can understand why the authors chose these particular problems. They might post stick-on notes with their initials on any sets they do not understand; resolve any such questions in a brief whole-group discussion.

$$10 \times 31 = 310 \quad \text{add zero because} \times \text{by 10}$$
$$20 \times 31 = 620 \quad \text{twice as much}$$
$$\text{half} \quad 25 \times 31 = (620 + 155) = 775$$
$$5 \times 31 = 155$$
$$1 \times 31 = 31$$
$$26 \times 31 = (775 + 31) = 806$$

The student who wrote the above cluster explained it this way: "To figure out 26×31 you can add up the answers to 20×31 and 5×31 and 1×31 because $20 + 5 + 1 = 26$. I started with 10×31 because I knew it automatically. Then 20×31 is double 10×31, so add $310 + 310$. And 5×31 is half of 10×31, so divide 310 by 2. You get 25×31 by adding the answers to 20×31 and 5×31. Then add 1 more 31 to get 26 31's."

Sessions 1, 2, and 3 Follow-Up

Homework

Writing About Multiplication Clusters After Session 1, students complete Student Sheet 21, Writing About Multiplication Clusters. Collect these papers so you can get a sense of how students are thinking about cluster problems.

Writing Multiplication and Division Situations After Session 2, students write a multiplication situation based on the final problem in one of the clusters they have solved. They record the problem they choose on Student Sheet 22, Writing Multiplication and Division Situations. Then they write a division situation that corresponds to their multiplication situation and write the equation with division notation. After Session 3, send home another copy of Student Sheet 22 for more practice.

❖ **Tip for the Linguistically Diverse Classroom** Students can use pictures with symbols and words to communicate their multiplication and division situations.

Students might ask an adult to solve their multiplication situation *without* using a standard algorithm or calculator. Students can then demonstrate how they used the problems in the cluster to find the answer.

Estimation: Emphasizing Strategies

Estimating is an important skill with useful applications both in and out of school. Practicing and talking about estimation develops good number sense and can also help students develop strategies for performing exact calculations. When students estimate, they use relationships among numbers that are familiar to them. For example, to estimate the answer to 27×8, students might think of $25 \times 8 = 200$, $27 \times 10 = 270$, or $30 \times 8 = 240$. Any of these familiar relationships can serve as fruitful starting places for exact calculations.

Some students believe that an estimate must be a "round" number, or that a better estimate is one that is closer to the answer. When asked to estimate the answer to 27×8, some students will first find the exact answer, 216, and then approximate it to a number such as 200, 210, or 220. These students are not estimating; they are simply approximating numbers.

Here are some ways that you can help students approach estimation in a meaningful way and recognize the importance of estimation:

■ As students discuss their strategies, draw their attention to approaches that yield estimates expressed as *less than* or *more than* rather than exact numbers. For example: "The answer to 27×8 is a little less than 240 because 27 is a little less than 30, and 30×8 is 240."

■ When students are sharing estimation strategies, focus the discussion on how they made their estimates rather than how close their estimates are to the exact answer. That way, students will not be tempted to first find the exact answer and then share an "estimation" strategy that yields a closer answer. To help students evaluate different estimation strategies, present a problem and two or three strategies for estimating the answer. Ask students if they can determine which would yield a closer estimate and why, without doing any calculations. For example: "Which is a closer estimate for the answer to 47×32: 40×32 or 50×32? Why?" Encourage reasoning such as "50×32 is a closer estimate because it is three 32's away from the answer, while 40×32 is seven 32's away."

■ Ask students to estimate as part of the problem-solving process. Making an estimate *first* can help them determine the reasonableness of the answer they find by exact calculation (with or without a calculator). Similarly, making an estimate *after* solving a problem can give them a sense of whether their answer is about right.

■ Help students recognize that how close an estimate needs to be depends on why they are estimating. For example, if you notice a student has an extra 0 at the end of an answer (having written 8700 instead of 870), ask for an estimate of the answer. Explain that in this case, it doesn't matter whether the estimate is off by 1, 10, or even 25; it is valuable simply because it shows that the calculated answer is too large.

■ Encourage students to think of situations where an estimate is sufficient (perhaps because an exact answer is unnecessary, difficult, or impossible to find) and to think about how close an estimate should be in each such situation. For example, if we are about to go to the grocery store and want to know if we have enough money to buy everything on our shopping list, we might make an estimate of the total cost. If we are planning a party, we might make estimates based on the number of guests: how much we think they will eat, and how much that amount of food will cost. Many people in business, like carpenters, house painters, and landscapers, need to make estimates when bidding a job to determine what materials they will need and how much they will cost.

Cluster problems are groups of related problems. Students choose problems from the cluster to help them solve the final problem. Sometimes more than one strategy is suggested by the group of problems, depending on which problems are used. Students need not solve all the problems in the cluster, and they may add problems to the cluster that they find useful in solving the last problem.

The cluster problems in this unit are designed to help students become familiar with different strategies for multiplying and dividing. Through these clusters, they learn how they can pull apart problems into more manageable components, then combine the answers to each component; they learn to use their knowledge of factor pairs, multiples, and the relationship between multiplication and division; and they become familiar with what happens when we multiply a number by 10, 100, or their multiples.

Different clusters lead students toward different strategies. For example, here are three ways we might think about the problem 24×31, with a different cluster that reflects each way:

■ The problem 24×31 is the same as 24×10 plus 24×10 plus 24×10 plus 24. I can count up by 240's—240, 480, 720, and then add on 24 and get 744.

Cluster:	24×10	24×20
	24×30	24×1
	24×31	

■ I know 24 x 3 is 72, so 24 x 30 is 720. Add 1 more 24 and get 744.

Cluster:	24×3	24×30
	24×1	**24×31**

■ I know 31×2 is 62, so 31×20 is 620. Double 31×2 and get 124. Add that to 620, and get 744.

Cluster:	31×2	31×20
	31×4	**31×24**

We can think about a division problem, such as $767 \div 36$, in different ways as well:

■ There are ten 36's in 360, so there are twenty in 720. In 767, there are twenty-one 36's and a remainder of 11 ($767 - 756 = 11$), so one way of expressing the solution to $767 \div 36$ is 21 R 11.

Cluster:	10×36	20×36
	21×36	**$767 \div 36$**

■ I know 36 x 2 is 72, so 36 x 20 is 620 (or $720 \div 20 = 36$). Then $767 - 720$ is 47. Take away 1 more 36 (or twenty-one 36's in all) and you're left with 11.

Cluster:	36×2	36×20
	$767 \div 720$	**$767 \div 36$**

■ The problem $767 \div 36$ is the same as twice $360 \div 36$ plus $47 \div 36$. That's $10 + 10 + 1$, with 11 out of a group of 36 left over.

Cluster:	$360 \div 36$	$720 \div 36$
	$47 \div 36$	**$767 \div 36$**

As students solve multiplication and division problems in this unit, observe their strategies and ways of thinking about multiplication and division. Always encourage them to "use what they know" to find their solutions. As they learn to build on what they already understand well—familiar factor pairs, multiples of 10, and problems they can solve easily—they deepen their understanding of numbers and operations.

Sessions 4, 5, and 6

Division Clusters

What Happens

Students explore strategies for making close estimates in division, then solve division clusters that emphasize using multiplication to solve division problems and making use of multiples of 10 and 100. They also write and solve their own division cluster problems. Student work focuses on:

- using familiar multiplication and division problems to estimate answers to unfamiliar division problems

- using familiar multiplication and division problems (especially those involving multiples of 10) to solve unfamiliar multiplication and division problems

- using relationships between multiplication and division to solve problems

Materials

- Student Sheet 23 (1 per student, homework)

- Student Sheet 24 (1 per student, optional)

- Student Sheet 25 (1 per student, homework)

- Student Sheet 26 (1 per student, homework)

- Students' Multiple Towers

- Stick-on notes

- Chart paper (optional)

- Overhead projector (optional)

Activity

Making Close Division Estimates

Write the following problem on the board:

$200 \div 9$

What are some estimates for this problem? Would the answer be more than 10? more than 20? more than 30? What helps you make an estimate?

As students share their strategies for estimating, help the class recognize uses of these strategies:

- Using familiar multiplication or division pairs: "The answer is a little over 22, because there are twenty 9's in 180, and two 9's in 18."

- Multiplying or dividing by 10 or a multiple of 10: "The answer is about 20, because $200 \div 10$ is 20."

- Breaking the problem into parts: "There are eleven 9's in 100, so there are about twenty-two 9's in 200."

Students then find the exact answer to $200 \div 9$ (without using standard algorithms or calculators).

Repeat the activity with $200 \div 11$.

Many students will recognize that the answer to both problems (200 ÷ 9 and 200 ÷ 11) is about 10, but may have difficulty determining which answer is a little more than 10 and which is a little less than 10. It may be helpful to think about 200 ÷ 9 as "How many 9's are in 200?" and 200 ÷ 11 as "How many 11's are in 200?"

There are twenty 10's in 200. How many 9's are in 200? Do we need more than twenty 9's to get to 200? Do we need more than twenty 11's to get to 200?

Other students may find it helpful to think about the relationship between the number of groups 200 is being divided into and the size of those groups:

If you divide 200 into 10 groups, how big is each group? (20) If you divide it into only 2 groups, will each group be bigger or smaller than 20? What if you divide it into 4 groups? 9 groups? 11 groups?

Note that the two ways of thinking about 200 ÷ 9, above, reflects two distinct kinds of division situations. In the first, you are thinking about *how many groups* of a certain size you need to make up the total. A related story problem might be: I have 200 balloons. I'm going to tie them together in bunches of 9 to give out to my friends. How many groups can I make? In this situation, division is used to describe partitioning. In the second, you know how many groups, and you want to know *what size groups* you need to make up the total. Here, a story problem might be: I have 200 balloons. I'm going to give them out to 9 friends.

Activity

Reasoning About Division Estimates

Write the following on the board or chart paper:

Problem: 101 ÷ 3   Estimates: 90 ÷ 3   120 ÷ 3

***Without doing any calculations,* are these estimates larger or smaller than the exact answer? Which is a closer estimate?**

Students discuss these questions with a partner, then share their thinking with the class. For example:

> 90 ÷ 3 is too small because 90 is less than 101, and 120 ÷ 3 is too big because 120 is bigger than 101.

> 90 ÷ 3 is a closer estimate because 101 is 11 away from 90, and it's 19 away from 120.

> 90 ÷ 3 is closer because 101 is about one-third of the way from 90 to 120.

For more practice, repeat the activity with another problem and pair of estimates:

Problem: $185 \div 7$ Estimates: $140 \div 7$ $210 \div 7$

Note: If you make up your own problems and estimates, the dividend of each estimate should be a multiple of 10 times the divisor.

Different Divisors   For the next problem, give one estimate that involves a change in the divisor, and another that involves a change in the dividend:

Problem: $44 \div 5$ Estimates: $44 \div 4$ $40 \div 5$

When the two estimates use different divisors like this, it can be difficult to determine which is closer to the answer without doing any calculations. So, focus attention on deciding if the estimates are larger or smaller than the exact answer.

If students are having difficulty, encourage them to think about relationships between the size of the dividend and the number of groups it is being broken into.

If we break 44 into 4 equal groups instead of 5, are those groups going to be larger or smaller? If we break 40 instead of 44 into 5 equal groups, are those groups going to be larger or smaller?

Repeat the activity, again asking only if the estimates are larger or smaller than the exact answer.

Problem: $140 \div 13$ Estimates: $130 \div 13$ $140 \div 10$

For an extra challenge, students might find a way to tell which of the two estimates is closer to the exact answer without doing any calculations. This requires sophisticated reasoning about relationships between the size of the dividends and divisors in the problem and each estimate.

As students work on the problems in this activity, observe how they are solving them and making sense of the remainders. Make a note of any students who seem to be having difficulty. For the next activity, Solving Division Clusters, you might call together these students to work with you as a small group on Student Sheet 24, Thinking About Division, while the rest of the class works on Student Sheet 23, Division Cluster Problems.

Note: If many of your students need practice making sense of division with remainders, you may need to spend an extra session on this.

Teacher Checkpoint

Looking at Division Clusters

Using Cluster Problems for Division   Write a cluster of related division problems on the board and ask students to solve them, alone or with a partner, without using standard algorithms or calculators.

$$12 \div 12 \qquad 120 \div 12$$
$$132 \div 12 \qquad 133 \div 12$$

As in the multiplication clusters, students look for ways to use the first three problems to help solve the last one ($133 \div 12$). Students may record remainders in any format they choose, such as $11\frac{1}{12}$ or 11 R 1.

Observing the Students   As students work, circulate to see how they are solving the problems. Here are some ways you might help students who are having difficulty:

■ Some students may immediately think of using multiplication to solve this problem. This approach is introduced in the next example, but it is fine for students to begin using it here. For example, a student might add $10 \times 12 = 120$ to the cluster.

■ If some students do not recognize the strategy of breaking a problem into two components, encourage them to think more about relationships among the problems.

   If there are ten 12's in 120, and you add another 12 to get 132, how many 12's do you now have? How can knowing $12 \div 12$ is equal to 1 and $120 \div 12$ is equal to 10 help you to solve $132 \div 12$?

■ If some students have trouble judging whether an answer makes sense, suggest they make an estimate, solve the problem in a different way, or make up a situation to fit the problem.

■ If some students are having difficulty making sense of the remainder, ask them to think about how they would handle remainders in an easier problem. The **Dialogue Box,** Thinking About Remainders (p. 90), shows how students in one class worked to make sense of remainders.

   If you have presented the *Investigations* grade 5 unit *Name That Portion,* some students may be comfortable relating division and fraction notation. If that is the case, you might add $1 \div 12 = \frac{1}{12}$ to the cluster. Can they find a way to use the answer to $1 \div 12$ along with $132 \div 12$ to solve $133 \div 12$?

As students share solution strategies, look for the remainder written as a fraction. Review the **Teacher Note,** Remainders, Fractions, and Decimals (p. 54), if the students need help thinking about remainders as fractions.

Add $131 \div 12$ to the cluster.

How can 132 ÷ 12 = 11 help solve this new problem?

Some students will think of 131 ÷ 12 as eleven 12's with a 1 taken away
from a 12, leaving ten 12's and 11 left over. Others may think of 131 ÷ 12
as ten 12's and 11 more. Still others might break 131 ÷ 12 into two
problems: 120 ÷ 12 and 11 ÷ 12.

Using Multiplication to Solve Division Problems   Introduce a division
cluster that includes multiplication problems.

3×7 30×7

10×7 4×7

$$241 \div 7$$

**Can you find a way to use these multiplication problems to help solve the
last division problem, 241 ÷ 7?**

Students work on the cluster alone or with a partner; a few then share
their strategies with the class.

Solving Division Clusters

Meeting Individual Needs If you observed some students having difficulty in the previous activity, Looking at Division Clusters, call them together to work with you on Student Sheet 24, Thinking About Division, while the others in the class begin Student Sheet 23, Division Cluster Problems.

The problems on Student Sheet 24 involve smaller, more familiar numbers. Some students may want to use counters, such as square tiles or paper clips, to help solve them. Others may find it helpful to draw pictures or make up division situations to represent the problems. Once these students have a better sense of remainders, they can work with the rest of the class on Student Sheet 23.

Division Cluster Problems Distribute copies of Student Sheet 23, Division Cluster Problems. Students work alone or in pairs. Encourage them to talk about how they can use what they know to solve more difficult problems. Suggest making an estimate for the final problem in the cluster (or for any problems in the cluster they find difficult). Students may sometimes find it helpful to refer to the posted Multiple Towers.

Students who finish early can find a different way to solve the final problem in each cluster, or they can build a Multiple Tower for a number that has not been explored yet.

Sharing Strategies for Division Clusters Write the third division cluster from Student Sheet 23 on the board for a whole-class discussion of strategies.

$300 \div 3$	$120 \div 3$
$90 \div 3$	$15 \div 3$
$45 \div 3$	**$437 \div 3$**

Ask students to share other problems they added to the cluster to help them solve $437 \div 3$. Point out when a student is using relationships between multiplication and division or is multiplying or dividing by 10. Also talk about finding and recording remainders in different ways.

**Making a
Division Cluster**

Allow at least 30 minutes at the end of Session 6 for this activity. Write on
the board or overhead:

250 ÷ 11

Students work with a partner to create their own cluster of several problems. As they work, circulate to observe. For those having difficulty, ask
how they might use multiplication or division problems that they already
know.

When pairs finish their clusters, they write them on the board or post them
on a bulletin board. Share and discuss them, just as you did with the multiplication clusters students wrote (Session 3), giving students a chance to
use stick-on notes to question any of their classmates' clusters they don't
understand.

Sessions 4, 5, and 6 Follow-Up

 **Homework**

Division Cluster Problems   After Session 4, students choose a cluster
of problems on Student Sheet 23, Division Cluster Problems, that they
have not yet done. They solve the problems, and they write about how
they found each answer.

A Division Situation   After Session 5, students write a division situation
based on the final problem in one of the clusters they have solved on
Student Sheets 23 or 24, and write about what they would do with the
extras. Students record the problem they choose on Student Sheet 25, A
Division Situation, before taking it home.

❖ **Tip for the Linguistically Diverse Classroom**   Students can use
pictures with symbols and words to communicate their division situation
and what they would do with the remainders.

A Cluster of Problems   After Session 6, students make up a problem
cluster that would help someone solve 187 ÷ 13 on Student Sheet 26, A
Cluster of Problems. Their paper should include answers to all the problems. Collect this homework to get a sense of how students are thinking
about division clusters.

To introduce the activity Looking at Division Clusters (p. 85), the teacher presents this cluster:

$$12 \div 12 \qquad 120 \div 12$$
$$132 \div 12 \qquad 133 \div 12$$

These students are talking about how they handled the remainder for the last problem in the cluster, $133 \div 12$. Their discussion illustrates different ways they make sense of remainders: as a "leftover" (1 extra); as part of a group (1 of the next group of 12); and as a fraction ($\frac{1}{12}$ of a group). A common misconception also comes up: that the answer to a division problem is the sum of the quotient and the remainder.

Maricel: Well, $120 \div 12$ is 10, and $12 \div 12$ is 1. Put them together and get $132 \div 12$ is 11. Between 132 and 133 there's only 1 difference. We're looking for 12 difference, so it's 11 R 1.

Julie: I got 12 for the answer. I know $132 \div 12$ is 11, so $133 \div 12$ would be 12. Just add the 1.

Sofia: No, it's one-twelfth of another group. It's 1 out of a group of 12, so $\frac{1}{12}$.

Maricel: I think $133 \div 12$ is the same as "How many 12's are in 133?" We know there's 11 of them in 132, and then you have 1 more left.

Noah: You can think of it like $132 \div 12$ is 11, and then you need to do $1 \div 12$ because there's 1 difference between 132 and 133. So it's 11 and $\frac{1}{12}$. Anyway, it can't be 12, because 12×12 is 144 and we only want 133.

To present an easier problem with remainders, the teacher draws 5 circles on a piece of chart paper and writes $5 \div 2$.

$$\bigcirc \; \bigcirc \; \bigcirc \; \bigcirc \; \bigcirc \qquad 5 \div 2$$

If I divided these 5 circles into two groups, how many are in each group? How many are left over?

A student comes to the board and circles two groups, and records the answer: 2 R 1.

$$\bigcirc \; \bigcirc \bigcirc \; \bigcirc \bigcirc \qquad 5 \div 2 = 2\ R\ 1$$

Julie: There's 1 left, because you can't take out any more groups of 2.

Sofia: But you don't have to have a remainder. You could divide that 1 into halves, so it would be $2\frac{1}{2}$.

Maricel: That's how it is with $133 \div 12$. You take out all the groups of 12 that you can and then there's 1 left.

Noah: Or $\frac{1}{12}$ left. The $\frac{1}{2}$ is like the $\frac{1}{12}$. It's 1 out of 2, so it's $\frac{1}{2}$, but we have 1 out of 12, so it's $\frac{1}{12}$.

How Did I Solve It?

What Happens

The emphasis on multiplication and division continues in a new kind of problem, called How Did I Solve It? Students are challenged to complete partial solutions, each of which reflects a different solution strategy. They work in pairs on How Did I Solve It? problems, and they create their own How Did I Solve It? problems for homework. Student work focuses on:

- understanding different strategies for solving division problems
- solving multiplication and division problems in two or more different ways
- keeping track of steps used to solve multiplication and division problems

Materials

- Student Sheet 27 (1 per student)
- Student Sheet 28 (1 per student, optional)
- Student Sheet 29 (1 per student, homework)
- Student Sheet 30 (1 per student, homework)
- Stick-on notes (1 package)
- Students' Multiple Towers
- Chart paper (optional)

Activity

Practice with Estimating

The strategies that students use in making estimates are often useful for finding the exact answer to a problem as well. Continue to provide students with practice in making multiplication and division estimates. Encourage them to extend their estimation strategies to more difficult problems.

Write on the board the problem $400 \div 34$.

What are some estimates for this problem? How did you make your estimates?

As students share their strategies for estimating, draw their attention to those strategies that involve using familiar multiplication pairs, multiplying or dividing by 10 or a multiple of 10, or breaking the problem into parts. Then give them a few minutes to find an exact answer, without using standard algorithms or calculators. Circulate to see how students are recording and keeping track of their work. If time permits, ask students to solve the problem in a second way.

As students explain their solution strategies, record the strategies on the board or chart paper. Ask students to explain any similarities they notice among the strategies.

Repeat this activity using a multiplication problem, such as 46×21 or 103×52.

Solving a Problem with the First Step Given

Note: As students work on this activity, make a note of any who are having difficulty understanding different strategies or who might need more practice with division problems that use smaller numbers. There is an option in the next activity for helping such students.

Write the following problem on the board:

$133 \div 6$

We've been talking about different ways to solve division problems. You can probably think of at least one way to solve $133 \div 6$.

This time I want to start a certain way. Suppose someone said that when she solved this problem, the first thing she did was solve 6×10. [*Write 6×10 on the board.*] Think about it: How could solving 6×10 have helped her? What's one thing she could have done next? What's one way she could have finished solving $133 \div 6$? Talk to a partner, and see how you might finish this problem, starting from 6×10.

This introduces the How Did I Solve It? type of problem. It is the first time in this unit students have been asked to think through a strategy from a given starting point. Some may find it helpful to think of the task as writing a cluster for $133 \div 6$, using 6×10 as the first problem in the cluster. There may be several possible clusters. Students having difficulty might first solve the problem their own way (but not with a standard algorithm), then look for ways that any of their steps might be like solving 6×10.

After a few minutes, talk about all the ways students found to complete the problem. Record their solution methods on chart paper or on a part of the board you can leave on display for the rest of Sessions 7–9. Title this display *Strategies for Solving $133 \div 6$*. Six possible strategies are shown in the **Dialogue Box,** How Can 6×10 Help Us Solve $133 \div 6$? (p. 98).

Another way to solve $133 \div 6$ is to start out by solving $12 \div 6$. [*Write $12 \div 6$ on the board.*] What could you do next? With your partner, start with $12 \div 6$ and finish solving $133 \div 6$.

As before, discuss and record students' strategies and reasoning, looking for similarities among the approaches.

Who can think of another way to start out solving $133 \div 6$? What's the first thing you would do?

Write students' suggestions on the board. Other possible first steps include 6×20, $120 \div 6$, and 6×2.

How Did I Solve It?

Note: On the basis of your observations during the previous activity, decide which students are ready for Student Sheet 27, How Did I Solve It? and which would benefit from some preliminary work on Student Sheet 28, Different Strategies.

The problems on Student Sheet 28 involve smaller, more familiar numbers. Students might use counters (such as square tiles or paper clips) or may find it helpful to draw pictures or make up division situations to represent the problems. They do not need to do all of Student Sheet 28; when they seem ready to work with slightly larger numbers, they can begin Student Sheet 27.

How Did I Solve It? Students who are doing Student Sheet 27 work in pairs. Each problem gives the first step of three to five different solution methods. Students choose *two* first steps to complete for each problem. Some may need additional paper for recording their work.

A few of the problems involve numbers on the students' Multiple Towers; they may refer to the Multiple Towers as they work. Students may also refer to your class display of *Strategies for Solving 133 ÷ 6.*

If some students are having difficulty, suggest they first solve the problem their own way (but without using a standard algorithm), and look for similarities between their steps and the options given on Student Sheet 27. For example, a student who solves a multiplication problem with repeated addition may recognize that the repeated addition could be shown with multiplication notation. Students who have trouble completing two solution methods might be given the option of doing only one and recording their own way of solving the problem as well.

Students may not find a way to complete every first step. As they talk with partners and later share solution strategies with the class, encourage them to listen and learn from one another. Do not be concerned if some students do not understand the more sophisticated strategies; even without these, students will be developing a repertoire of strategies that make sense to them. The **Teacher Note,** Choosing Strategies for Computation (p. 97), offers ideas on helping students become fluent with a variety of strategies.

Throughout this activity, encourage students to work at their own pace. Those who finish early can go back to complete other first steps for each problem, or they can record additional first steps and solution methods for the same problems. Students who do not complete Student Sheet 27 will have a chance to finish during Choice Time in Investigation 5. At this point, the emphasis should be on developing a strong understanding of strategies for solving computation problems rather than on speed in finding answers.

Sharing Our Solution Strategies

Allow at least 20 minutes at the end of Session 9 for sharing How Did I Solve It? solution strategies in small groups (two pairs) and then as a class. Depending on the size of your class and the time available, you might organize class sharing in one of several different ways:

- **Option 1** Choose two of the problems from Student Sheet 27. Write each problem and all the corresponding "first steps" on the board or on separate sheets of chart paper. Leave enough room for students to record several solution methods for each first step. Each pair or group chooses one of the problems and records a way that they solved it. (You may need to remind students that there can be several solution methods for each first step.) Students also check that they understand the solution methods already on the chart, using stick-on notes to identify anything they don't understand or agree with. If your class is large, you may want to assign an order in which pairs come up to record their solutions. While some students are recording, others can compare solutions in their groups.

  When everyone has recorded a solution, give students a few minutes to look over the variety of methods for solving each problem. Hold a brief class discussion about any questions.

- **Option 2** Organize class sharing as above, but make a chart with sections for *all six* problems on Student Sheet 27. Each pair might record solutions for two or three problems.

- **Option 3** Choose one of the problems. Ask for volunteers to explain how they completed each first step. See how many different ways students can come up with. Record students' strategies, or invite them to record their strategies on the board themselves.

Focus on Difficult Solution Methods Take a few minutes to discuss any first steps that students did not know how to complete.

Were there any first steps that no one in your group could complete? Which ones? Was anyone else in the class able to complete them? How?

If there are some first steps that *no one* could complete, challenge students to continue to try to find a way to complete them in the next few days. You may want to post these first steps (and the associated problem) on a piece of chart paper headed *Challenge*. Students can record solution methods here as they find them.

14 × 9

a. Start with 10 × 9

$10 \times 9 = 90$
$4 \times 9 = 36$
$\begin{array}{r} 90 \\ +36 \\ \hline \boxed{126} \end{array}$

$10 \times 9 = 90$
Half it $= 45$
$\begin{array}{r} -9 \\ \hline 36 \end{array}$
$90 + 36 = 126$

b. Start with 7 × 9

$7 \times 9 = 63$
then 14 is
double 7, so
double 63 is
126

c. Start with 14 × 10

$14 \times 10 = 140$
$140 - 14 = 126$

499 ÷ 2

a. Start with 2 × 200

$2 \times 200 = 400$
$\begin{array}{r} +90 \\ 9 \\ \hline 499 \end{array}$ divide each by 2
$\begin{array}{r} 200 \\ +45 \\ 4r1 \\ \hline 249 r1 \end{array}$

b. Start with 400 ÷ 2

$400 \div 2 = 200$
$99 \div 2 = 49 \, r \, 1$ } add
$\overline{249 \, r \, 1}$

c. Start with 500 ÷ 2

$500 \div 2 = 250$ Then since it's one less you put a remainder of 1 and −1 from 250 so

249 R 1

d. Start with 100 ÷ 2

$100 \div 2 = 50$ round 499 to 500
$5 \times 100 = 500$
$5 \times 50 = 250$ $-\frac{1}{2} = 249\frac{1}{2}$ or $249 \, r1$

Sessions 7, 8, and 9 Follow-Up

🏠 **Homework**

Two Ways   After Session 7, Students find *two ways* to solve one of the following from Student Sheet 29, Two Ways:

$87 \div 3$ $175 \div 8$ $263 \div 12$ $357 \div 15$

Students may not use calculators. Encourage them to find two solution methods that do not involve standard algorithms. Collect students' work to get a sense of their strategies for division.

My Own How Did I Solve It? Problem   After Session 8, students make up their own How Did I Solve It? problem on Student Sheet 30, My Own How Did I Solve It? Problem. They start by choosing one of the following:

$98 \div 5$ $176 \div 6$ $197 \div 4$ $243 \div 11$ $685 \div 27$

$989 \div 49$ 112×9 55×32 16×26 24×12

Adjust the numbers if you think students need more challenge or more practice. Students solve the chosen problem in at least two ways, and they write their solutions clearly, as if explaining to someone else. Then, on a separate piece of paper, they record the problem and the first step of each solution method they found, creating a How Did I Solve It? problem.

Collect students' written solutions to the problems to get a sense of the strategies they are using for solving multiplication and division problems. Return page 2 of Student Sheet 30 to students for use as Session 9 homework.

$176 \div 6 =$

start with $120 \div 6$	start with $174 \div 6 =$
you could break up the problem and say how many times does 6 go into 120 (20) and there's 56 more and 6 goes into that 9 with 2 more (54+2) and add that together and get 29 R2.	Start with the closest number to 176 that six goes into evenly. Which is 174. Now 174 is 2 away from 176 and 6 does not go into 2. So the answer is 29 R2.

Another How Did I Solve It? Problem   After Session 9, students use their completed page 2 of Student Sheet 30 to ask an adult (a friend or family member) to finish the How Did I Solve It? problem they wrote. Remind students to be patient teachers; many adults will be unfamiliar with the students' methods for solving multiplication and division problems.

Choosing Strategies for Computation

One goal of this unit is for students to explore many different computation strategies. The more strategies they come to understand well, the deeper their sense of computation will be and the more choices they will have when solving problems. Following are some ways that you can help students to become familiar with a variety of strategies and learn how to choose appropriate ones.

Allow students plenty of time to work with different strategies. When students first meet a new strategy, they need opportunities to try it with a range of problems before they begin to see how efficient it is in different situations. Students also need practice with several strategies before they can think about which one is most appropriate for a given problem. Through their work in this unit, some students will develop a wide repertoire of strategies; others only a few. What's important is that students understand why their strategies work and be able to use them with confidence, however many strategies they develop.

Encourage students to find similarities among strategies. Comparing strategies can help students understand new approaches. For example:

Yu-Wei found 4×253 by adding 253 four times. Rachel doubled 253 and then doubled it again. How are those two strategies similar? Which one is easier for you to do?

Amir started out solving $256 \div 12$ by adding 12 + 12 to get 24, and then multiplying by 10. Cara used a standard algorithm. She began by saying "There's two 12's in 25." How are those two approaches similar?

Comparing strategies can also highlight the efficiency of different approaches.

Encourage students to *think through* different ways to approach a problem. Help students see that they can think about how easy it would be to use different strategies without actually carrying out all the steps. For example, you might

suggest a first step (as in How Did I Solve It?) and ask students to talk in pairs about what else they would need to know in order to find the answer:

Robby wanted to solve 253×46. He started by finding the answer to 200×40. How would that help? What other products would he need to find?

You might also ask students to work in pairs to brainstorm possible strategies for a problem and talk about which of them would be easiest to use and why.

Emphasize strategies over answers. When students are sharing solution strategies, keep the focus on different ways to think about the problem, rather than who got the correct answer. As one teacher reminded her class before they shared strategies: "I want to hear all the ways you're thinking about the problem. If I just wanted to know the correct answer, I'd ask someone to take out a calculator and do the problem."

Emphasize different "meanings" of operations. Help students to see that we can think about operations in different ways. A deep understanding of what it means to multiply, or to divide, can help students make sense of different strategies. For example, consider the following three different ways to think about the same division problem, $800 \div 32$.

- $800 \div 32$ means how many 32's in 800. Since ten 32's are 320, there are twenty 32's in 640. Half of 320 is 160, so there are five 32's in 160, and 25 in 640 + 160, or 800.

- You can think of $800 \div 32$ as a fraction (800/32) or ratio and find equivalent fractions or ratios until you have one with a denominator of 1. I cut 800 and 32 in half: 400 and 16. Then I did it again: 200 and 8. And again: 100 and 4. So the problem is the same as $100 \div 4$, which I know is 25.

Continued on next page

■ 800 ÷ 32 means sharing 800 things among 32 people. If everyone got 10 things, you would take away 32 × 10, or 320, from 800 to find out how many left. That's 480 things left. If everyone got 10 more things, you would take away another 320 things, so there would be 160 things left. Since 160 is half of 320, you would give everyone 25 things and there would be none left.

Help students to think about why and when certain strategies are easy to use. Students need to understand that there is no one best strategy for every person and every problem. Encourage them to begin evaluating strategies:

Which number in this multiplication problem is easier for you to find multiples of? Why?

Would it be easier for you to solve this division problem using multiplication? Is there a factor pair involving multiples of 50 that could help you solve this problem more easily?

As you listen to students talking through possible strategies for solving a problem, gather examples of different students using different approaches. Share some of the examples you gather with the class, or ask students to share their own thinking and reasoning. As they reflect on why and when strategies are easy to use and share their thinking with others, they come to see that choice of strategy depends on the numbers in the problem, the kinds of computations a person is most comfortable with, and the factor pairs a person knows very well.

How Can 6 × 10 Help Us Solve 133 ÷ 6?

After students found a way to use 6 × 10 to help solve 133 ÷ 6, a few of them recorded their solution strategies on chart paper. As they explain the strategies they have recorded, they find similarities and differences among them.

Alani: *[Strategy A]* OK, 6 times 10 is 60. Double it to get 120. 120 is the closest you can get to 133 with 60, so add 6's to get as close as you can with 6. 126. And 1 more. 132. So you have 20 6's to get to 120. Then you have to add 2 more 6's to get to 132 because it's the closest you can get to 133. So your answer is 22 with 1 left over.

Rachel: *[Strategy B]* I did it almost the same as Alani except at the end I divided. I thought, there's 13 left between 120 and 132, and 6 fits into 13 twice.

So Alani added up to find out how many more 6's go in after 120, and you divided.

Cara: *[Strategy C]* It's hard for me to use multiplication to solve a division problem, so I turned 6 × 10 into division, 60 ÷ 6 = 10. Double it and you get 120 ÷ 6 = 20. Then there's 13 ÷ 6. I made that into two division problems, 12 ÷ 6 equals 2 and 1 ÷ 6 equals ⅙. Add the three problems together and you get 22⅙.

Yu-Wei: *[Strategy D]* Well, maybe division is harder for you, but I know multiplication better so I like to use it. I took the 10 from 6 times 10 and then added 12 because I know 6 times 12 is 72. That's 132. Then the 1 extra is R 1.

Continued on next page

$$133 \div 6 = \qquad \text{Start by solving } 6 \times 10$$

A
$6 \times 10 = 60$
$(6 \times 10) \times 2 = 120$
$6 \times 20 = 120$
$6 \times 21 = \dfrac{+6}{126}$
$6 \times 22 = \dfrac{+6}{132}$
$132 \div 6 = 22$
$133 \div 6 = 22\,\frac{1}{6}$

B
$6 \times 10 = 60$
$6 \times 20 = 120$
$133 - 120 = 13$
$13 \div 6 = 2\,r1$
$133 \div 6 = 22\,r1$

C
$6 \times 10 = 60 \rightarrow 60 \div 6 = 10$
$120 \div 6 = 20$
$12 \div 6 = 2$
$1 \div 6 = \frac{1}{6}$
$133 \div 6 = 22\,\frac{1}{6}$

D
1) $6 \times 10 = 60$
2) $6 \times 12 = 72$
3) $6 \times 22 = 132$ (add #1 and 2)
4) $133 \div 6 = 22\,R1$

E
$6 \times 10 = 60$
$6 \times 20 = 120$ double
$120 \div 6 = 20$ 1 more 6
$+6\ \ 126 \div 6 = 21$ 1 more 6
$+6\ \ 132 \div 6 = 22$ 1 leftover
$+1\ \ 133 \div 6 = 22\,r1$

F
$6 \times 10 = 60 \quad 6 \times 20 = 120 \quad 6 \times 2 = 12$
$6 \times 22 = 132 \quad 132 \div 6 = 22$
$133 \div 6 = 22\,R1$

We have some different ways of breaking up the problem: 120 and 13, 60 and 72 and 1, 120 and 12 and 1.

Duc: *[Strategy E]* I did it like way C, except I got to $120 \div 6$ is 20 and then I added on 6; $126 \div 6$ is 21, and 6 more is $132 \div 6$ equals 22, and then add 1 and it's $133 \div 6$. It's a remainder 1 because you can't take out another 6.

Alani: That's a little like what I did *[Strategy A]*. Seeing how many 6's you can take out.

Lindsay: *[Strategy F]* We did 6×10 equals 60 so 6×20 equals 120, and then 6×2 is 12 and add them together to get 6×22 is 132. And then turn it into a division problem and it's $132 \div 6$ is 22, and then $133 \div 6$ is 22 with 1 left.

Noah: I did it like that, but I didn't use 6×22. You can do it in your head. You don't have to write it down.

Lindsay: But I think that's what clusters are, saying everything you're doing in your head.

Ways to Multiply and Divide

Materials

■ Paper and pencil

What Happens

As an assessment, students show the strategies they use to solve one multiplication problem and one division problem, without standard algorithms or calculators. Student work focuses on:

■ explaining division and multiplication and strategies using equations and words

---

Activity

Assessment

Ways to Multiply and Divide

Write two problems on the board, adjusting the numbers if they seem too difficult for your students:

$42 \times 51 \qquad 374 \div 12$

Explain that today you want to see how each of them are thinking about multiplication and division problems and what kinds of strategies they are using, so they will work alone on these problems, without using a standard algorithm or calculator. Emphasize recording each step as if explaining their solution methods to someone else.

Depending on what your emphasis in class has been, you can extend this assessment by asking students to write a situation that reflects each of the problems, or by asking them to solve each problem a second way.

As you observe students working and later, as you review their papers, consider these questions:

■ What types of strategies are students using? Are they repeatedly multiplying the divisor or one of the factors by 10? reasoning about multiples? breaking up the problem into smaller or more familiar components?

■ Do students recognize and use relationships between multiplication and division?

■ How do students keep track of and record their steps in the problem? How are they making sense of and recording remainders?

■ Do students have strategies for checking whether their answer makes sense? For example, do they make up a situation to fit the problem? use estimation? solve the problem in a different way?

If you have asked students to write a situation:

■ Are students able to create a division situation that reflects the problem? Do they deal with remainders sensibly, given the context of their situation?

The **Teacher Note,** Assessment: Ways to Multiply and Divide (p. 102) contains samples of student work and things to look for as you evaluate their papers. The important thing to evaluate is not how fast are students finding the answers, but rather, do they have strategies for solving computation problems? If some students are taking much longer than others, ask them to first write what steps they would take to solve the problem. Later they can carry out the steps to finish the problem. (One example in the assessment **Teacher Note** shows a student who has a correct strategy for dividing but needs more time to carry it out.)

When everyone has finished, collect the work and invite students to share their solution strategies and division situations with the class.

Note: If students finish this assessment before the end of Session 10, repeat the activity Practice with Estimating (p. 91), using problems that you make up yourself or that students suggest.

Assessment: Ways to Multiply and Divide

Students use a wide range of strategies for solving the problems 42×51 and $374 \div 12$. This is just a small sample of the many possible approaches, including some that are incomplete or only partially correct.

Multiplication: 42 × 51

The first three examples show the problem solved correctly by students who each used a different strategy.

$42 \times 51 =$

$40 \times 50 = 2000$ (cluster)

$50 \times 2 = 100$
$42 \times 1 = 42$

$\begin{array}{r} 2000 \\ 100 \\ +\ \ 42 \\ \hline 2142 \end{array}$

Answer:
2142

I did a cluster
rounded 42-40
51-50, 40×50=2000
Need 2 more 50s
for 42 so 50×2=100
then 1 more 42 for
the 51. Add all
together = 2142

$\begin{array}{ll} 42 \times 10 = & 420 \\ 42 \times 10 = & 420 \\ 42 \times 10 = & 420 \\ 42 \times 10 = & 420 \\ 42 \times 10 = & 420 \\ 42 \times 1 & 42 \end{array}$

$\boxed{2142}$

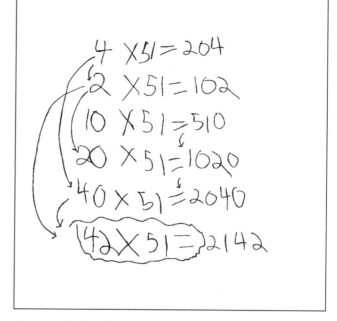

$4 \times 51 = 204$
$2 \times 51 = 102$
$10 \times 51 = 510$
$20 \times 51 = 1020$
$40 \times 51 = 2040$
$\boxed{42 \times 51 = 2142}$

Computational Errors   A few students may have correct strategies and a solid grasp of multiplication and division, but will arrive at the wrong answer because they made an addition or subtraction error, or because they recorded the answer to a factor pair incorrectly. For example, Danny recorded the answer to 50×40 as 4000, instead of 2000, so his final answer was incorrect.

$51 \times 42 =$ I knew 40 50s = 4000
and I need 2 more 50s. 50 +
50 = 100 = 4,100 add 42 more
because it is 51 not 50
answer 4,142

In reading over Danny's work, the teacher notes that he demonstrates the ability to solve a difficult multiplication problem by breaking it into more manageable pieces and then recombining the parts. The teacher also makes a note to remind Danny to continue practicing factor pairs he finds difficult.

Continued on next page

Errors in Breaking a Problem into Smaller Parts You may have some students who do not break a problem into parts correctly. Sometimes it can be difficult to tell whether the student simply lost track of the steps, or if there is more fundamental confusion. For example, Natalie wrote a cluster containing each of the four "partial products" of 42×51 and an extra problem, $20 \times 25 = 500$. To solve the problem, she added three of the four partial products, and did not use $20 \times 25 = 500$.

The teacher does not know whether Natalie understood how to break 42×51 into parts and simply forgot to add the answer to 1×2 to find her answer, or whether she was uncertain of how to break the problem into parts. The teacher decides to meet with Natalie and ask her to talk through her solution process.

Division: 374 ÷ 12

The following examples show three different approaches to this division problem, each correct.

Continued on next page

$$374 \div 12$$

start with: $12 \times 10 = 120$
$12 \times 20 = 240$
$12 \times 30 = 360$
$\cancel{12 \times 40 = 480}$ +12
$12 \times 31 = 372$

$\boxed{31 \text{ R2}}$

Trevor explained to the teacher that he broke $374 \div 12$ into three division problems, and that he plans to solve each of the problems and then add the answers together. He said he chose this approach because he knew there are twelve 25's in 300. He noted that he will need to add the remainders, and that if the total remainder is greater than 12, he will need to subtract 12 from the remainder and add 1 to "the answer."

Although Trevor's strategy is less efficient than some others for this particular problem, he demonstrates sound reasoning about division. The teacher suggests that he take more time to complete the problem, and makes a note to encourage Trevor to explore other division strategies in the future.

Incomplete Work A few of your students may have solid strategies but simply need more time to carry them out. They may take longer because they perform the computations more slowly, or because their strategies are less efficient. By the time most students had finished this assessment, Trevor was still working on $374 \div 12$. When the teacher observed him working at the end of class, he had recorded the work shown below.

If you notice some students working much more slowly than the others, ask them to record the steps they would take to solve the problem, as Trevor did. Check that their reasoning is sound, and then give them extra time to carry out the steps and bring the problem to completion.

Trevor

$$374 \div 12$$

$300 \div 12 = 25$ I know $12 \times 25 = 300$ because we did it
a lot $4 \times 25 = 100$ and there are 3 of them

$70 \div 12$ $(12 + 12) + (12 + 12) + 12$
  24 $+$ 24
  $48 + 12 = 60$

$4 \div 12 =$
$=$ answer

Continued on next page

Representing Remainders Incorrectly   Some students may be able to make sense of the remainder (that is, recognize that there are 2 left over) but will record it incorrectly. For example, after noting that there are 2 left over, Danny records the remainder of 2 as point 2 (.2) rather than as a fraction (2/12) or as "2 left over."

$374 \div 12 = $ I know $12 \times 5 = 60$ another $12 \times 5 = 60$ another $12 \times 5 = 60$ and $60 \times 3 = 180$ You know you have 15 12's. $180 + 180 = 360$ another 15 12's = 30 12's and one more 12 so 31.2

If you find that several students are representing remainders incorrectly, you might call together a small group to review this (refer to the **Teacher Note,** Remainders, Fractions, and Decimals, p. 54).

A Million Dots

What Happens

Session 1: Arrays of Dots Students determine how many dots are on a page that contains a 7-by-9 array of blocks of 100 dots. They use sheets of this paper to construct rectangles of 10,000 dots. As they share their strategies for making the rectangle, they explain what they know about 10,000, its factors, and its multiples.

Session 2: How Big Is a Million? Students begin making the class display of one million dots, putting together sheets of paper containing 5000 dots each. They label the "start" and "end" numbers of the dots on each sheet to keep track of how many dots are posted in the display.

A Note on Investigation 4

This investigation introduces a class project: making a display of a million dots. Although only two sessions are spent introducing the arrays of dots and starting the project, students will continue to work on the project in pairs throughout the remainder of this unit. These hands-on activities complement the work with numbers and computation that students are doing. They help students extend their understanding of rectangular arrays, factor pairs, and number relationships as they think about numbers up to a million, in multiples of 5000. You will need to allocate time after these two sessions for students to work on the project and to share their thinking about the growing display. Two **Teacher Notes,** The Million Dots Display (p. 113) and Have We Reached a Million Yet? (p. 119), offer tips on integrating this project into the unit.

Mathematical Emphasis

- Developing a sense of quantities in the thousands, ten thousands, and hundred thousands
- Using a rectangular array model to represent factor pairs of numbers 10,000 and larger
- Developing a sense of the size of 1,000,000

What to Plan Ahead of Time

Materials

- Scissors: 1 per pair (Session 1)
- Tape: a few rolls to share (Sessions 1–2)
- Stick-on notes: 1 package (Session 1)
- Calculators
- Chart paper (optional)
- Overhead projector (Session 1)
- Overhead pens and blank transparencies (Session 1, optional)

Other Preparation

- Before students begin working on the million dots display in Session 2, you will need to plan where the display will be located and how students will work on it. Read the **Teacher Note,** The Million Dots Display (p. 113), for points to consider.

- Duplicate student sheets and teaching resources (located at the end of this unit) in the following quantities. If you have Student Activity Booklets, copy only the item marked with an asterisk.

For Session 1

How Many Dots? (p. 197): 3–5 sheets per pair, and 1 transparency*

Student Sheet 31, Counting Up from 10,000 (p. 194): 1 per student (homework)

Student Sheet 32, Counting Down from 10,000 (p. 195): 1 per student (homework)

For Session 2

Million Dots Display Sheet (p. 198): about 250 sheets total for the million dots display. You will need about 50 for Session 2 and can make the rest available gradually over the next week or so.

Student Sheet 33, Our Million Dots Display (p. 196): 1 per student (homework)

Arrays of Dots

Materials

- How Many Dots? (3–5 sheets per pair, and 1 transparency)
- Scissors (1 per pair)
- Tape (to share)
- Stick-on notes (1 package)
- Student Sheet 31 (1 per student, homework)
- Student Sheet 32 (1 per student, homework)
- Calculators
- Overhead projector
- Overhead pens and blank transparencies (optional)

What Happens

Students determine how many dots are on a page that contains a 7-by-9 array of blocks of 100 dots. They use sheets of this paper to construct rectangles of 10,000 dots. As they share their strategies for making the rectangle, they explain what they know about 10,000, its factors, and its multiples. Student work focuses on:

- using a rectangular array model to represent factor pairs of numbers 10,000 and larger
- developing a sense of the size of 10,000

Activity

How Many Dots on a Page?

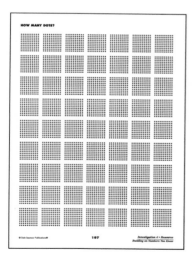

Distribute one How Many Dots? sheet to each pair.

Some of the problems you've been solving in the last couple of weeks have involved large numbers. You've worked with numbers like 2415, 4500, and 15,480, and some even larger. Now we're going to use dots to show how big those numbers really are.

How many dots do you think there are on your sheet of paper? How could we find out?

Students work in pairs to determine and record how many dots are on the sheet. Encourage them to work without calculators, but allow calculators if students feel they need them.

As students work, circulate to observe how they approach the problem. If some students are having difficulty counting the number of dots in a block, you might tell them that each block contains 10 dots across and 10 down. If some students think the page shows 700 dots across and 900 down, help them to see the page is composed of 7 rows of 900 (or 9 rows of 700, or 70 rows of 90). You might circle the first row of 900 and ask how many in that row; circle the second row of 900 and ask how many in the row and the total circled so far, and so on. Encourage students to imagine how much larger a page with 700 rows of 900 dots would be.

Students who finish early try to "prove" they have accurately found the number of dots on the page by finding the answer a different way.

How did you figure out how many dots are on the page? Did anyone do it a different way?

Invite students to come to the overhead and use the transparency of How Many Dots? to demonstrate their solution strategies. They might use overhead markers to show how they grouped the dots in order to solve the problem (for example, in rows or columns). On a blank transparency or on the board, they record any calculations they made. Possible student strategies include these:

- Finding the total number of blocks ($7 \times 9 = 63$) and then multiplying by the number in a block ($63 \times 100 = 6300$)

- Finding the number of dots in a row of blocks ($7 \times 100 = 700$) or a column of blocks ($9 \times 100 = 900$) and then multiplying by the number of columns ($700 \times 9 = 6300$) or rows ($900 \times 7 = 6300$).

- Finding the number of dots across the page ($7 \times 10 = 70$) and the number down the page ($9 \times 10 = 90$) and then multiplying them together ($70 \times 90 = 6300$).

As students give their explanations, listen for the way they say numbers in the thousands and hundreds. That is, some students may say 6 thousand 3 hundred, while others may call the same number 63 hundred. Ask students if both names represent the same number, and how they know.

Rectangles with 10,000 Dots

We're going to use this dot paper to make rectangles that have 10,000 dots. Can you see in your mind how many dots that will be? What can you tell me about 10,000?

Take a few minutes for students to share what they know about the number 10,000. Those who have worked through the *Investigations* unit *Mathematical Thinking at Grade 5* will have had experience with factors and multiples of 10,000. Encourage students to think about characteristics of 10,000 like these: How much larger is 10,000 than 10? how much larger than 100? than 1000? What are the factor pairs of 10,000? Is 10,000 a square number? Record students' ideas on the board.

How many of these sheets of dots do you predict you will need to make a rectangle filled with 10,000 dots?

Making the Rectangles   Distribute scissors and two additional How Many Dots? sheets to each pair. Have extra sheets available for students who need them. Distribute rolls of tape to share. As students begin work, remind them that it's hard to count lots of little dots accurately, so they should be sure to doublecheck before they cut. On the back, they record the size of their rectangle: the number of dots across and the number of dots down. They also write about how they know the rectangle they made has 10,000 dots. Students who finish early can make another 10,000-dot rectangle with different dimensions. You might challenge them to use some blocks cut so that they contain fewer than 100 dots.

Displaying the Rectangles   When every pair has completed one rectangle, discuss the rectangles they made and their strategies for making them. Record the dimensions of rectangles that students suggest. Then ask for volunteers to share their strategies for making them. Possible strategies include these:

- Choosing a factor of 10,000, and then figuring out the number of times we need to count by that number to reach 10,000.
- Building on factor pairs of 1000, 100, or 10 (for example, finding a factor pair of 1000 and multiplying one of the factors by 10).
- Using a calculator to find numbers that divide 10,000 evenly.

As students explain their strategies, listen for how they make sense of multiplying by numbers such as 10 and 100. Some students may talk about multiplying by "adding on" 0's, or dividing by "taking away" 0's:

> 10,000 is 100×100 because you multiply the 1's and then add on the 0's.

Ask these students to show why this procedure works by finding the answer in a different way:

> 100×100 is 10,000 because 10,000 is the same as one hundred 100's—ten 100's make 1000, and ten of those make 10,000.

Point out that the dimensions of rectangles with 10,000 dots are factor pairs of 10,000. Ask if anyone can think of factor pairs of 10,000 for which no one has made rectangles.

Display the students' rectangles on a bulletin board, wall, or section of the classroom floor. As students circulate to look at them, they post stick-on notes questioning any they do not understand or agree with. Take a few minutes to discuss any such questions with the class.

Write 10,000 on the board. Direct attention to the 10,000-dot rectangles they just made and indicate two of the rectangles in the display.

How many dots are in these two rectangles together?

Ask how to write the corresponding number, and record it on the board. Continue asking students how many dots there are when more and more rectangles are added:

How many dots are in three rectangles? four rectangles? five rectangles? How many dots are in all the rectangles we made? How do you know?

Students find the answer with a partner, writing down the number they find. They may use calculators. As students work, circulate to see how they write the total number of dots and how they say that number.

Ask for volunteers to explain how they found the total number of dots. Some students will add 10,000 repeatedly; others will multiply 10,000 by the number of students in the class; still others will use what they know about smaller numbers to find the answer. For example, a student might say that because 10×16 is 160, 10 *thousand* times 16 is 160 *thousand*. Record students' strategies on the board.

We have [16] rectangles with 10,000 dots each. That's 160,000 dots in all. Can that help us figure out what number we will end up on if we count around the class by 10,000? How would it help?

Some students may recognize that since the class worked in pairs to make rectangles, doubling the total number of dots in the rectangles gives the final number of the count. Others may use strategies similar to those they used for finding the total number of dots in the rectangles.

Counting Forward and Backward from 10,000 Count around the class by 10,000. Stop the count periodically and ask students how to write the number just counted. Record the number on the board.

When you have gone all around the class, start the count again. Begin at 10,000 and count *forward* by a multiple of 100 or 500, such as 200 or 1000. For a third count, begin at 10,000 and count *backward* by the same number. Again, stop the counts periodically and ask students how to write the number just counted, then record it on the board. If time permits, stop partway through each count, asking the class how many students have counted so far and how they know.

Session 1 Follow-Up

 **Homework**

Counting Up and Down From 10,000   Students complete Student Sheet 31, Counting Up from 10,000, and Student Sheet 32, Counting Down from 10,000. These sheets ask them to write the numbers they would say if they begin at 10,000 and count forward and backward by a given number. Encourage students not to use calculators, but they may if they feel it is necessary. Students who do not have calculators at home may need to borrow one or to take time at school to complete the sheets.

Extensions

Counting to Say Large Numbers   Students find numbers they could count by so that somewhere in the count, someone would say 100,000 or 1,000,000 (or another multiple of 10,000 or 100,000).

Counting to Say 0   Students choose a starting number for their counts and find numbers by which they could count backward so that they say 0. For example, if they begin at 30,000 and count backward by 5000, they say 0, but if they count backward by 4000, they do not.

Factor Pairs of 100,000   Students find and list factor pairs of 100,000. They might build rectangles from dot paper to represent some of the factor pairs.

The Million Dots Display

The class display of a million dots, when completed, consists of 200 copies of the Million Dots Display Sheet (5 rows of 10 hundred dots, or 5000 dots per sheet). Students keep track of the total number of dots by labeling the "start" and the "end" numbers of the dots on each sheet they add to the display. The first sheet starts at 1 and ends at 5000; the second starts at 5001 and ends at 10,000; the third starts at 10,001 and ends at 15,000; and so on, up to the final sheet, which starts at 995,001 and ends at 1,000,000.

Student pairs take turns working on the display. Each pair labels a few sheets, then either adds them to the display or gives them to you to add at the end of the session. Each ensuing pair picks up where the previous pair left off: If the last sheet ended at 135,000, the next begins at 135,001.

Before introducing the activity to the class, decide where you will post the million dots display and how students will work on it. Following are some questions to consider.

Where will the display fit? Depending on the size of your classroom, you might plan to post the sheets in two or three rows all around the room, or in another arrangement on the classroom walls (you may need to completely cover more than one wall). Another possibility is a long row or large rectangular area in a corridor. Assuming that you overlap the sheets so the dots are closer together, and that you post the sheets oriented vertically, these are the general dimensions of different arrangements:

- A 20 × 10 array of sheets would be about 9 feet (2.75 meters) square.
- A 40 × 5 array would be about 18 feet (5.5 meters) long and 5 feet (1.5 meters) down.
- A 100 × 2 array would be about 46 feet (14 meters) long and 2 feet (0.5 meters) down.
- A single row of sheets would be about 92 feet (28 meters) long.

The area you choose must be available throughout the rest of the unit, since your class will add to the display gradually. You will also need to plan the order in which successive sheets will be posted; for example, beginning in the upper left corner of the back wall of the classroom, and continuing across the wall in left-to-right-rows.

How much will each pair do during their turn at the display? Depending on the size of your class and the time you have available for students to work on the display, you might allot a time period, such as 10 minutes, for each turn. Or, you might tell students how many sheets they may complete at each turn, somewhere between 5 and 10 sheets. You may need to adjust the time period or number of sheets as you see how students work. Pairs need at least two turns so that they have a chance to label sheets with numbers of different sizes.

What will students need in order to work on the display? Students will need copies of the Million Dots Display Sheet and pencils for labeling. Some teachers leave about 50 blank sheets out at all times, so that students do not think that the number of blank sheets remaining corresponds to the number of sheets needed to complete the display. Calculators should be available for student use.

Continued on next page

When will pairs work on the display? You might decide to allow students to work on the display throughout the school day: when they finish an activity early in math or another class, during a few free minutes before lunch, or at the end of the school day. You might also include working on the display as one of the choices during Choice Time in Investigation 5.

In what order will pairs work on the display? You could assign an order in which students work on the display, or allow a pair to work on the display when they have free time or finish an activity early. (If you do not assign an order, you might need to allocate time for certain pairs, such as those who are unlikely to finish an activity early.) In either case, post a list of the students in your class. Students check off their names once they have had a turn. When everyone has had a turn, pairs can begin taking a second turn and checking off their names again.

Who will post the sheets? Depending on where the display is located, students might post their own completed sheets, or you might set aside a time each day when students gather around as you post them. If students will not be posting the sheets themselves, set up a box where students can place their labeled sheets, ready for display.

What about monitoring students' work on the display? At least once every day that students work on the display, check that the new sheets are labeled correctly. You might take a few minutes at the end of each day to go over how to say and write the numbers on that day's new sheets.

When will students share their thinking about the growing display? The Teacher Note, Have We Reached a Million Yet? (p. 119), lists questions you might use as a focus for class sharing about the display; these might be used for whole-class discussion, as homework assignments, or for in-class writing work.

How Big Is a Million?

What Happens

Students begin making the class display of one million dots, putting together sheets of paper containing 5000 dots each. They label the "start" and "end" numbers of the dots on each sheet to keep track of how many dots are posted in the display. Student work focuses on:

- skip counting by 5000 to 5- and 6-digit numbers
- beginning to develop a sense of the relative size of 1000, 10,000, and larger powers of 10

Materials

- Million Dots Display Sheets (200–250 total; at least 50 to start with)
- Student Sheet 33 (1 per student, homework)
- Tape (1 roll)
- Calculators
- Chart paper (optional)

Activity

When we put together all the rectangles of 10,000 dots we made, do you remember how many dots we had altogether? That was lots of dots, but now we're going to put together even more. Over the next couple of weeks, you'll be spending a little time almost every day working on a display of a million dots. Can anyone tell me how we write the number one million?

Record students' suggestions on the board. If no one gives you the correct way to write the number, supply it yourself.

What can you tell me about a million? What things do you know that come in millions? Are there a million pencils in the school? Are there a million blades of grass in the park?

How much larger is a million than ten thousand? How many ten thousands make a million? How much larger is a million than a hundred thousand? How many hundred thousands make a million?

Students talk briefly with their neighbors about what they know about a million, then share their ideas with the class.

Most students will know that a million is a very large number, but only some will be able to suggest things that there are millions of, or will know how much larger a million is than 10,000 or 100,000. Some students may at first assume that it is just as far from 1 to 100,000 as it is from 100,000 to 1,000,000. As students work on the million dots display, they will gain a better understanding of the relative sizes of ten thousand (10,000), one hundred thousand (100,000), and one million (1,000,000).

How Big Is a Million?

The Million Dots Display

As you introduce the million dots display and discuss it throughout the rest of the unit, do not give away information such as the size of the completed display or how long you think it will take to finish it. Many students are surprised to discover just how large the final display is and how long it takes to create. Some students may calculate exactly how many sheets of paper will be needed for the display, or the size of the completed display. Encourage them to explain their reasoning, but do not tell them whether they are "correct."

Distribute a copy of the Million Dots Display Sheet to each pair.

We'll be making our display of a million dots from copies of this sheet. How many dots are on this one page?

Pairs may use calculators as they determine and record how many dots there are. Circulate to see how students are writing the number 5000 and to observe the strategies they are using. After a few minutes, call the class together briefly to share strategies.

Do you think our display of a million dots will fit on the bulletin board? on the chalkboard? on the longest wall of the classroom? along the hall?

Allow only enough time for quick estimates. Record students' predictions on a piece of chart paper or on a part of the board where they can remain for a couple of weeks.

Tell the class where the million dots display will be located and how the sheets will be posted. Then explain how they'll be keeping count of the dots so they know when they get to a million. Hold up a Million Dots Display Sheet.

You figured out that there are 5000 dots on a sheet like this. So we'll fill in 1 for the start number and 5000 for the end number. Since this is the first sheet, we'll number it 1.

Fill in the start and end numbers, the sheet number, and today's date on the sheet. Then hold up a second sheet.

Here's the second sheet in our million dots display. We went up to 5000 on the last sheet. This sheet has 5000 more dots. It starts at the number after 5000. What number comes after 5000? What should we write for the start number? What do we end at? How do you know?

Some students may find their answers by adding 5000 to the start and end numbers on the first sheet. Others may observe that just as there are 5000 numbers from 1 to 5000, there are 5000 numbers as we go from 5001 to 10,000.

If some students think that the end number is 5000 more than 5001, or 10,001, you might suggest that they think about more familiar numbers: When we count from 1 to 50, we say 50 numbers, and when we count from 51 to 100, we say 50 more numbers. Some students may find it helpful to think about the number of dots on two sheets: if there are 5000 dots on one sheet, there are 10,000 on two sheets.

Again, fill in the start and end numbers, the sheet number (2), and the date. Repeat until you have filled several sheets and are confident that students understand the task. Then, post all the sheets you have labeled as students gather around to observe.

At this point, students return any Million Dots Display Sheets that they have not written on.

Are We Close to a Million?

With just the first sheets posted, students compare the number of dots in the display to one million.

Are we close to a million? How many more do we need?

After students discuss this with a partner, a few volunteers share their thinking with the class.

Would we have a million if we made about twice as many? About ten times as many? How do you know?

Do you want to change any of your predictions about how much space a million dots would take up? Do you want to change any of your predictions about how long it will take us to make the display? Why?

Students give reasons for any changes; they may want to change their predictions because they recognize that a million is much larger than they thought.

Update students' recorded predictions. If students are interested and if time permits, they can explore some of the predictions. For example, students could estimate about how large the display is so far and use that as a basis for refining their predictions about the final size of the display.

Launching the Project   Explain the procedures you have established for the project, as discussed in the **Teacher Note,** The Million Dots Display (p. 113). For example:

■ How are pairs to take turns working on the display? (in a specified order, or when they finish an activity early)

■ How much does each pair do during their turn at the display? (they work for a certain amount of time, or complete a certain number of sheets)

■ How will the sheets be posted? (by pairs or by the teacher)

■ Where do students find blank sheets, and what do they do with completed sheets?

Explain that at the start of each turn, a pair determines the number at which they are to begin labeling by checking the last sheet completed—either on the display itself, or in a box you have set aside for sheets that are ready to be added to the display. You might suggest that students look through the last 2 or 3 sheets completed to be sure they agree with the way they are labeled. They discuss any disagreements with the pair that completed those sheets (or with you), and if necessary, relabel them.

This ongoing project continues until the display is complete, even as you proceed with Investigation 5. Refer to the **Teacher Note,** Have We Reached a Million Yet? (p. 119), to plan how students might share their thinking about the display as it grows.

Session 2 Follow-Up

 **Homework**

Our Million Dots Display   Distribute Student Sheet 33, Our Million Dots Display. Before students leave for the day, they fill in the total number of dots already in the class display. For homework, they answer the questions on the sheet.

Extension

How Long Would It Take to Count to a Million?   Each student estimates how long it would take someone to count to a million. Students begin by planning what information they will need in order to make their estimates. For example: How many numbers can they say in a minute? Does it take them longer to say some numbers than others? How long does it take them to count to 100? Would it take them just as long to count from 99,900 to 100,000, or longer?

Different students, pairs, or groups might approach the problem in different ways. Once students develop their plans, they gather the information they need, make their calculations, and write about how they arrived at their answers.

Have We Reached a Million Yet?

Three or four times during the ongoing million dots project, bring the class together for 10 to 20 minutes to share their thinking on the growing display. Each time, choose a few questions as a focus for discussion, perhaps asking students to discuss them in pairs or small groups first. For homework, periodically hand out new copies of Student Sheet 33, Our Million Dots Display, to provide practice with larger and larger multiples of 5000.

Students may use calculators as they explore any of these questions.

Questions About How Close We Are to a Million   Students will be eager to know, at any point, whether the display yet contains close to a million dots. Exploring questions like the following can help students understand the size of 5- and 6-digit numbers compared with a million:

- Are we close to a million yet? How do you know?
- Are we halfway there yet?
- What number is halfway there? How do we write it?
- How many more dots do we need to reach a million?
- How many more days do you think it will take us to finish?

Questions About How the Display Is Growing
As students consider how much the display has grown in the last couple of days, they work with relative and absolute size of 5- and 6-digit numbers: how many more dots are in the display, and how many times as many dots are in the display. You might pose questions like the following:

- When we checked last [Wednesday], we had [30,000] dots. Today, we have [185,000] dots. How many dots have we added since [Wednesday]?
- How many sheets have we added to the display? How do you know?

- Do we have twice as many dots as we had on [Wednesday] yet? If not, how many more do we need?
- Do we have three times as many yet? About how many times as many dots do we have now?
- About how many times as many dots do we need to get to a million?

Questions About Numbers on the Display   As students locate numbered dots on the display, they practice reading, writing, and sequencing numbers up to a million.

- *[Indicate one of the sheets in the display.]* This sheet starts at 90,001 and ends at 95,000. What number sheet is this? How do you know?
- *[Indicate the next sheet in the display.]* This next sheet starts at 95,001 and ends at 100,000. Imagine all the dots on the sheet are numbered. On which sheet is the number 94,985?
- What number is 10 more than 94,985? What sheet is it on?
- What number is 10 more than that? What sheet is it on?
- What number is 100 more than that? What sheet is it on?

Questions About Our List of Predictions
When the display contains close to a million dots, encourage students to share any surprises about the size of a million dots. They can review their recorded predictions to determine if they are true.

- Is the display as large as you predicted?
- Did it take as long as you thought to make it?
- Did it take as many sheets as you predicted?

If the display does not yet contain close to a million dots, ask students if they want to change any of their predictions. Encourage them to give reasons for any changes they make; then revise their recorded predictions for them.

Understanding Operations

What Happens

Sessions 1 and 2: The Estimation Game
Students first practice making close estimates for multiplication and division problems. They then play the Estimation Game, in which their score depends on how closely they can estimate the answers to problems created from randomly drawn numerals.

Session 3: Solving Difficult Problems Students solve a difficult multiplication problem and a difficult division problem without using calculators or standard algorithms.

Sessions 4, 5, and 6: Exploring Operations
During Choice Time, students work in pairs on at least three activities: How Did I Solve It? Challenges (an extension of the type of problem introduced in Investigation 3); Problems About You (a series of problems that represent multiplication and division situations); and the game Different Paths to 10,000 (using calculators to create numeric problems with an answer of 10,000). Classes making the million dots display (Investigation 4, Excursion) work on that project as a fourth choice, and may spend an extra session on this Choice Time.

Session 7: Assessing Students' Understanding
As an assessment, students solve a difficult multiplication problem and a difficult division problem without standard algorithms or calculators. If you are doing the Excursion, students continue to assemble the million dots display.

Mathematical Emphasis

- Applying computation strategies to more difficult problems, including both numeric and situational problems
- Developing strategies for estimating answers to difficult multiplication and division problems
- Reading, writing, and sequencing multiples of 5000 up to 1,000,000
- Developing a sense of the size of 1,000,000
- Understanding relationships among the four basic operations

Estimate 600×6 is 3600, plus $6 \times 25 = 150$... so 3750.

627×6

What to Plan Ahead of Time

Materials

- Numeral Cards from Investigation 1 (Sessions 1–2)
- Class clock or watches that show seconds (Sessions 1–2)
- Million Dots Display Sheets (available as needed)
- Overhead projector (Sessions 1–2)
- Chart paper (Sessions 1–2 and 4–6, optional)
- Calculators (Sessions 1–2 and 4–6)

Other Preparation

- Duplicate student sheets and teaching resources (located at the end of this unit) in the following quantities. If you have Student Activity Booklets, copy only the item marked with an asterisk.

For Sessions 1–2

Student Sheet 34, How to Play the Estimation Game (p. 199): 1 per student (homework)

Student Sheet 35, Estimation Game Score Sheet (p. 200): 2 per student (1 for class, 1 for homework) and 1 transparency*

For Session 3

Student Sheet 36, Another Division Problem (p. 201): 1 per student (homework)

For Sessions 4–6

Student Sheet 37, How Did I Solve It? Challenges (p. 202): 1 per student

Student Sheet 38, Problems About You (p. 206): 1 per student. Be prepared to supply the information for the blanks on each page, for students to fill in before they begin work.

Student Sheet 39, Different Paths to 10,000 (p. 209): 2 per student (1 for class; 1 for homework)

Student Sheet 40, A Multiplication Problem (p. 210): 1 per student (homework)

Student Sheet 41, How Can This Help? (p. 211): 1 per student (homework)

The Estimation Game

Materials

- Numeral Cards (from Investigation 1)
- Transparency of Student Sheet 35
- Class clock or watches that show seconds
- Student Sheet 34 (1 per student, homework)
- Student Sheet 35 (1 per student, class; 1 per student, homework)
- Overhead projector
- Chart paper (optional)
- Calculators

What Happens

Students first practice making close estimates for multiplication and division problems. They then play the Estimation Game, in which their score depends on how closely they can estimate the answers to problems created from randomly drawn numerals. Their work focuses on:

- developing strategies for estimating answers to difficult multiplication and division problems

 Ten-Minute Math: Quick Images   Two or three times in the next few days, outside of math time, continue to present the Quick Images activity with a focus on geometric shapes, using Power Polygons, pattern blocks, or other regular polygon shapes to create simple designs on the overhead projector. For example:

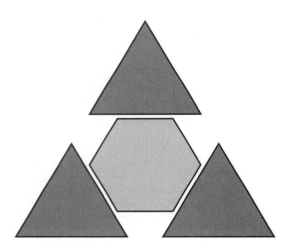

Flash one design for 3 seconds, and give students time to try to draw or create what they remember. Flash it for another 3 seconds and let students revise their work. Then, leave the design visible for further revision.

For more challenge, you can either use more pieces in the design, or leave no spaces between the pieces so that the individual shapes are not clear.

For variations on the Quick Images activity, see p. 149.

Write the following problem on the board:

971 ÷ 38

Ask students to estimate the answer. Acknowledge that this problem is more difficult than those they have been solving for the past two or three weeks.

What are some estimates for this problem? Would the answer be about 5? About 10? About 50? What helps you make an estimate?

Listen for the following possible strategies:

- Approximating 38 to 40, and then using multiplication pairs involving 40: "It's about 25 because 25 × 40 is 1000, and 971 is close to 1000."

- Approximating 38 to 40 and then using multiplication pairs involving 4: "It's about 25 because 4 × 2 is 8, so 40 × 20 is 800, and 4 × 3 is 12, so 40 × 30 is 1200. 971 is almost in the middle of 800 and 1200."

- Approximating 38 to 30 and then using multiplication pairs involving 3: "It's about 30, because 3 × 3 = 9, and 30 × 30 = 900."

- Using multiples of 10 × 38: "I did 10 × 38 to get 380, and then doubled that to get 760— that's twenty 38's. You need about 200 more to get up to 971. Half of 380 is 190, so there's a little more than five 38's in 200. The answer is a little more than 25."

Ask for a couple of volunteers to use calculators to find the exact answer and report it to the class. If you have students who want to try finding the exact answer *without* calculators or conventional algorithms, encourage them, and ask calculator users to hold their report until these students have found their answers.

Repeat the activity once or twice, using both multiplication and division problems. For example:

273 × 96	62 × 89	4605 × 6
609 ÷ 7	2704 ÷ 5	909 ÷ 147

You may want to gradually reduce the amount of time you give students to make their estimates.

Estimating Answers to Difficult Problems

Introducing the Estimation Game

Introduce The Estimation Game by playing a sample round with the class.

We're going to use our Numeral Cards *[hold up a deck]*, with the Wild Cards removed, to play the Estimation Game. In every group, one person starts out as the leader. The leader sets up and times the game for the other players. You'll take turns being leader. I'll be the leader for a sample round to show you how the game is played and what the leader's role is.

Display the transparency of Student Sheet 35, Estimation Game Score Sheet, and write a 3-digit × 1-digit multiplication problem template somewhere on the overhead or on a piece of chart paper:

$$\_\ \_\ \_ \times \_$$

As needed, explain that a *template* is like a pattern for a problem—the pattern stays the same even when the numerals change. To clarify further, you might show a variety of problem templates and sample problems that fit them.

Here's what I do as the game's leader: After I mix up the Numeral Cards, I'll secretly deal out four numerals to make up a multiplication problem with this template. The first numeral will go in the first slot, the second one in the second slot, and so on. Making up the problems is the leader's job, and none of the players can watch. When the problem is ready, the leader shows it to the other players. Then you'll have exactly 30 seconds to estimate the answer.

If you are using the overhead, turn the light off while you create the problem. If you are using chart paper, work where the class cannot see. Deal four Numeral Cards and record the numerals on the template in the order dealt. For example:

$$\boxed{7}\ \boxed{4}\ \boxed{1}\ \boxed{3} \qquad \underline{7}\ \underline{4}\ \underline{1} \times \underline{3}$$

Reveal the problem and start timing with a watch or clock. Allow students exactly 30 seconds to estimate the answer. When the time is up, gather their estimates on the board. Briefly discuss their strategies for making them. A few students may be able to find the exact answer within 30 seconds. This is great, as long as they work *mentally*. However, there are bound to be some problems that will be too difficult for them to solve mentally in 30 seconds, so they will need to estimate.

Note: Some students will be accustomed to expressing their estimates in approximate terms. For scoring the Estimation Game, though, they will need to express their estimates as an exact number. So, instead of "a little more than 25," they would need to specify a number like 26; instead of "a little less than 100," they might say 97.

Scoring the Game   Explain that a player's score for each round is the *difference* between his or her estimate and the actual answer. Ask for volunteers to find the actual answer with calculators; record it on the board.

How close is your estimate to the actual answer? How do you know?

Students then find the difference between their estimates and the actual answer, again without using calculators. As a few volunteers explain their strategies, write their numbers on the board as subtraction expressions to demonstrate how to find their score. For example, for an estimate of 2200 and the answer 2223, you would write:

$$2223 - 2200 = 23$$

Always write the expressions horizontally, to help students focus on the difference between the numbers rather than use the traditional algorithm.

Choose estimates both above and below the actual answer.

We said the actual answer is 2223. Suppose you estimated 2250. How far apart are 2250 and 2223? (27) Your score would be 27.

Suppose you estimated 2100. How far apart are 2223 and 2100? (123) Your score is 123. Your goal is to get the lowest score, so 27 is better than 123.

Demonstrate recording the scores on the Estimation Game Score Sheet transparency.

Play another sample round, setting up a template for a division problem:

$$\_\ \_\ \_ \div \_$$

You'll need to discuss what to do about remainders, so be sure the problem you make here does not divide evenly. For example, present the problem $491 \div 5$. If necessary, adjust the amount of time students have to make their estimates.

After students have made their estimates and determined the exact answer (in this example, 98.2, or $98\frac{1}{5}$, or 98 R 1), decide as a class how to handle remainders in determining the score. Choose from the four options listed with the game rules on Student Sheet 34, How to Play the Estimation Game.

- Approximate answers to the next-lowest whole number: "The answer is 98.2, so we will approximate it as 98. My estimate was 100, so my score is 100 – 98, or 2."

- Approximate answers to the next-highest whole number: "The answer is 98.2, so we will approximate it as 99. My estimate was 100, so my score is 100 – 99, or 1."

- Approximate answers to the next-highest whole number if the remainder is 0.5 or greater, otherwise to the next-lowest number.

- Include the remainder in determining the score: "The answer is 98.2. My estimate was 100, so my score is 100 – 98.2, or 1.8." (This option is suitable for students who are comfortable with decimals.)

Activity

Playing the Estimation Game

Student groups of 3 or 4 play the Estimation Game for the remainder of Sessions 1 and 2. Each group needs a deck of Numeral Cards (from Investigation 1) and a calculator for the leader. Students remove the Wild Cards from each deck for this game. Give each student a copy of Student Sheet 35, Estimation Game Score Sheet. For more than three games, suggest that students use notebook paper to record each problem, their estimates, the actual answers, and the difference (their score). They can use the printed score sheet as a model.

On the board or overhead, list templates for the first four games.

Game 1 template	_ _ × _ _
Game 2 template	_ _ _ ÷ _
Game 3 template	_ _ _ × _ _
Game 4 template	_ _ _ ÷ _ _

If time permits, students play additional games with templates of their own choice.

Decide whether or not you want to distribute the rules now (Student Sheet 34, How to Play the Estimation Game) for use in class; in either case, you will send the sheet home with students to help them teach the game to their families. Remind students how remainders are to be handled in determining the score with division problems.

Note: Because of the random way Numeral Cards are dealt, players may sometimes get 0 as the leftmost digit of a number. Explain that 090 is the same as 90, and 03 is the same as 3. If they end up with a problem that requires dividing by 0 or 1 (such as 491 ÷ 0), the leader should deal a new card to replace the 0 or 1.

Observing the Students As students begin playing in small groups, circulate quickly to make sure everyone understands the basic directions. Then, observe what strategies students are using to estimate and to determine how close they are to the target. As necessary, remind students that they are to make their estimates mentally; they are not to write down the problem or anything else while they are estimating. Similarly, they are not to use standard algorithms or calculators to find the difference between their estimates and the actual answer.

If necessary, adjust the difficulty level of the problem templates for particular groups, or reorganize some students into pairs or small groups working at the same pace. Watch for these situations:

■ Some students might need more time to make their estimates. One possibility is to provide a longer time, such as 1 minute, for the whole group. Another option is for players to raise their hands when they have an estimate. The leader asks all players to share their estimates (and strategies) only when everyone in the group has a hand raised.

■ Students who need more practice might play additional games with the templates that involve fewer digits (_ _ × _ _ or _ _ _ ÷ _).

■ Students ready for more challenge might make their estimates in a shorter time, such as 20 or 15 seconds. They might try templates involving larger numbers, fractions, decimals, addition, or subtraction. For example:

$$\_\,\_\,\_ \times \_\,\_\,\_ \qquad \_\,\_\,\_\,\_ \div \_ \qquad \_\,.\,\_ \times \_ \qquad \_\,\_\,\_\,\_\,\_ - \_\,\_\,\_\,\_$$

You may want to work with some students in smaller groups to share strategies for making estimates.

Sessions 1 and 2 Follow-Up

The Estimation Game Students play the Estimation Game with family members or a small group of friends. Send home copies of Student Sheet 34, How to Play the Estimation Game and Student Sheet 35, Estimation Game Score Sheet. Students should have the cards they prepared for playing the Digits Game at home during Investigation 1. If not, they can easily make another set from paper cut in small squares, or use another method to generate random digits (such as page numbers in a book, as suggested on p. 33).

Homework

Solving Difficult Problems

Materials

■ Student Sheet 36 (1 per student, homework)

What Happens

Students solve a difficult multiplication problem and a difficult division problem without using calculators or standard algorithms. Their work focuses on:

■ applying strategies for multiplying and dividing to more difficult problems

---

Activity

Teacher Checkpoint

How Do We Solve Difficult Problems?

Throughout the unit, students have been developing their own strategies for solving multiplication and division problems without using a calculator or standard algorithms. This activity gives you an opportunity to observe how they apply those strategies to more difficult multiplication and division problems. If necessary, adjust the numbers in the problems to make them easier or more challenging (the **Teacher Note,** Creating Your Own Multiplication and Division Problems, p. 55, talks about what makes a problem more or less difficult).

Write the following two problems on the board:

$$253 \times 46 \qquad 701 \div 27$$

As you've been playing the Estimation Game, you've had to work with problems that are sometimes very difficult to multiply or divide without a calculator. These problems are like that. In the game, you got to use a calculator to find the exact answer. Now we're going to try finding the answers to these harder problems *without* a calculator.

Write these two problems on your paper and work alone to solve them— no calculators, no standard algorithm. Show me how you would think about them, and what strategies you would use to solve them. Write down each step of your work so that when I look at it, I can understand exactly how you solved the problems.

As you observe students working and as you review their papers, consider the following:

- What strategies do students use? Do they repeatedly multiply the divisor or one of the factors by 10? reason about multiples? break the problem into smaller or more familiar components? use repeated addition? use relationships between multiplication and division?

- How do students choose which strategy to use? Do they consider which strategies are efficient, given the particular numbers in the problem? Do they consider what strategies they are most comfortable with? If the students seem to need help, review the **Teacher Note,** Choosing Strategies for Computation (p. 97), for suggestions on how to help students evaluate strategies.

- Do students recognize that they can use the same types of strategies they developed earlier in the unit, with simpler problems?

- What strategies do students have for determining if the answer is reasonable? Do they estimate the answer? try solving the problem in a different way?

- How do students keep track of and record the steps in the problem?

- How are they making sense of and recording remainders?

This checkpoint will help you identify students who are having difficulty applying their strategies to larger numbers. You might want to call these students together to work with you in a small group during Choice Time in Sessions 4–6.

Students who finish early can find another way to solve each problem. They might also play the Estimation Game in small groups, or start on the homework.

Session 3 Follow-Up

Another Division Problem Students make up a situation that would be represented by 720 ÷ 34. They solve the problem without using a standard algorithm or calculator, writing their solutions out in full on Student Sheet 36, Another Division Problem. They also write about what they would do with the extras.

 **Homework**

❖ **Tip for the Linguistically Diverse Classroom** Students make simple sketches to supplement and clarify their writing, both in their situation and in their discussion of the remainder.

Review students' work to get a sense of their strategies for solving division problems and how they are thinking about remainders.

Exploring Operations

Materials

- Student Sheet 37 (1 per student)
- Student Sheet 38 (1 per student)
- Student Sheet 39 (1 per student, class; 1 per student, homework)
- Student Sheet 40 (1 per student, homework)
- Student Sheet 41 (1 per student, homework)
- Million Dots Display Sheets (available as needed)
- Calculators
- Chart paper (optional)

What Happens

During Choice Time, students work in pairs on at least three activities: How Did I Solve It? Challenges (an extension of the type of problem introduced in Investigation 3); Problems About You (a series of problems that represent multiplication and division situations); and the game Different Paths to 10,000 (using calculators to create numeric problems with an answer of 10,000). Classes making the million dots display (Investigation 4, Excursion) work on that project as a fourth choice, and may spend an extra session on this Choice Time. Student work focuses on:

- applying computation strategies to more difficult numeric and situational problems
- understanding relationships among the four basic operations
- reading, writing, and sequencing multiples of 5000 up to 1,000,000 (in work on the million dots display)

Activity

Choice Time: Exploring Operations

How to Set Up the Choices For the next three sessions, students work in pairs on several activities going on in the classroom simultaneously. If you have presented other units in the *Investigations* curriculum, students will be familiar with Choice Time. Remind students of your expectations or explain the Choice Time format to them, as necessary. Pairs are to work on each activity, but will decide themselves on the order in which they do them. List the choices on the board as you introduce the activities. Students might also make their own lists to keep track of the choices available and the ones they have completed.

You might give each student a complete set of Student Sheets 37–39 at the beginning of Session 3, or keep copies where students can help themselves as they are ready.

Choice 1: How Did I Solve It? Challenges—Student Sheet 37 (1 per student). Some students may need additional sheets of paper on which to record their work. Note that students may *not* use calculators for this choice.

Choice 2: Problems About You—Student Sheet 38 (1 per student). Note that students may *not* use calculators for this choice.

Choice 3: Different Paths to 10,000— Student Sheet 39 (1 per student), calculators needed

If your class is making the million dots display, offer that work as Choice 4 and plan on an extra session for Choice Time. As time permits, you may want to add other choices, such as the Estimation Game (directions on p. 199), the Digits Game (directions on p. 162), or building a Multiple Tower for a number that has not been explored yet (perhaps 59, 87, 248, or 3097).

Briefly explain to students what you expect them to do in order to complete each choice, and how they will take their turns working on the million dots display.

Choice 1: How Did I Solve It?

Both students in a pair work on their own copy of the How Did I Solve It? Challenges on Student Sheet 37. These are similar to the problems on Student Sheet 27, but they involve larger and less familiar numbers. For each problem, students are given the first step of three or four different solution methods. Students complete any *two* of these. Remind students that there can be more than one way to complete each first step.

There are several different ways you might structure the activity, depending on the skills of your students and the amount of time available:

- Students might complete the first two steps for all eight problems.

- You might assign one problem that all students will solve; pairs then choose three others to solve, being sure to do some multiplication and some division.

- Students might do one problem that you assign and then choose one other to solve completely. For the remaining problems, they record *the steps* they would take to find the answers, but they do need to carry out those steps. For example, for problem 1, 37×86, a student might write:

    I would solve 86×10. Then I would times the answer by 3. Then I would solve 7×86 by solving 80×7 and 6×7. Then I would add the answers to 80×7, 6×7, and 860×3.

- Students who did not complete Student Sheet 27, How Did I Solve It? can work on those problems first. Then they continue on Student Sheet 37, doing a problem you assign plus one multiplication and one division problem of their own choice.

Students who are having difficulty may find it helpful to solve problems their own way, then think about how *their* solution method might be like one of those listed. You might decide to permit students having difficulty to complete only one first step, and then to record their own way of solving the problem as well. Or you might suggest some possible *second steps*. The **Dialogue Box,** A Challenging Problem: 37×86 (p. 138), shows how one pair solved a problem that was difficult for them.

When pairs finish, they compare solutions with another pair. Those ready for more challenge might go on to complete some of the remaining first steps, or make up their own solution methods. They could also create their own How Did I Solve It? problems and trade them with partners to solve.

Choice 2: Problems About You

Student Sheet 38, Problems About You, presents three hypothetical situations involving boxes of pencils, pads of paper, and earning money from recycling. The problems use the actual numbers of students in your class, in all classes at the same grade, and in the entire school. You might list these numbers on the board for students to fill in the blanks on the student sheet. Although students work on these problems in pairs, each should complete his or her own student sheet. Remind them to record every step of their thinking.

❖ **Tip for the Linguistically Diverse Classroom** As you read each problem aloud, students sketch a rebus for any key word they might have trouble reading. For the Pads of Paper problems on page 2, be sure students link the numbers for *class, grade,* and *school* with the corresponding problems, perhaps by writing the number of students above those words in the problems.

In order to solve the first Pads of Paper problem, students need to think about relationships among *three* quantities: the number of sheets in a pad, the number of pads in a package, and the total number of packages. If you notice that students are having difficulty, work with a small group or call the class together to talk about strategies for thinking about the problem, without actually solving it. Following are some possible approaches:

- Working with two quantities at a time; for example, first finding the total number of sheets in one package, then the number of sheets in all the packages, or first finding the total number of pads, then the total number of sheets in the pads.

- Drawing a diagram to help visualize the situation.

- Making a chart that shows the number of sheets in 1 package, 2 packages, and so on.

sheets in 1 package	sheets in 2 packages	sheets in 3 packages
$4 \times 85 = 340$ 320×20	$2 \times 340 = 680$	$680 + 340 = 1020$

Choice 3: Different Paths to 10,000

Students play the calculator game, Different Paths to 10,000. To start, each player in a pair or small group enters the same number on a calculator. The players work to find at least two ways to get 10,000 showing on the calculator display. For example, from the starting number 1025, here are two possible paths:

Path 1: $1025 \times 10 = 10{,}250$ $10{,}250 - 250 = 10{,}000$
Path 2: $1025 \div 25 = 41$ $41 + 9 = 50$ $50 \times 2000 = 10{,}000$

Players may use as many different operations as they want, but at least one path should include multiplication or division. Students may use any keys except those that clear the calculator display.

Briefly review the directions on Student Sheet 39, Different Paths to 10,000. If necessary you might plan to play one round with the class, using the starting number 1000. If students have trouble understanding what they are to do, suggest one simple path to 10,000: After entering 1000, they can enter ×, then 10, then =.

Challenge students to find other paths using addition, or both addition and multiplication. Remind students to press the equals key after each operation and number, and to record their work as *separate* equations.

Note: Because of the way the numbers come up on the calculator, students find it tempting to record each path using several equals signs within a single expression like this: $1000 + 3000 = 4000 \times 3 = 12{,}000 - 2000 = 10{,}000$. Point out that this sets up statements that are not true. Demonstrate how to separate such a path into steps, each showing a true equality:

$1000 + 3000 = 4000$ $4000 \times 3 = 12{,}000$ $12{,}000 - 2000 = 10{,}000$

As you watch students play, notice those who are sticking to addition and subtraction, and encourage them to find paths that involve multiplication and division. Also encourage them to find paths with several steps, even though these solutions may be inefficient.

After finding two paths for the five given starting numbers on Student Sheet 39, students play the game with starting numbers of their own choice. Guide those who need more practice toward numbers such as 500, 720, 2000, and 10,100 (multiples of 1000, 100, or other familiar numbers). For students who are ready for more challenge, suggest 5- and 6-digit starting numbers (such as 57,391 or 207,000), or starting numbers that have one or more decimal places (such as 700.25 or 4999.97). These students might also look for paths to 100,000 or 1,000,000, or another large number.

Starting number	Paths to 10,000
1025	$1025 \times 6 = 6150$ $6150 \times 4 = 24600$ $24600 - 14000 = 10600$ $10600 - 600 = 10000$
	$1025 \times 9 = 9225$ $9225 + 8075 = 17300$ $17300 - 7300 = 10000$
73	$73 \div 1 = 73$ $73 \times 9 = 657$ $657 \times 50 = 32850$ $32850 - 22850 = 10000$
	To find out what times 73 is 10000 I did $10000 \div 73 = 136.9863$ So $73 \times 136.9863 + .0001 = 10000$
9974	$9974 \times 38 = 379012$ $379012 - 279012 = 100000$ $100000 - 90000 = 10000$
	$9974 \times 8 = 79792$ $79792 - 78792 = 1000$ $1000 + 9000 = 10000$
21,681	$21681 \div 2 = 10840.5$ $10840.5 - 840.5 = 10000$
	$21681 - 681 = 21000$ $21000 - 11000 = 10000$
130.5	$130.5 \times 5 = 652.5$ $652.5 + 452.5 = 1105$ $1105 + 900 = 2005$ $2005 - 1005 = 1000$ $1000 \times 10 = 10000$
	$130.5 \times 8 = 1044$ $1044 + 9000 = 10044$ $10044 - 44 = 10000$

Observing the Students

While students are working on the Choice Time activities, circulate and talk with them to see what strategies they are using, how they are keeping track of their work, and how they are dealing with remainders. Observe how students are working together. Are all students participating? Are they explaining their reasoning so that others can understand? listening to one another? learning about new strategies from others? You might take some whole-group time toward the end of Session 7 for students to share some of the things they have learned from one another. You could begin by reporting some of the instances you saw in your conversations with students.

Small-Group and Whole-Group Discussions   During these sessions, you might want to work with a small group of students who are having difficulty with specific activity choices. While you are occupied in this way, enlist the help of students in the room who understand the activities to act as resources or helpers for their peers who might have questions.

At some point later on in Choice Time, take about 15 minutes for a whole-group discussion, to share strategies for one of the How Did I Solve It? Challenges. At another point, spend 10 minutes with the group sharing strategies for the first two or three Pads of Paper problems on Student Sheet 38, page 2. Before each such discussion, check to be sure students have completed the problems you have chosen as the focus for sharing. More detail for each discussion is given below.

On the board or on chart paper, record the one How Did I Solve It? problem you chose for class sharing. Leave enough room for students to record several solution methods for each first step. (You may need to remind them that each first step can have several solution methods.)

When students have recorded as many different solution methods as they can, ask them to check that they understand each solution method listed. Pairs briefly explain their methods to the class, and the group discusses any questions. Then refer the class to the remaining seven problems.

Were there any first steps that you could not complete? Which ones? Was anyone else in the class able to complete them? How?

If there are some first steps that no one could complete, challenge students to continue working on them for the next few days. You might post these first steps (with each associated problem) on a piece of chart paper. Students can record solution methods as they find them.

Discussion: How Did I Solve It?

$899 \div 7 =$

a. Start by solving 100×7

$100 \times 7 = 700$
$700 \div 7 = 100$
$100 \div 7 = 14 \, R2$ —add
$99 \div 7 = 14 \, R1$
$128 \, R3$

$100 \times 7 = 700$
$20 \times 7 = 140$
$59 \times 7 = 8 \, r3$

$700 \div 7 = 100$
$+ 140 \div 7 = 20$
$840 \div 7 = 120$
$+ 59 \div 7 = 8 \, r3$
$899 \div 7 = 128 \, r3$

b. start by solving 7×12

c. Start by solving $700 \div 7$

$700 \div 7 = 100$
$140 \div 7 = 20$
$59 \div 7 = 8 \, r3$
$899 \div 7 = 128 \, R3$

$70 \div 7 = 10$
$70 \div 7 = 10$
$140 \quad 59 \div 7 = 8 \, 3/7$

$700 \div 7 = 100$
$199 \div 7 = 28 \, 3/7$
$100 + 28 \, 3/7 = 128 \, 3/7$

Discussion: How Many Sheets of Paper?

When everyone has completed page 2 of Student Sheet 38, Problems About You, students then share solution strategies for the first two or three problems. Invite students to come to the board to demonstrate any diagrams, charts, or equations they used. Ask them to represent each problem using multiplication or division notation, in addition to explaining how they solved it.

Sessions 4, 5, and 6 Follow-Up

Homework

A Multiplication Problem   After Session 4, students make up a situation for 518×42 on Student Sheet 40, A Multiplication Problem. Then they solve the problem without using a standard algorithm or a calculator, and they write their solutions to show every step. Collect students' work to get a sense of their multiplication strategies.

There are 42 dogs in our town. Each dog has exactly 518 fleas. How many fleas live on all our dogs?

42×518

$2 \times 518 = 1036$
$4 \times 518 = 2072$
$40 \times 518 = 20,720$
$42 \times 518 = 21,756$

How Can This Help?   After Session 5, send Student Sheet 41, How Can This Help?, home with students. Students show how the answer to 25×40 can help them find the answer to two problems they choose from the list.

Different Paths to 10,000   After Session 6, students who have calculators at home play Different Paths to 10,000 with an older family member. They play with at least two different starting numbers of their own choice. They record all the expressions both players make on Student Sheet 39, Different Paths to 10,000. If possible, you might lend calculators to students who need them.

Rewriting Multiplication Expressions Challenge students to rewrite a multiplication expression so that it has a different number of factors. For example, present an expression with two composite factors (factors that are not prime), such as 36×45. Ask students to find different ways to rewrite the expression with three factors (for example, $9 \times 5 \times 36$ or $9 \times 30 \times 6$), four factors (for example, $6 \times 6 \times 9 \times 5$), or some other number of factors. You might also give students an expression with several factors, at least *some* of which are composite, such as $5 \times 9 \times 7 \times 24 \times 3$. Students find different ways to rewrite the expression so it has only two or three factors.

How Many Factors? Students choose a number and rewrite it as a multiplication expression with the *greatest possible* number of factors, excluding the number 1. For example, 100 can be expressed as $2 \times 2 \times 5 \times 5$. Encourage students to do this with a series of numbers, for example: the first few powers of 10 (10, 100, 1000, 10,000...); the first few square numbers (4, 9, 16, 25...); the first few multiples of 6 (6, 12, 18, 24...). They then look for patterns in the factors and in the number of possible factors for each number in the series.

Multiplication and Division Practice For more practice with multiplication and division strategies, students generate problems the same way they do for the Estimation Game: They choose a template (such as $\_\,\_\,\_ \div \_\,\_$) and deal out Numeral Cards to fill in the slots. In addition to estimating the answers, they solve the problems without using standard algorithms or calculators.

 **Extensions**

A Challenging Problem: 37×86

Jasmine and Katrina are working on 37×86, the first How Did I Solve It? challenge on Student Sheet 37. They decide to complete the first step 10×86. When the teacher visits them, they have written the steps they would take to solve the problem, but they seem stuck. The following dialogue shows how, with the teacher's encouragement, they complete the problem.

$$37 \times 86$$
$$10 \times 86 = 860$$
Do 860×3
Then do 86×7
Then add the two answers.

Tell me about what you've written down.

Jasmine: We solved 10×86. That equals 860. Then, here's what we'd do *[she reads what she has written]*.

That looks like a good plan.

Jasmine: I know we have to do 860×3. We aren't sure how to start.

Katrina, do have any ideas how you might start solving 860×3?

Katrina: *[after a short pause]* We could just add it. Add the 800's, that's 8, 16, 24 … 24 hundred, and the 60's: 6, 12, 18 … 180 *[she writes down 2400 + 180]*. Add it up and you get 2580.

Jasmine: OK, so that's 2580. Then we have to do 7×86. That is so hard!

Can you make up a cluster that could help you?

Jasmine: Um…we could do a cluster with 6×7 and 80×7. We could add some other problems to make it a little easier. We could do the half and double thing. Like, if you didn't know 6×7 you could do 3×7 equals 21 and then do two times it.

$$860 \times 3 = 2580$$
$$86 \times 7$$

6×7 80×7
$3 \times 7 = 21$ 40×7 then $\times 2$
42 $20 \times 7 = 70 \times 2$
     $70 + 70 = 140$
     560 then $\times 4$

$$42 + 560 = 602$$

$$2580 + 602 = 3182$$

Jasmine *[continuing]*: So, for 80×7 I can do half of 80 is 40×7 and then do times 2, and I don't know that, so I can do 20×7 and then do it times 4. So 20×7 is … *[after a few seconds]* 20×7 is the same thing as 70×2, and that's 70 plus 70 equals 140.

Katrina: Then you can double 14 and get 28 and then double 28 and get 56, so it's 560. Then add the 42, and then add that to the answer to 860×3, 2580.

Session 7

Assessing Students' Understanding

What Happens

As an assessment, students solve a difficult multiplication problem and a difficult division problem without standard algorithms or calculators. If you are doing the Excursion, students continue to assemble the million dots display. Student work focuses on:

- writing about strategies for solving difficult multiplication and division problems
- developing a sense of the size of 1,000,000

Materials

- Paper and pencil

Activity

Assessment

Solving Harder Problems

Write the following problems on the board:

$$803 \times 41 \qquad 663 \div 26$$

If you feel that these problems are too difficult for some students, adjust the numbers accordingly.

Tell students that you would like to get an idea of how they are thinking about multiplication and division problems and what kinds of strategies they are using. Students work alone, solving each of the problems on the board without using a standard algorithm or calculator. Explain that they are to record each step of their work so that someone looking at their papers would understand their solution methods.

Depending on what your emphasis in class has been, you can extend this assessment by asking students to write a situation that reflects each of the problems, or by asking them to solve each problem a second way.

As you observe and talk with students, and as you later read their papers, think about the following:

- What types of strategies are students using?
- How do students choose which strategy to use? Do they consider which strategies are efficient, given the particular numbers in the problem? Do they consider which strategies they are able to carry out well?
- How do students determine whether their answer is reasonable? Do they make up a situation to fit the problem? Do they use estimation? Do they solve the problem in a different way?

Session 7: Assessing Students' Understanding ■ **139**

■ How do students keep track of and record their steps in the problem? How are they making sense of and recording remainders?

The **Teacher Note,** Assessment: Solving Harder Problems (p. 141), includes some samples of student work and suggestions for evaluating their papers. As in the earlier assessment activity (p. 102), you are interested in the students' strategies for working computation problems, not in how rapidly they are able to find the answers. Students who are taking much longer than others might first write what steps they would take to solve the problem. These students can begin to carry out the steps and can bring the problem to completion as time permits.

When everyone has finished, collect students' work. If there is time, invite students to share their solution strategies and division situations with the class.

Activity

How Far to a Million?

If you are doing the Excursion, A Million Dots, repeat the activity Are We Close to a Million? (p. 117), asking students to share ideas on their progress on the million dots display. Choose some of the questions listed in the **Teacher Note,** Have We Reached a Million Yet? (p. 119), to explore with the class. If the display does not yet contain a million dots, allow more time during math or use free time to complete the display. Repeat this activity again when the students have reached a million.

Activity

Choosing Student Work to Save

As the unit ends, you may want to use one of the following options for creating a record of students' work:

■ Students look back through their folders or notebooks and write about what they learned in this unit, what they remember most, and what was hard or easy for them. Students could do this during their writing time.

■ Students select one or two pieces of their work as their best, and you also choose one or two pieces, to be saved in a portfolio for the year. You might include students' written solutions to the two assessments, Ways to Multiply and Divide (p. 100), and Solving Harder Problems (p. 139), along with any other tasks you have used for assessment in this unit. Students can create a separate page with brief comments describing each piece of work.

■ You may want to send a selection of work home for families to see. Students write a cover letter, describing their work in this unit. This work should be returned if you are keeping year-long portfolios.

Assessment: Solving Harder Problems

As you review student work on the final assessment in this unit, you will see many different strategies for working the problems 803×41 and $663 \div 26$. Shown here are a few of the many possible approaches.

Multiplication: 803×41

The three students whose work is shown on this page all solved the problem correctly, using different strategies.

803×40

I would take 800 and X it by 40 and thats 32,000 because 8 x 4 = 32 and X it by 100. And then X 3 X 41 and 1 X 800

= 123
  800

  923

 32,000
+   923

 32,923

803×41 First I would round 41 off to 40. Then I would do 803×40 which is 32,120. Then since I had 1 leftover I did 803×1 which I knew without doing it out is 803. For the last step I did 32,120 + 803 and I got my answer, 32,923.

$803 \times 41 =$

Start with $41 \times 10 = 410$ then do $410 \times 10 = 4100$. That means that $4100 = 41 \times 100$. If I then do $4100 \times 8 = 32800$ which means $32800 = 41 \times 800$ Then add $3 \times 41 = 123$ to get $803 \times 41 = 32923$ which is my answer.

Continued on next page

"Order of Magnitude" Errors Some students may make errors that involve multiplying or dividing by an extra 10 or 100. For example, Alani used a correct strategy but neglected to multiply by 10 in one of the steps. To go from her second equation (2×803) to her third (40×803), she would need to double the answer to 2×803 and then multiply by 10. However, the answer she recorded, 3212, shows that she only doubled. Thus, to find the answer to 41×803, she adds 3212 (instead of 32,120) to 803.

Alani

$$803 \times 41 = 4015$$
$$1 \times 803 = 803$$
$$2 \times 803 = 1606$$
$$40 \times 803 = 3212$$
$$41 \times 803 = 4015$$

If you notice students making this kind of error, encourage them to think about whether their answer is reasonable by making an estimate or by solving the problem in a second way. Give them an opportunity to look over their work and make revisions.

Incomplete Work Some students will work more slowly than others to solve difficult problems. They may need more time to organize and keep track of their work, or they may need more time to add or subtract parts of the problem. Because you need to evaluate whether students have good strategies, rather than how rapidly they can find answers, ask students who are taking longer to begin by recording the steps they would take to solve each of the problems.

The teacher took this approach with Manuel, who has difficulty adding large numbers quickly and accurately. While the teacher knew that addition is an important skill that Manuel needs to work on, the goal here was to evaluate his understanding of multiplication and division. So, Manuel was told to concentrate on recording the steps he would take. When the teacher visited him partway through the session, he had recorded *how* he would solve 803×41, without actually finding the answer.

Manuel

$$803 \times 41$$
$$803 \times 10 = 8030$$
$$803 \times 41 = \text{is } 4 \text{ } 8030\text{'s}$$
to get 40 and you need 1 more to get 41.
So do
$$8030 + 8030 + 8030 + 8030 + 803$$

The teacher asked Manuel to talk through what he wrote and was satisfied that he demonstrated sound reasoning about multiplication. Manuel was told to make an estimate and then to find the answer, finishing his work outside of class time if necessary. At the same time, the teacher made a note to include Manuel in a group for extra practice with addition and subtraction strategies.

Continued on next page

Division: 663 ÷ 26

Each of these students used a different correct
approach for the division part of the assessment.

$663 \div 26$

$26 \times 10 = 260$

$260 \times 2 = 520$

$520 \div 26 = 20$

after finding this out I
knew I needed to find
out $193 \div 26$ and add
that to 20.

$260 \div 2 = 26 \times 5 (130) \rightarrow 5 + \frac{13}{26}$

$5\frac{13}{26}$
$20\frac{0}{26}$
—————
$25\frac{13}{26}$

$663 \div 26$

round 26 to 25, 25 goes
into 100 4 times so
$4 \times 6 = 24) + 24$ because
for every 25 that goes
into 600 (you need to
add one) because your
number is 26 insted of
25 - 624 Then go back
to 26 and add that
to $624 + 26 = 650$
which takes 25 26s to get
there. But theres
thirteen more so

(25 with 13 leftover)

$663 \div 26$

What you do to solve this problem is:

Start by solving
25×26 which is 650

$25 \times 12 = 300$
$25 \times 24 = 600$
$25 \times 2 = 50$

Now find the
difference between 50 and 63 $= 13$ If it is under
which it is. The inbetween number is the
remainder and the solid answer is 25 R13.

Continued on next page

Solving the Wrong Problem Some students start out explaining that they will solve the problem by finding the number of 25's in 663 and then adjusting. But in the process of carrying this out, they lose track of the original problem (663 ÷ 26) and find the answer to 663 ÷ 25 instead.

Round 26 to 25

$663 \div 25 = (600 \div 25) + (63 \div 25)$

There are 4 25s in 100
So there are 24 25s in 600

Then $63 \div 25$ is 2R13 because there are 2 25s in 50 and 13 left over.

$600 \div 25 = 24$

$63 \div 25 = \underline{\quad 2R13 \quad}$

answer $\longrightarrow$ 26 R13

When this happens, ask the students to talk through with you how they would solve 663 ÷ 26, even if they have a solid strategy for solving 663 ÷ 25. For many students, 663 ÷ 26 will be more difficult because the divisor, 26, is not as familiar as 25. Another approach would be to ask these students if they can explain how they intended to use their work on the problem 663 ÷ 25 to help them find the answer to 663 ÷ 26.

Errors in Breaking a Problem into Smaller Parts When students incorrectly break a problem into parts, meet with them to probe how they are thinking about the problem. In one such error, Tai broke 663 ÷ 26 into two parts: 663 ÷ 25 and 663 ÷ 1.

663÷26 First I would round 26 off to 25. Then I did 663÷25 which is 26 R13. Then since there is 1 left over I did 663÷1 which I knew without doing it out is 663. Then for the last step I did 663 + 26R13 and I got my answer 689 R13.

In earlier sessions, the teacher had observed Tai breaking down division problems in appropriate ways, and thus was surprised at what he wrote for this assessment. Had he been intending to solve 663 ÷ 25 and then adjust, but lost track of the steps he needed to take? Or was he really unsure of how to break the problem into parts? As a follow-up to the assessment, the teacher met with Tai, first asking him to estimate the answer, to see if he recognized that his answer was much too large. Then, the teacher asked Tai to talk through his solution process and to solve the problem in a different way.

Continued on next page

Julie

$663 \div 26 = 25 \ R23$

First I would do $20 \times 33 = 660$ then for every twenty I used another 6 which is 33 6's (because $33 \times 6 = 188$) and I would put them together.

$660 + 188 = 848$ so $33 \times 26 = 848$

Then take away 26's to fill up the difference. $26 \times 5 = 130$. $848 - 130 = 718$. Minus one more 26 is 692 and minus one more is 666 and minus one more is 640. That's minus 8 from my answer 33 which gives me 25 26's is 640. The problem is $663 \div 26$ so its <u>25 with 23 left over.</u>

A Creative Solution with a Computational Error   A few students may demonstrate a solid grasp of multiplication and division but will arrive at the wrong answer because of a computational error. Julie's strategy shows sophisticated reasoning about division. She has strong mental computation skills and enjoys creating new ways to solve problems. However, because of an incorrect computation (she recorded $6 \times 33 = 188$, rather than 198), she ends up with a remainder of 23 instead of a remainder of 13.

The teacher was impressed with Julie's complex approach to the problem and her deep understanding of relationships among the four basic operations. After a reminder to Julie to check her computations more carefully, the teacher encouraged the girl to continue finding new strategies for multiplication and division, and to share them with her classmates.

What Is Likely?

Basic Activity

Students make judgments about drawing objects of two different colors from a clear container. They first decide whether it's likely that they'll get more of one color or the other. Then they draw out 10 objects, one at a time, recording the color of each and replacing that object before picking the next one. Students then discuss whether what they expected to happen did happen. They repeat the activity with another sample of 10 objects.

What Is Likely? involves students in thinking about ratio and proportion, and in considering the likelihood of the occurrence of a particular event. Ideas about probability are notoriously difficult for children and adults. In the early and middle elementary grades, we simply want students to examine familiar events in order to judge how likely or unlikely they are. In this activity, students' work focuses on:

- visualizing the ratio of two colors in a collection
- making predictions and comparing predictions with outcomes
- exploring the relationship between a sample and the group of objects from which it comes

Materials

- A clear container, such as a fishbowl or large glass or clear plastic jar
- Objects that are all very similar in size and shape, but come in two colors (wooden cubes, beans, beads, marbles)

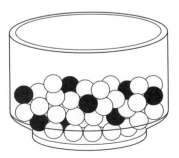

Procedure

Step 1. Fill the container with cubes, beads, or beans of two colors. When you first do this activity, put much more of one color into the container. For example, for every 10 cubes, you might use 9 yellow and 1 red. Thus, if you used 40 cubes, 36 would be yellow and 4 would be red. Mix these well inside the container. Continue to use these markedly different proportions for a while.

Step 2. Students predict which color will be taken most often if they draw 10 objects out of the container. Carry the container around the room so that all students can get a good look at its contents. Then ask students to make their predictions. "What is likely to happen if we draw out 10 objects? Will we get more yellows or more reds? Will we get a lot more of one color than the other?"

Step 3. Students draw 10 objects from the container, immediately replacing them after each draw. Ask a student, with eyes closed, to draw out one object. Record its color on the board before the student puts the object back. Ask nine more students to pick an object, then replace it after you have recorded its color. Record the colors with tallies.

> YELLOW ~~////~~ ///
> RED //

Step 4. Discuss what happened. "Is this about what you expected? Why or why not?" Even if you have a 9:1 ratio of the two colors, you won't always draw out a sample that is exactly 9 of one color and 1 of the other. Eight yellow and 2 red or 10 yellow and 0 red would also be likely samples. Ask students whether what they got is likely or unlikely, given what they can see in the container. What would be *unlikely*, or surprising? (Of course, surprises can happen, too—just not very often.)

Continued on next page

Step 5. Try it again. Students will probably want to try drawing another 10 objects to see what happens. "Do you think it's likely that we'll get mostly reds again? Why? About how many do you think we'll get?" Draw objects, tally their colors, and discuss in the same way.

Variations

Different Color Mixes Try a 3:1 ratio—3 of one color for every 1 of the second color. Also try an equal amount of the two colors.

Different Objects Try two colors of a different kind of object. Does a change like this affect the outcome?

The Whole Class Picks See what happens when each student in the class draws (and puts back) one object. Before you start, ask, "If all [28] of us pick an object, about how many reds do you think we'll get? Is it more likely you'll pick a red or a yellow? A *little* more likely or *a lot* more likely?"

Students Fill the Container Ask students to help you decide what proportions of each color to put in the container. Set a goal. For example:

- How can we fill the container so that's it's *very likely* we'll get mostly reds when we draw 10?

- How can we fill the container so that it's *unlikely* we'll get more than one red?

- How can we fill the container so that we'll get close to the same number of reds and yellows when we draw 10?

After students decide how to fill the container, draw out objects, as in the basic activity, to see if their prediction works.

Three Colors Put an equal number of two colors (red and yellow) in the container, and mix in many more or many fewer of a third color (blue). "If 10 people pick, about how many of each color do you think we will get? Do you think we'll get the same number of red and yellow, or do you think we will get more of one of them?"

Expected Percent, Actual Percent When predicting what is likely, ask students to state their predictions as percents; for example, "I think it will be about 25% yellow and 75% red." They then express the actual results as percents, and discuss in Step 4 what percents would be unlikely or surprising.

Quick Images

Basic Activity

Students are briefly shown a design or a picture of a figure. Depending on the kind of figure, they either draw it or build it.

For each type of figure—geometric shapes, pattern block arrangements, dot patterns, or cube images—students must find meaningful ways to see and develop a mental image. They might see the figure as a whole ("It looks like a window, three cubes high and five cubes wide"), or decompose it into memorable parts ("It looks like a pinwheel with a square in the middle"), or use their knowledge of number relationships to remember a pattern ("There were 6 groups of 5 dots, so it's 30"). Their work focuses on:

- organizing and analyzing visual images
- developing concepts and language needed to reflect on and communicate about spatial relationships
- using geometric vocabulary to describe shapes and patterns
- using number relationships to describe patterns

Materials

- Overhead projector
- Power Polygons, pattern blocks, or other regular polygon shapes (either transparent or regular)
- Pencil and paper
- Interlocking cubes, dot patterns for the variations

Procedure

Step 1. Flash an image for 3 seconds. It's important to keep the figure showing for as close to 3 seconds as possible. If you show the figure too long, students will draw or build from the actual figure rather than their image of it; if you show it too briefly, they will not have time to form a mental image. Suggest to students that they study the figure carefully while it is visible, then try to draw or build it from their mental image.

Step 2. Students draw or build what they saw. Give students a few minutes with their pencil and paper or the manipulatives to try to draw or construct a figure based on the mental image they have formed. After you see that most students' activity has stopped, go on to step 3.

Step 3. Flash the image again, for revision. After you show the figure for another 3 seconds, students revise their building or drawing, based on this second view.

It is essential to provide enough time between the first and second flashes for most students to complete their attempts at drawing or building. While they may not have completed their figure, they should have done all they can until they see the picture on the screen again.

Step 4. Show the image a final time. When student activity subsides again, show the picture a third time. This time leave it visible so that all students can complete or revise their solutions.

Step 5. Students describe how they saw the figure as they looked at it on successive "flashes."

Variations

In this unit, the Ten-Minute Math activities focus on geometric designs. Following is a description of these Quick Images and some other options.

Quick Image Geometric Designs Create designs on the overhead out of Power Polygons, pattern blocks, or other regular polygon shapes. Arrange three or four shapes on the overhead to form a larger shape or design. Follow the usual procedure. Students create the shapes they see using their own set of shapes or by drawing the figure.

Continued on next page

You might suggest this strategy for students having difficulty: "Each design is made from familiar geometric shapes. Find these shapes and try to figure out how they are put together."

As students describe their figures, you can introduce correct terms for the shapes: *parallelogram, rhombus, trapezoid, equilateral triangle,* and so forth. As you use these terms naturally as part of the discussion, students will begin to use and recognize them.

For more challenge, construct a figure using more pieces. Or, continue to use only a few shapes, but leave no spaces between them.

Quick Image Cubes   Each student should have a supply of 15–20 cubes. Flash a drawing of a three-dimensional cube figure, like this:

Follow the same procedure, giving students time to build what they saw.

Quick Image Dot Patterns   Draw dots on a transparency in several same-size groups, arranged in some pattern. For example:

The procedure is the same, except that now students are asked two questions: "Can you draw the dot patterns you see? Can you figure out how many dots you saw?"

When students answer only one question, ask them the other again. You will see different students using different strategies. For instance, some will see a multiplication problem, 6×5, and will not draw the dots unless asked. Others will draw the dots, then figure out how many there are.

Using the Calculator   You can integrate the calculator into the Quick Image Dot Patterns. As you draw larger or more complex dot patterns, students may begin to count the groups and the number of groups. They should use a variety of strategies to find the total number of dots, including mental calculation and the calculator.

Creating Quick Images   Students can make up their own Quick Images to challenge the rest of the class. Talk with students about keeping these reasonable—challenging, but not overwhelming. If they are too complex and difficult, other students will just become frustrated.

The following activities will help ensure that this unit is comprehensible to students who are acquiring English as a second language. The suggested approach is based on *The Natural Approach: Language Acquisition in the Classroom* by Stephen D. Krashen and Tracy D. Terrell (Alemany Press, 1983). The intent is for second-language learners to acquire new vocabulary in an active, meaningful context.

Note that *acquiring* a word is different from *learning* a word. Depending on their level of proficiency, students may be able to comprehend a word upon hearing it during an investigation, without being able to say it. Other students may be able to use the word orally, but not read or write it. The goal is to help students naturally acquire targeted vocabulary at their present level of proficiency.

We suggest using these activities just before the related investigations. The activities can also be led by English-proficient students.

Investigation 1

strategy, strategies

1. Place a pencil on one edge of the table. Explain that the problem is how to move the pencil from this edge of the table to the other edge, without using any hands.

2. Blow the pencil so that it rolls across the table. Explain that blowing is one *strategy* for moving the pencil without using any hands.

   Did my strategy work?
   Who has another strategy?

3. As students suggest other approaches—such as pushing the pencil with another object, or with another body part, verbalize each strategy for them. Ask:

   Did that strategy work?
   How many strategies have we thought of so far?

4. List all the strategies on the board with simple words and sketches. Write a heading for the list: *Our Strategies for the Pencil Problem.*

Investigation 2

situation

1. Write on the board $2 \times 4 = 8$. Then draw two animals with four legs each:

2. Explain that you have drawn a *situation* that matches the problem 2×4: Two animals with four legs gives us eight legs altogether.

3. Now draw four people, each with two balloons:

   Then ask:

   Does this situation match $2 \times 4 = 8$?
   Who can draw another situation that matches $2 \times 4 = 8$?

4. Write another problem on the board, such as $18 \div 3 = 6$. Challenge students to sketch a real-life situation that matches this problem.

imaginary, coin, dollar, worth

1. As you show different U.S. coins, ask simple questions that can be answered with a one-word response.

   Is this coin worth more or less than that coin?
   Which coin is worth the most?
   Which coin is worth the least?

2. Repeat the activity with dollar bills of different denominations.

3. Display all the coins. Identify them by name as you emphasize that these are real coins.

Continued on next page

4. Tap your head to indicate you are thinking. Explain that you are *imagining* a new coin. Show a button or a round chip to students, and tell them that this is your *imaginary* coin. Explain that you will call it a Dooper, and it is worth 7 cents.

5. Ask questions about the Dooper and the displayed U.S. coins.

   Could I use a Dooper at the store?
   Is the Dooper a real coin? Is it an imaginary coin?
   Is my imaginary Dooper worth more or less than this coin [point to a dime]?
   Is my imaginary Dooper worth more or less than this coin [point to a nickel]?

6. Ask students to decide on a name for their own imaginary coin, and how much their imaginary coin is worth. Choose a volunteer to share the name of his or her coin, *without* saying what it is worth. The group tries to guess its value by asking more-than and less-than questions.

   Is it worth more than 10 cents? Is it worth less than 20 cents?

share or divide equally, extra

1. Have a collection of small counters, chips, or cubes that will divide evenly among the group. Distribute them equally to the students and ask:

   How many counters did you get? Did everyone get the same amount? Were the counters equally divided?

2. Collect the counters and redistribute them unequally. Give some students twice or three times the amount you give others, and then ask about this distribution.

   How many counters did you get this time? Did everyone get the same amount? Were the counters equally divided?

3. Challenge students to figure out how to share the counters equally. Ask questions as necessary:

   Would [name] have to give up some of his counters to give everyone an equal share? How much will he have to give up? Who should he give it to?

4. Collect the counters once more. Add just enough so that they can no longer be divided evenly among the group. Distribute them again, placing the extras in one place. Ask questions about these:

   Are these counters extra? How many extra counters are there? If I gave these extra counters to some people, would the counters still be equally divided? What could I do with the extra counters?

Blackline Masters

_____ , 19 ___

Dear Family,

In mathematics, our class is starting a new unit called *Building on Numbers You Know*. We will be working on computation and estimation skills as we do harder problems in multiplication and division, as well as addition and subtraction.

As the children solve these problems, they develop a variety of strategies, all based on good number sense. These strategies may not look the same as those you learned in school. For example, take the problem $463 \div 75$. We might use what we already know about 75 to solve it: We know two 75's are 150, so four 75's are 300, and six 75's are 450—we're getting close to 463 now. So, there are six 75's in 463, with a remainder of 13.

Here's another example: 59×13. One person in class might think of it this way: 59×13 means 59 groups of 13. That's the same as 60 groups of 13 minus 1 group of 13. We can calculate $60 \times 13 = 780$. Subtract 13 from that, and the result is 767.

Someone else in the class might do the same problem this way: 59×13 is the same as 10 groups of 59, plus 3 groups of 59. Tens are easy: $10 \times 59 = 590$. The 3×59 will be easier if we break it down a bit more: It's the same as 3 groups of 50 (or 150) plus 3 groups of 9 (or 27). So the answer is $590 + 150 + 27$, or 767.

While these methods may at first look complicated, they are actually easy to keep track of, result in numbers that are easy to work with, are not prone to calculation errors, and don't take too long to carry out. When children understand from the beginning the strategies they are using, they develop confidence as well as skill, fluency as well as accuracy.

While the class is working on this unit, you can help in several ways:

- Notice when you use multiplication and division in your everyday life. Enlist your child's help. For example, if you are planning a picnic, have your child help figure out what you need to buy. If there are 20 slices in a loaf of bread, how many loaves will we need if each person eats two sandwiches?

- Play the games your child brings home. In the Digits Game, you'll be finding the difference between two large numbers. The Estimation Game focuses on making estimates for multiplication and division problems.

- Ask your child to tell you about how he or she is multiplying and dividing. Show that you are interested in these approaches. Because these strategies may be unfamiliar to you, listen carefully to your child's explanation; you might even try to do a problem or two, using the new procedure. Let your child be the teacher!

Sincerely,

How Many People Counted?

Find your answers without counting.

1. Mr. Lu's class counted by 25's. The first person said 25, the second said 50, and the third said 75.

   How many people counted to get to 300? How do you know?

2. Ms. Patterson's class counted by 20's. The first person said 20, the second said 40, and the third said 60.

   How many people counted to get to 300? How do you know?

3. Mrs. Gomez's class counted by 10's, starting at 100. The first person said 110, the second said 120, and the third said 130.

   How many people counted to get to 300? How do you know?

What's the Counting Number?

For each puzzle, find three numbers I could have counted by.

1. I started counting at 0.
I stopped counting at 180.
I said fewer than 12 numbers when I counted.

2. I started counting at 240.
I stopped counting at 360.
I said between 5 and 15 numbers when I counted.

3. I started counting at 423.
I stopped counting at 523.
I said more than 7 numbers when I counted.

4. I started counting at 0.
I stopped counting at 3000.
I said more than 10 numbers when I counted.

5. I started counting at 2000.
I stopped counting at 2500.
I said fewer than 10 numbers when I counted.

What's In Between?

For each puzzle, find three numbers that fit all the clues.

1. This number is between 1000 and 2000.
   You say this number if you start at 1000 and count by 125.
   This number is closer to 2000 than it is to 1000.

2. This number is about halfway between 0 and 480.
   You say this number if you start at 0 and count by 24.

3. This number is between 7900 and 8100.
   You say this number when you start at 7900 and count by 10.
   This number is closer to 8100 than it is to 7900.

4. This number is between 11,000 and 12,000.
   This number is even.
   This number is closer to 11,000 than it is to 12,000.

5. This number is between 18,998 and 22,998.
   You say this number if you start at 18,000 and count by 500.
   This number is closer to 22,998 than it is to 18,998.

6. This number is between 0 and 30,000.
   This number is odd.
   This number has five digits.
   This number is closer to 0 than it is to 30,000.

Different Ways to Count

Part 1

For each problem, find three numbers you could count by to go from the **Start** number to the **End** number. For problem 6, you need to count backward.

	Start	Count by	End
1.	0		240
2.	70		140
3.	1100		1200

	Start	Count by	End
4.	0		12,000
5.	7493		8493
6.	800		0

Part 2

For each question below, find a counting number and write about how you found it.

- If you start at 0 and count by this number, you never say 10,000.

- If you start at 1000 and count backward by this number, you never say 0.

Using Multiples to Solve Problems

Choose a problem about 21 to solve. Record the problem in the box below:

Now solve the problem without using a standard algorithm or a calculator. Record your strategy so that someone else could follow your thinking.

Multiple Towers

Answer these questions about the Multiple Tower you made in class.

1. What number did you find multiples of?

2. Copy your Multiple Tower into the tall box.

3. What multiples of 10 are in your tower?

4. If you kept building your tower until it reached the next multiple of 10, how many numbers would be in your tower? How do you know?

5. Does your tower include any multiples of 100? Which ones?

6. If you kept building your tower until it reached the next multiple of 100, how many numbers would be in your tower? How do you know?

7. What patterns do you see in your tower?

8. Write a multiplication or division problem that you can solve by using what you know about the multiples in your tower. Show how you can use multiples to solve the problem.

How to Play the Digits Game

Materials: Numeral Cards (with Wild Cards removed)
Digits Game Score Sheet for each player

Players: 2 or 3

How to Play

1. Decide on the target number to use.

   Example: The target is 1000.

2. Deal the Numeral Cards. Deal out one more card than there are digits in the target.

   Example: The target has four digits, so you deal out five cards: 3, 8, 0, 1, and 5.

3. Players use the numerals on the cards to make a number as close as possible to the target.

   Example: You can use 3, 8, 0, 1, and 5 to make 1035, 853, or other numbers.

4. Write the target and the number you made on your score sheet. Find and record the difference between them.

   Example: $1000 - 853 = 147$. The difference is your score.

5. When everyone has finished, compare answers. Which number is closest to the target? Is it possible to make a number even closer?

   Example: Player A made 853. Player B made 1305. Who is closer? Can you make a number with these digits that is even closer to 1000?

6. For the next round, mix up all the cards and deal a new set.

7. After three rounds, total your scores. Lowest total wins.

Digits Game Score Sheet

For each round you play, record the target number and the closest number you can make with your digits. Put the larger one first. Then find and record the difference between them.

Game 1 target: _____   Difference

Round 1:_____ − _____ = _____

Round 2:_____ − _____ = _____

Round 3:_____ − _____ = _____

Total score: _____

Game 2 target: _____   Difference

Round 1:_____ − _____ = _____

Round 2:_____ − _____ = _____

Round 3:_____ − _____ = _____

Total score: _____

Game 3 target: _____   Difference

Round 1:_____ − _____ = _____

Round 2:_____ − _____ = _____

Round 3:_____ − _____ = _____

Total score: _____

Problems from the Digits Game

Pretend you are dealt these cards in the Digits Game.
Consider your target for each round. What numbers
would you make to get as close to the target as possible?

Round 1 target: 7306   Difference

Digits dealt:

| 1 | 7 | 4 | 8 | 0 |

_____ − _____ = _____

Round 2 target: 5029

Digits dealt:

| 8 | 2 | 6 | 9 | 3 |

_____ − _____ = _____

Round 3 target: 1015

Digits dealt:

| 4 | 0 | 7 | 5 | 2 |

_____ − _____ = _____

Total score: _____

0	0	1	1
0	0	1	1
2	2	3	3
2	2	3	3

© Dale Seymour Publications®

Investigation 1 • Resource
Building on Numbers You Know

4	4	5	5
4	4	5	5
<u>6</u>	<u>6</u>	7	7
<u>6</u>	<u>6</u>	7	7

8	8	<u>9</u>	<u>9</u>
8	8	<u>9</u>	<u>9</u>
WILD CARD	WILD CARD		
WILD CARD	WILD CARD		

Ringles

For each problem, show how you found your solution.
Suppose that there is a new coin called the ringle.
A ringle is worth 21 cents.

1. How many ringles are in 1 dollar?

2. How many ringles are in 2 dollars?

3. How many ringles are in 5 dollars?

Boxes of Markers

For each problem, show how you found your solution.

Number of students in your class: _____

Suppose that markers come in boxes of 70.

1. Suppose your class has 1 box of markers. How many would each person get if the markers were shared equally among the students in your class?

2. Suppose your class has 2 boxes of markers. How many would each person get if the markers were shared equally among the students in your class?

3. Suppose your class has 5 boxes of markers. How many would each person get if the markers were shared equally among the students in your class?

Zennies

For each problem, show how you found your solution.

Suppose that there is a new coin called the zenny.
A zenny is worth 3 cents.

1. How many zennies are in 1 dollar?

2. How many zennies are in 2 dollars?

3. How many zennies are in 3 dollars?

4. How many zennies are in 10 dollars?

My Coin

Make up a new coin.

How much is your coin worth?

Coin name: _____

Coin value: _____

For each problem, show how you find your solution.

1. How many of your coins are in 1 dollar?

2. How many of your coins are in 2 dollars?

3. How many of your coins are in 5 dollars?

4. How many of your coins are in 10 dollars?

A Division Problem

Solve one of the following problems *without* using a standard algorithm or calculator.

$$67 \div 7 = \qquad 98 \div 12 = \qquad 175 \div 15 =$$

$$245 \div 8 = \qquad 363 \div 24 = \qquad 477 \div 21 =$$

Show how you solved the problem.

Division Situations

For each problem, show how you found your solution.

1. Five people picked up shells at the beach. They found 171 shells. They want to share them equally. How many shells will each person get?

2. Five friends earned 171 dollars with a car wash. They want to share the money equally. How much will each person get?

3. A group of 171 children are going to the zoo. They will travel in cars that hold 5 passengers. How many cars will they need?

4. There are 171 fifth graders. They need to form 5 teams for a field day. How many fifth graders should be on each team?

Milk Cartons

For each problem, show how you found your solution.

Suppose that milk cartons come in boxes of 12.

1. If there are 15 boxes in the cafeteria, how many milk cartons are there in all?

2. If there are 30 boxes in the cafeteria, how many milk cartons are there in all?

3. If there are 75 boxes in the cafeteria, how many milk cartons are there in all?

Mimi's Mystery Multiple Tower

This is the top part of Mimi's Multiple Tower.

```
264
253
242
231
220
```

1. What number did Mimi count by?

2. How many numbers are in Mimi's tower so far? How do you know?

3. If Mimi kept adding numbers to her tower, what is the next multiple of 10 she would reach?

4. How many numbers would be in her tower then? How do you know?

5. Write a multiplication problem that you can solve by using what you know about the multiples in Mimi's tower. Show how you can use multiples to solve the problem.

6. Write a division problem that you can solve by using what you know about the multiples in Mimi's tower. Show how you can use multiples to solve the problem.

Relating Multiplication and Division Situations

Write a multiplication situation about **one** of the following problems.

$21 \times 14 =$ $51 \times 23 =$ $125 \times 36 =$

$144 \times 25 =$ $212 \times 9 =$ $21 \times 288 =$

Show how you solved the problem *without* using standard algorithms or calculators.

Now write a division situation that corresponds to your multiplication situation. Record your equation with division notation.

176

A Problem About Large Quantities

Look at home or in a store for items that are packaged in groups. Use what you find to make up and solve a "how many in all?" problem. Make sure you include the number of items in the package and the total number of packages found at home or the store.

My problem:

This is how I solved it:

Ask someone at home to solve your problem too. What strategy did that person use to solve your problem?

(handwritten: 3)   *(handwritten: 15)*   *(handwritten: 40)*

1	2	3	4	5	6	7	8	9	10
11	12	13	14	15	16	17	18	19	20
21	22	23	24	25	26	27	28	29	30
31	32	33	34	35	36	37	38	39	40
41	42	43	44	45	46	47	48	49	50
51	52	53	54	55	56	57	58	59	60
61	62	63	64	65	66	67	68	69	70
71	72	73	74	75	76	77	78	79	80
81	82	83	84	85	86	87	88	89	90
91	92	93	94	95	96	97	98	99	100
101	102	103	104	105	106	107	108	109	110
111	112	113	114	115	116	117	118	119	120
121	122	123	124	125	126	127	128	129	130
131	132	133	134	135	136	137	138	139	140
141	142	143	144	145	146	147	148	149	150
151	152	153	154	155	156	157	158	159	160
161	162	163	164	165	166	167	168	169	170
171	172	173	174	175	176	177	178	179	180
181	182	183	184	185	186	187	188	189	190
191	192	193	194	195	196	197	198	199	200
201	202	203	204	205	206	207	208	209	210
211	212	213	214	215	216	217	218	219	220
221	222	223	224	225	226	227	228	229	230
231	232	233	234	235	236	237	238	239	240
241	242	243	244	245	246	247	248	249	250
251	252	253	254	255	256	257	258	259	260
261	262	263	264	265	266	267	268	269	270
271	272	273	274	275	276	277	278	279	280
281	282	283	284	285	286	287	288	289	290
291	292	293	294	295	296	297	298	299	300

Multiplication Cluster Problems

Solve each cluster of problems. Look for ways that
the problems in each cluster are related.

10×123	20×123
2×123	**22×123**

10×18	5×18
50×18	2×18
20×18	40×18
45×18	**47×18**

400×9	500×9
90×9	8×9
2×9	**498×9**

2×72	10×72
5×72	20×72
200×72	210×72
215×72	

Investigation 3 • Sessions 1–3
Building on Numbers You Know

Writing About Multiplication Clusters

Solve this cluster of problems and write about how you solved it. Tell how you used one answer to help you find another answer.

10×21 2×21

5×21 50×21

52×21

Writing Multiplication and Division Situations

Choose the final problem from one of the clusters you
solved and record it here.

_____ × _____

Write a multiplication situation based on the final problem
in the cluster.

Now write a division situation that relates to the multiplication situation you wrote above. Write the equation using
division notation.

Division Cluster Problems

Solve each cluster of problems. Look for ways that
the problems in each cluster are related.

30 ÷ 15	150 ÷ 15
60 ÷ 15	**181 ÷ 15**

75 × 2	75 × 4
75 × 6	450 ÷ 75
463 ÷ 75	

300 ÷ 3	120 ÷ 3
90 ÷ 3	15 ÷ 3
45 ÷ 3	**437 ÷ 3**

10 × 21	5 × 21
20 × 21	30 × 21
738 ÷ 21	

Thinking About Division

Solve each cluster of problems. Look for ways that
the problems in each cluster are related.

$60 \div 6$	$66 \div 6$	**$65 \div 6$**
$30 \div 3$	$12 \div 3$	**$44 \div 3$**
10×7 2×7	12×7 **$86 \div 7$**	
10×4 20×4	9×4 **$79 \div 4$**	
10×11 11×11	3×11 2×11	**$146 \div 11$**
$100 \div 25$ $75 \div 25$	$200 \div 25$ **$282 \div 25$**	

A Division Situation

Choose the final problem from one of the clusters you solved and record it here.

_____ ÷ _____

Write a problem about a situation that uses the final problem in the cluster. Write about what you would do with the extras.

A Cluster of Problems

Make up a problem cluster that would help someone
solve:

$$187 \div 13 =$$

Include answers to all the problems in your cluster.

How Did I Solve It? (page 1 of 3)

For each problem, choose **two** first steps to complete.

1. $14 \times 9 =$

    a. Start by solving $10 \times 9 =$

    b. Start by solving $7 \times 9 =$

    c. Start by solving $14 \times 10 =$

2. $499 \div 2 =$

    a. Start by solving $2 \times 200 =$

    b. Start by solving $400 \div 2 =$

    c. Start by solving $500 \div 2 =$

    d. Start by solving $100 \div 2 =$

How Did I Solve It? (page 2 of 3)

For each problem, choose **two** first steps to complete.

3. $22 \times 37 =$

  a. Start by solving $22 \times 10 =$

  b. Start by solving $37 \times 10 =$

  c. Start by solving $20 \times 30 =$

4. $754 \div 30 =$

  a. Start by solving $30 \times 10 =$

  b. Start by solving $30 \times 2 =$

  c. Start by solving $300 \div 30 =$

  d. Start by solving $25 \times 30 =$

  e. Start by solving $75 \div 3 =$

How Did I Solve It? (page 3 of 3)

For each problem, choose **two** first steps to complete.

5. $105 \times 23 =$

   a. Start by solving $105 \times 10 =$

   b. Start by solving $100 \times 23 =$

   c. Start by solving $105 \times 2 =$

6. $300 \div 24 =$

   a. Start by solving $24 \times 10 =$

   b. Start by solving $240 \div 24 =$

   c. Start by solving $24 + 24 = 48$ and $48 + 48 =$

Different Strategies (page 1 of 2)

For each problem, choose **two** first steps to complete.

1. $59 \div 5 =$

   a. Start by solving $10 \times 5 =$

   b. Start by solving $11 \times 5 =$

   c. Start by solving $12 \times 5 =$

   d. Start by solving $50 \div 5 =$

2. $111 \div 9 =$

   a. Start by solving $10 \times 9 =$

   b. Start by solving $12 \times 9 =$

   c. Start by solving $90 \div 9 =$

Different Strategies (page 2 of 2)

For each problem, choose **two** first steps to complete.

3. $151 \div 7 =$

    a. Start by solving $10 \times 7 =$

    b. Start by solving 2×7 and $20 \times 7 =$

    c. Start by solving $70 \div 7 =$

4. $13 \times 11 =$

    a. Start by solving $13 \times 10 =$

    b. Start by solving $10 \times 11 =$

    c. Start by solving $10 \times 10 =$

Two Ways

Find **two ways** to solve one of the following problems without using a calculator.

$$87 \div 3 = \qquad 175 \div 8 = \qquad 263 \div 12 = \qquad 357 \div 15 =$$

My Own How Did I Solve It?
Problem (page 1 of 2)

Choose one of the following:

$98 \div 5 =$	$176 \div 6 =$	$197 \div 4 =$	$243 \div 11 =$	$685 \div 27 =$
$989 \div 49 =$	$112 \times 9 =$	$55 \times 32 =$	$16 \times 26 =$	$24 \times 12 =$

Solve the problem you choose in *at least two ways*.

Write your solutions clearly, so that someone else could follow your strategy.

First Way:

Second Way:

On page 2, record the problem and the first step of each solution method you found.

My Own How Did I Solve It?
Problem (page 2 of 2)

Record the problem and the first step of each solution method you found.

Problem:

First Step:

First Step:

First Step (if you have more than two ways to solve it):

Counting Up from 10,000

Fill in the numbers you say if you start at 10,000 and count up by each counting number.

Count up by 1000	Count up by 500	Count up by 100	Count up by 50	Count up by _____ (your choice)
10,000	10,000	10,000	10,000	10,000
_____	_____	_____	_____	_____
_____	_____	_____	_____	_____
_____	_____	_____	_____	_____
_____	_____	_____	_____	_____
_____	_____	_____	_____	_____
_____	_____	_____	_____	_____
_____	_____	_____	_____	_____
_____	_____	_____	_____	_____
_____	_____	_____	_____	_____
_____	_____	_____	_____	_____
_____	_____	_____	_____	_____
_____	_____	_____	_____	_____
_____	_____	_____	_____	_____

Counting Down from 10,000

Fill in the numbers you say if you start at 10,000 and count down by each counting number.

Count down by 1000	Count down by 500	Count down by 100	Count down by 50	Count down by _____ (your choice)
10,000	10,000	10,000	10,000	10,000
_____	_____	_____	_____	_____
_____	_____	_____	_____	_____
_____	_____	_____	_____	_____
_____	_____	_____	_____	_____
_____	_____	_____	_____	_____
_____	_____	_____	_____	_____
_____	_____	_____	_____	_____
_____	_____	_____	_____	_____
_____	_____	_____	_____	_____
_____	_____	_____	_____	_____
_____	_____	_____	_____	_____
_____	_____	_____	_____	_____
_____	_____	_____	_____	_____

Investigation 4 • Session 1
Building on Numbers You Know

Our Million Dots Display

1. Our class is making a display of one million dots. So far, we have _____ sheets and _____ dots in our display.

2. How many groups of 1000 dots are in the display?

   How do you know?

3. How many groups of 100 dots are in the display?

   How do you know?

4. How many groups of 10 dots are in the display?

   How do you know?

5. How many groups of 5000 dots are in the display?

   How do you know?

HOW MANY DOTS?

MILLION DOTS DISPLAY SHEET

Names _____

Sheet number _____   Date _____

Start _____   End _____

How to Play the Estimation Game

Materials: Estimation Game Score Sheet for each player
Calculator, watch, or clock
Numeral Cards

Players: 3–4

How to Play

1. Choose a problem template. **Example:** _ _ _ × _ _

2. Take turns being the leader. The leader deals one card for each slot in the template and records the digits in order without showing anyone.

Example: Deal [7] [4] [1] [0] [3]   Write $\underline{7}\ \underline{4}\ \underline{1} \times \underline{0}\ \underline{3}$

3. The leader uncovers the problem and starts timing. You have exactly 30 seconds to estimate the answer mentally, without pencil and paper. The leader finds the actual answer with a calculator.

4. Record your estimate and the actual answer on your score sheet. The difference between them is your score.

5. The leader deals new Numeral Cards for Rounds 2 and 3. Use the same problem template.

6. After three rounds, total your scores. Lowest score wins.

Variations

■ Make your estimates in just 15 seconds.

■ Use problem templates with 4- or 5-digit numbers, decimals, fractions, addition, or subtraction.

■ Find the actual answer without using a calculator.

Note: How will you handle remainders? Check one:

_____ Approximate to the next-lowest number (98.2 becomes 98).

_____ Approximate to the next-highest number (98.2 becomes 99).

_____ Approximate to the next-lowest number if less than 0.5; otherwise to the next-highest number (98.2 becomes 98; 98.7 becomes 99).

_____ Include the remainder in determining the score.

Estimation Game Score Sheet

For each round you play, record your estimate and the
solution. Put the larger number first. Find and record
the difference between them.

Game 1   Difference

Round 1: _____ – _____ = _____

Round 2: _____ – _____ = _____

Round 3: _____ – _____ = _____

Total score: _____

Game 2   Difference

Round 1: _____ – _____ = _____

Round 2: _____ – _____ = _____

Round 3: _____ – _____ = _____

Total score: _____

Game 3   Difference

Round 1: _____ – _____ = _____

Round 2: _____ – _____ = _____

Round 3: _____ – _____ = _____

Total score: _____

Another Division Problem

1. Make up a situation that would be represented by $720 \div 34$.

2. Solve the problem without using a calculator.
   Explain how you solved the problem.

3. What would you do with the extras?

How Did I Solve It? Challenges (page 1 of 4)

For each problem, choose **two** first steps to complete.

1. $37 \times 86 =$

   a. Start by solving $10 \times 86 =$

   b. Start by solving $10 \times 37 =$

   c. Start by solving $30 \times 80 =$

   d. Start by listing the first few multiples of 86 and using them to find 30×86 and 7×86.

2. $899 \div 7 =$

   a. Start by solving $100 \times 7 =$

   b. Start by solving $7 \times 12 =$

   c. Start by solving $700 \div 7 =$

How Did I Solve It? Challenges (page 2 of 4)

For each problem, choose **two** first steps to complete.

3. $980 \div 46 =$

    a. Start by solving $10 \times 46 =$

    b. Start by solving $2 \times 46 =$

    c. Start by solving $460 \div 46 =$

4. $248 \times 71 =$

    a. Start by solving $100 \times 71 =$

    b. Start by solving $2 \times 71 =$

    c. Start by solving $200 \times 70 =$

    d. Start by solving $250 \times 71 =$

How Did I Solve It? Challenges (page 3 of 4)

For each problem, choose **two** first steps to complete.

5. $543 \times 59 =$

    a. Start by solving $543 \times 10 =$

    b. Start by solving 543×100 and $543 \times 50 =$

    c. Start by listing the first few multiples of 543 and using them to find 543×50 and 543×9.

    d. Start by solving $543 \times 60 =$

6. $703 \div 17 =$

    a. Start by solving $10 \times 17 =$

    b. Start by solving $170 \div 17 =$

    c. Start by listing the first few multiples of 17 and finding the largest one less than 70.

How Did I Solve It? Challenges (page 4 of 4)

For each problem, choose **two** first steps to complete.

7. $1904 \div 6 =$

    a. Start by solving $100 \times 6 =$

    b. Start by solving $3 \times 6 =$

    c. Start by solving $250 \times 6 =$

8. $2401 \times 27 =$

    a. Start by solving $2 \times 27 =$

    b. Start by solving $2401 \times 10 =$

    c. Start by finding the first few multiples of 2401.

Problems About You (page 1 of 3)

Boxes of Pencils

Number of students in your class: _____

Suppose that pencils come in boxes of 19.

For each problem, show how you found your solution.

1. How many boxes of pencils do you need to open
to give 2 pencils to each student in your class?

2. How many boxes of pencils do you need to open
to give 4 pencils to each student in your class?

3. How many boxes of pencils do you need to open
to give 10 pencils to each student in your class?

Problems About You (page 2 of 3)

Pads of Paper

Number of students in your class: _____

Number of students in your grade: _____

Number of students in your school: _____

Suppose that pads of paper have 85 sheets. They come in packages of 4 pads each. You have 3 packages in the classroom.

For each problem, show how you found your solution.

1. How many sheets of paper do you have in all?

2. If you share the paper equally among the students in your class, how many sheets will each person get?

3. If you share the paper equally among the students in your grade, how many sheets will each person get?

4. If you share the paper equally among the students in your school, how many sheets will each person get?

Investigation 5 • Sessions 4–6
Building on Numbers You Know

Problems About You (page 3 of 3)

Recycling

Number of students in your class: _____

Suppose you get 6¢ for each bottle you return for recycling.

For each problem, show how you found your solution.

1. You have collected 149 bottles. How much will you earn?

2. If you share what you earn with one friend, how much will each person get?

3. If you share what you earn with two friends, how much will each person get?

4. Find the fairest way to share what you earned with everyone in your class, so there is no money left over. How much will each person get?

Different Paths to 10,000

Your goal is to get 10,000 on your calculator display. Start
with each of the numbers listed below and find two ways
to get to 10,000. At least one path must use multiplication
or division. You may not use keys that clear the calculator
display. Record each path you find.

Starting number	Paths to 10,000
1025	
73	
9974	
21,681	
130.5	
your choice	
your choice	

A Multiplication Problem

Make up a situation that would be represented by 518×42.

Solve the problem without using a calculator. Record all the steps you used to solve the problem.

How Can This Help?

Select **two** of the following problems.

$25 \times 41 =$ $24 \times 40 =$ $25 \times 39 =$ $26 \times 41 =$

$24 \times 41 =$ $26 \times 39 =$ $24 \times 29 =$

First problem: _____

How would the answer to **25 × 40** help you find the answer to this problem? Show your thinking.

Second problem: _____

How would the answer to **25 × 40** help you find the answer to this problem? Show your thinking.

Practice Pages

This optional section provides homework ideas for teachers who want or need to give more homework than is assigned to accompany the activities in this unit. The problems included here provide additional practice in learning about number relationships and in solving computation and number problems. For number units, you may want to use some of these if your students need more work in these areas or if you want to assign daily homework. For other units, you can use these problems so that students can continue to work on developing number and computation sense while they are focusing on other mathematical content in class. We recommend that you introduce activities in class before assigning related problems for homework.

Close to 0   This game is introduced in the unit *Mathematical Thinking at Grade 5*. If your students are familiar with the game, you can simply send home the directions, score sheet, and Numeral Cards so that students can play at home. If your students have not played the game before, introduce it in class and have students play once or twice before sending it home. Students ready for more challenge can try the variation listed at the bottom of the sheet. You might have students do this activity four or five times for homework in this unit.

Solving Problems in Two Ways   Students explore different ways to solve computation problems in the units *Mathematical Thinking at Grade 5* and *Building on Numbers You Know*. Here, we provide 2 sheets of problems that students solve in two different ways. Problems may include addition, subtraction, multiplication, or division. Students record each way they solved the problem.

Counting Puzzles   In this kind of problem, introduced in the unit *Mathematical Thinking at Grade 5*, students are given a clue about a set of numbers. Students find three numbers that match the clue (there may be many numbers that would work). If necessary, you might distribute 300 charts for students to use. Provided here are 2 problem sheets and one 300 chart, which you can copy for use with the problem sheets. Because this activity is included in the curriculum only as homework, it is recommended that you briefly introduce it in class before students work on it at home.

How to Play Close to 0

Materials

- One deck of Numeral Cards
- Close to 0 Score Sheet

Players: 2

How to Play

1. Deal out eight numeral cards to each player.

2. Use any six cards to make two numbers. For example, a 6, a 5, and a 2 could make 652, 625, 526, 562, 256, or 265. Wild Cards can be used as any numeral. Try to make two numbers that, when subtracted, give you a difference that is close to 0.

3. Write these numbers and their difference on the Close to 0 Score Sheet. For example: $652 - 647 = 5$. The difference is your score.

4. Put the cards you used in a discard pile. Keep the two cards you didn't use for the next round.

5. For the next round, deal six new cards to each player. Make two more numbers with a difference close to 0. When you run out of cards, mix up the discard pile and use them again.

6. After five rounds, total your scores. Lower score wins.

Variation   Deal out ten Numeral Cards to each player. Each player uses eight cards to make two numbers that, when subtracted, give a difference that is close to 0.

Close to 0 Score Sheet

Player 1   Score

Round 1:   ___ ___ ___ + ___ ___ ___ = _____   _____

Round 2:   ___ ___ ___ + ___ ___ ___ = _____   _____

Round 3:   ___ ___ ___ + ___ ___ ___ = _____   _____

Round 4:   ___ ___ ___ + ___ ___ ___ = _____   _____

Round 5:   ___ ___ ___ + ___ ___ ___ = _____   _____

                                            TOTAL SCORE   _____

Player 2   Score

Round 1:   ___ ___ ___ + ___ ___ ___ = _____   _____

Round 2:   ___ ___ ___ + ___ ___ ___ = _____   _____

Round 3:   ___ ___ ___ + ___ ___ ___ = _____   _____

Round 4:   ___ ___ ___ + ___ ___ ___ = _____   _____

Round 5:   ___ ___ ___ + ___ ___ ___ = _____   _____

                                            TOTAL SCORE   _____

0	0	1	1
0	0	1	1
2	2	3	3
2	2	3	3

Practice Page
Building on Numbers You Know

4	4	5	5
4	4	5	5
<u>6</u>	<u>6</u>	7	7
<u>6</u>	<u>6</u>	7	7

Practice Page
Building on Numbers You Know

8	8	9	9
8	8	9	9
WILD CARD	WILD CARD		
WILD CARD	WILD CARD		

Practice Page A

Solve this problem in two different ways and write about how you solved it:

$$37 \times 42 =$$

Here is the first way I solved it:

Here is the second way I solved it:

Practice Page B

Solve this problem in two different ways and write about how you solved it:

126 ÷ 14 =

Here is the first way I solved it:

Here is the second way I solved it:

1	2	3	4	5	6	7	8	9	10
11	12	13	14	15	16	17	18	19	20
21	22	23	24	25	26	27	28	29	30
31	32	33	34	35	36	37	38	39	40
41	42	43	44	45	46	47	48	49	50
51	52	53	54	55	56	57	58	59	60
61	62	63	64	65	66	67	68	69	70
71	72	73	74	75	76	77	78	79	80
81	82	83	84	85	86	87	88	89	90
91	92	93	94	95	96	97	98	99	100
101	102	103	104	105	106	107	108	109	110
111	112	113	114	115	116	117	118	119	120
121	122	123	124	125	126	127	128	129	130
131	132	133	134	135	136	137	138	139	140
141	142	143	144	145	146	147	148	149	150
151	152	153	154	155	156	157	158	159	160
161	162	163	164	165	166	167	168	169	170
171	172	173	174	175	176	177	178	179	180
181	182	183	184	185	186	187	188	189	190
191	192	193	194	195	196	197	198	199	200
201	202	203	204	205	206	207	208	209	210
211	212	213	214	215	216	217	218	219	220
221	222	223	224	225	226	227	228	229	230
231	232	233	234	235	236	237	238	239	240
241	242	243	244	245	246	247	248	249	250
251	252	253	254	255	256	257	258	259	260
261	262	263	264	265	266	267	268	269	270
271	272	273	274	275	276	277	278	279	280
281	282	283	284	285	286	287	288	289	290
291	292	293	294	295	296	297	298	299	300

Practice Page
Building on Numbers You Know

Practice Page C

Find three numbers that fit each clue.

1. If you count by this number, you will say 27, but you will not say 37.

2. If you count by this number, you will say 128, but you will not say 131.

3. If you count by this number, you will say 144, but you will not say 164.

Practice Page D

Find three numbers that fit each clue.

1. If you count by this number, you will say 64, but you will not say 63.

2. If you count by this number, you will say 240, but you will not say 250.

3. If you count by this number, you will say 105, but you will not say 100.